W9-CHS-368

# MY GOD! WHAT A LIFE!

# My God! What A Life!

Monsignor James A. O'Callaghan, P.A.

Copyright © 2013 The Estate of Monsignor James A. O'Callaghan, P.A.

ISBN 978-0-615-71994-8

All rights reserved. No part of this publication may be reproduced, stored in a retrieval system, or transmitted in any form or by any means, electronic or mechanical, recording or otherwise, without the prior written permission of the author's estate.

Cover art designed by Paco Garcia

Dictated by Monsignor James A. O'Callaghan, P.A., 2001

Printed in the United States of America by Booksource On Demand, St. Louis, MO

For additional copies or inquiries, contact FatherOBook@gmail.com

# DEDICATION

I dedicate this book to my brothers. Ours is a glorious and challenging vocation, binding us in a special camaraderie dedicated to Christ's service. I include all my brother shepherds "in the mist," trusting that the will and subsequent peace of Christ will be theirs. My hope is that many future candidates will follow the Master's call.

# TABLE OF CONTENTS

# ABOUT THE AUTHOR

Praised by colleagues for his devotion to the priesthood, Monsignor James A. O'Callaghan, born May 31, 1917, was a native Angeleno. He attended St. Patrick's Seminary, Menlo Park, CA, and St. John's Seminary, Camarillo, CA. In April, 1943, he was ordained by Archbishop John Cantwell.

Considered a powerful and charismatic speaker with a no-nonsense approach to preaching and living the Word of God, many priests cite him as having had a significant influence on their lives and decision to enter the seminary.

In January, 2000, Pope John Paul II elevated Monsignor O'Callaghan to Protonotary Apostolic, the highest rank of monsignor and one of only four such priests in the Los Angeles Archdiocese. Soon after, Father O dictated this autobiography. It has been published posthumously.

# FORWARD
# BY FATHER JOSEPH SHEA

This book is an attempt to capture the greatness of a man who was one of the finest persons and priests I had ever met.

The inspiration for this book first came from the people and the priests who knew and worked with Monsignor James Aloysius O'Callaghan—known by most as Father O—during his 59 years of priesthood. We encouraged Father O to record some of the fascinating stories of his life in order to preserve his incredible spirit, joy, zeal, and wisdom. I often told him that even if I had lived four lifetimes, I never would have met the number of famous people nor had the number of incredible experiences he had; his life was that unique and extraordinary.

Father O only agreed to share his memories and reflections because he wanted to inspire people to completely commit their lives to Christ and His Church and for young people to seriously consider serving Christ and His Church full time as priests or religious. That's how blessed and grateful he was that Jesus called him to be a Catholic priest.

For those who knew him, Father O was a man's man and a priest's priest. He had a passionate love for life, for all sports— fishing, hunting, golfing, football (especially Notre Dame football)—and spending time with family and friends, priest and lay alike.

As passionate as his love for life was, he had an even more passionate life of love. He loved God the Father. He loved Jesus Christ, God's Son and the Savior of the world. He loved the Holy Spirit, who moved powerfully in Father O's life and especially in his preaching. He loved the Holy Catholic Church, the Catholic Faith, the Catholic Priesthood, and the people he served.

Father O always felt indebted to Jesus Christ and the Church, often saying, "The Catholic Church owes me nothing. I owe the Catholic Church everything!" He viewed his life as a priest in the profoundly simple way that all of us should see our lives—to bring Christ to people and people to Christ, to bring people to heaven and heaven to people. This is accomplished through the Holy Eucharist ("A day without the Eucharist is a dead day for me."), through the Sacrament of Reconciliation (to which Father O was so dedicated in imitation of St. John Vianney, the patron of the parish he built and fathered), and through his passionate preaching, teaching, and pastoral service. It didn't matter the cost or the sacrifice. All that mattered was to win souls for Christ. That's why it was not unusual to see Father O rushing to a hospital or chasing an ambulance through the streets of his parish or stopping by an accident scene just to see if someone needed a priest.

Father O lived the words of Father Henri-Dominique Lacordaire in his famous meditation on the Catholic priesthood:

*To live in the midst of the world*
*without wishing its pleasures;*
*To be a member of each family,*
*yet belonging to none;*
*To share all suffering;*
*to penetrate all secrets;*
*To heal all wounds;*
*to go from men to God*
*and offer Him their prayers;*
*To return from God to men*
*to bring pardon and hope;*
*To have a heart of fire for Charity,*
*and a heart of bronze for Chastity*
*To teach and to pardon,*
*console and bless always.*
*My God, what a life;*
*and it is yours,*
*O priest of Jesus Christ.*

Yes! What a life it was, O priest of Jesus Christ. And it truly was yours, Monsignor James Aloysius O'Callaghan. And for that, we thank God and you!

# PREFACE: PRIESTLY HANDS BY FATHER O

During the evening's silent meditation in the rotunda of the New Camaldoli Hermitage in Big Sur, I looked at my eighty-five-year-old hands. In the chapel shadows they appeared dark as though clasped in death, old worn out hands, hopefully used well in Christ's ministry.

In youth these hands gripped a baseball bat, felt the seams while passing a football, developed the touch in releasing a basketball jump shot, felt the whip of the shaft in a solid golf hit, and knew the struggle of striving to reel in a fighting marlin. These are the hands that pulled the trigger to bring down a duck or dove in full flight, that plied the shovel in controlled brush burning, that pushed the mop in janitorial service, that stocked the trunks in Southern Pacific Railroad boxcars, that massaged and worked and trained greyhounds for the track, that cleaned the garage and weeded the garden for my father, and that picked pears in the desert heat as a migrating fruit picker. These were Jack-of-all-trade hands, with no great future for them foreseen.

Then came the call to the priesthood!

What a challenge to these hands! Books, compositions, term papers, exams, cassocks, sacred vessels, vestments, and liturgical objects became familiar to them. All were handled awkwardly, clumsily, but reverently, with no great finesse. And yet, like fearfully passing the Department of Motor Vehicles' written and driving tests, somehow I made it. I qualified and was ordained a priest!

During the past fifty-nine years, countless times these hands have held the body and blood of Jesus Christ in consecration, fed myself and the faith-filled communicants. These hands have made the sign of the cross in absolving the sins of the people of God, anointed and consoled many sick and dying faithful; they have blessed multiple people as well as animals and religious objects–from rosaries, medals, and automobiles to ships at sea.

Happily God's blessings go through these hands to people and things. These blessings are for the good of the person and objects blessed. The priest enjoys the gratitude of the recipient and God's appreciation of his priestly conduit.

Today's world is impressed with the productive hands of a Phil Mickelson, Michael Jordan, Barry Bonds, Venus Williams, and Annika Sorenstam. The results of their hands benefit first themselves and then the egos and pride of those possessing their friendship and autographs or other memorabilia. But all in time must pass as did Bill Tilden, Babe Ruth, Helen Wills, and Babe Didrikson. As St. Paul says, "Theirs is a perishable crown but ours an eternal one."

Thus priests' hands prepare souls not for the current time or egocentric self but simply for God's glory. This is the beauty and richness of the **SELFLESS HANDS OF THE PRIESTS!** *April 19, 2002*

# PART ONE:
# BECOMING A PRIEST

# EARLY YEARS

I felt rather uncertain as I approached the adobe-colored Spanish building and rang the doorbell. I had never been in the rectory before. The housekeeper, a typical kind of dried up person, let me in.

"I'd like to talk to the pastor," I began.

"Wait right here."

I stood in a little hall. After a few minutes the pastor came downstairs. "Well, son, what do you want?"

"I want to talk to you. I don't know exactly why I am here except that I feel like maybe I should be a priest."

"What's your name?"

"My name is Jim O'Callaghan."

"Oh, I think I know a little about you," he said. "Didn't you go to the grammar school here a few years ago?"

"I did, but I didn't stay. That's the problem. I wanted to transfer to 66th Street School."

"Didn't you also have some difficulty when you attended confirmation classes?"

"Yes. I was kicked out of class for insubordination, but after a public apology I was allowed back. My father threatened me with a good whipping until I made an apology to the pastor, sister in charge, and the class." (These were the stipulations upon my being reinstated.)

"Were you ever an altar boy?"

"No, I never was. I didn't care to be an altar boy."

"Well, do you ever come to any of our High Masses?"

"Oh no, they are too long. I do not care for High Masses."

He looked at me very skeptically and finally he said, "I know about you. You know what you are?"

"What am I, Father?"

"You're kind of an athletic bum."

That really turned me off because the only thing I was really good at was athletics. I was a poor student so my grades weren't so hot, and he had just put me down for the only thing I felt I was fairly good at.

My anger rose up. I put my hand on the doorknob, saying, "Well, you know everything, and I don't know what else to say. I just asked if I should be a priest or not."

"Your name is O'Callaghan. By any chance are you related to Father James O'Callaghan, the pastor at Mother of Sorrows?"

"Yes, Father, I am. In fact, he's my uncle."

"Oh," he said. "I'll tell you what I'll do. I will recommend you to the seminary on your bloodline."

So that's how I was recommended to the junior seminary.

As far as my origin is concerned, I know that my father, William Ferris O'Callaghan, was from Tralee, County Kerry, and my mother, Hannah O'Brien, from Middleton, County Cork. They were about thirty years of age when they met at St. Mary's Academy. It's where my father was assigned as a stationary engineer; my mother was a friend of one of the Sisters. From what I understand, somehow Sister Ligouri persuaded my mother to marry my father, and that is how my brother John, my sister Mary, and I came into being. I have always said that the Sisters of St. Joseph of Carondelet are responsible for my existence.

I don't recall much of my early youth except that we lived near St. Patrick's Parish, across from the church at 34th & Central Avenue in Los Angeles. At that time, my uncle, Father James A. O'Callaghan, a very benevolent man, was its pastor.

He died at age fifty-two, but I always remember him being rather old. He was very interested in birds and flowers, and he had an aviary and all sorts of beautiful plants in his garden. He was a dignified, handsome man, very good to us kids and our family.

St. Patrick's often held dances in its hall for its many Irish immigrant people. As chairman, my father participated in lots of them. I remember one time my uncle came into the dance carrying Jackie Coogan—who was a tremendous child star at the time—in his arms.

My uncle greatly encouraged vocations to the religious life. Two of his young parishioners, Alden Bell and Joseph McGucken, became bishops. Joseph McGucken eventually became archbishop of San Francisco, while Bishop Alden Bell served in Los Angeles and later became bishop of Sacramento.

After a few years, we moved to the South Central area of Los Angeles and became members of St. Columbkille parish. That's where John and I began school. I didn't do too well in their grammar school. I seemed to be a constant thorn in the side of Sister Gertrude of the Notre Dame de Namur. I recall many instances of coming up to the front of the class and being slapped on the hands with a ruler.

I also very vividly recall preparing for my First Communion. While waiting for confession, I found a woman's hat pin lying in the pew. I got the enormous temptation to stick that into the behind of Bill Stack, the young man in front of me. I took that hat pin, shoved it in, and he jumped nearly ten feet high off the pew. Of course, I was disciplined severely for that.

Later on, because of various difficulties, I left St. Columbkille School and went to 66th Street School. I don't remember much about it except one thing: the fifth and sixth grade teacher, Mrs. Glover, used to tell us that her husband was so cheap that he wouldn't take her to a nickelodeon. (I didn't know what a nickelodeon was, but at that time it was a five-cent show.)

After 66th Street School I went on to Edison Junior High School, which I liked. I frequently bummed rides and occasionally got there by walking on the railroad tracks. Bumming rides was forbidden by school rule. Mr. Gilett, the principal, said if I continued to bum rides to school he would send me to Jacob Reis High School, which was the school for delinquent boys. I wouldn't have minded that too much because they had the only swimming pool in town, but I never got that lucky.

I was not much of a student, but I did participate a lot in athletics. Our teams were the Wolves, Wildcats, Pirates, and Tigers. I happened to be a Pirate. We had great athletic competitions which promoted lots of fun.

When I finished junior high school, my folks thought it might be a good idea if I went to Cathedral High School. I agreed that maybe a Catholic high school would be good for me. My brother, John, who was going to Fremont High School, joined me at Cathedral. I started in the tenth grade; he was an eleventh grader.

I wasn't in school but one day before I got into trouble. They had inserted glass windows in the room doors for class control reasons, and some kid hit me. I hauled off and hit him back, and, of course, the principal, Brother Victor, happened to see me. I was called into his office and told that, coming in from a public school, I had to behave myself or I would be out on my ear.

You'd have thought I would learn from that, but I didn't.

My English teacher and varsity football coach was Dick Hassler, who later became president of Pasadena City College. When I first came into his classroom he walked down the aisle and asked, "Is your name Jim O'Callaghan?"

"Yeah!"

"Don't you say 'yeah' to me."

"Yeah!"

Suddenly he bent over, and I took a short swift punch right to the jaw that landed me out in the aisle. "Don't say 'yeah' to me," he repeated. "Did you say your name was Jim O'Callaghan?" he curtly asked.

"Yes, sir!"

And I said "Yes, sir" for the rest of my time there.

When I got home my father saw my jaw and asked me what had happened. "A Mr. Hassler hit me," I said.

"Let me see that jaw."

He put his hand lightly on my jaw. All of a sudden a punch came from the right and knocked me down again. "Anytime you're struck by a teacher you'll get double from me."

So I always said, "Please, teachers, don't let my folks know about any of my disciplinary actions. I'll do anything you want, but keep me from going home to face more problems."

I liked Cathedral High School very much. Jerry Cahill was the senior varsity quarterback and student body president when I went out for B football. Jerry was a marvelous football player and later became one of my greatest buddies. They had splendid teams in those days, and so did the seminary, which went undefeated for two years. That was about all I knew about the seminary at that time. My grades were not good; I just barely maintained an average which allowed me to participate in sports. I liked basketball, football, and baseball, but I wasn't that great in any of them, although I certainly enjoyed playing.

I remember my first encounter with death.

We practiced our games on what was called Tombstone Field. (The field had formerly been a cemetery.) Grave diggers were continually digging up the graves and removing the bodies to another cemetery. Every time it rained the graves would sink, sometimes two or three inches. One of our pastimes at lunch would be to go to the quad where the workmen had brought out the remains to place in redwood boxes. We would open up the covers to see what kind of bones were inside, or whatever else might be there. Then we would eat our lunch.

Cathedral was a great school with much spirit and a lot of wonderful people; the Christian Brothers of La Salle were magnificent brothers. I began to feel some indications that maybe I was being called to the priesthood.

One day a Monsignor Edward Kirk came to talk to the student body about vocations. He even said, "When I was an altar boy I heard a voice behind the tabernacle say to me, 'Edward, I want you to be a priest.'"

Of course, my reaction was that there must have been some guy behind the curtain pulling his leg. I didn't give it much thought at the time, but later it kept bugging me.

I was not attracted to the priesthood for two simple reasons: I didn't know much about priests, and I was not very religious. I even felt a little bit embarrassed being around my uncle, although he was a wonderful, gentle, dignified man. The only real talent or virtue that I had was that I was an honest person. The thought of the priesthood kept challenging me, however. Even though I never talked to my parents or anyone, the desire was there. I would be playing sports or I would be with other boys and girls, and in the back of my mind somehow I knew that one day I would be a priest. I would wonder, "Where did that come from?" I didn't understand then, but this was a call from God, and a call from God is not merely a choice, it is a call. Since I was an honest person and it was all I had going for me, I thought, *Well, I better answer that call.* That's what prompted me to talk to my pastor.

It was toward the end of my first year at Cathedral. I had not been getting along too well with the principal, but I went into his office and said, "I want to transfer."

Brother Victor seemed quite upset when he replied, "So you're leaving us?"

"Yes."

"Where you are going?"

"I don't want to tell you."

"Unless you tell me where you're going, I can't send your transcripts. You have to tell me."

Finally, I confessed, "I'm going to enter the junior seminary."

"Oh, wonderful!" He beamed delightedly.

I wanted to keep this quiet.

During the course of the following week the student body was holding elections for next year's officers. I will never forget the moment somebody nominated me for junior vice president. "Oh, no, I said. "Don't do that."

All of a sudden Brother Victor announced, "Jim O'Callaghan cannot accept the nomination for the simple reason that he is going to the seminary to become a priest and he will be leaving at the end of this year."

I was so embarrassed that I wanted to get down under the chairs, but the student body stood up and gave me a resounding cheer. I will never forget how really remarkable it was. After that Brother Victor and I became better friends, and he helped me prepare to enter the junior seminary.

At first I didn't tell my parents much about wanting to go to the seminary, but I finally broke the news to them. Both were agreeable but not terrifically enthusiastic. Maybe they had some doubts about whether I would be able to handle it. I had no idea what I was going to run into. I thought perhaps the guys in the seminary would be walking around with surplices on and lighted candles in their hands.

The only other contact I had with the seminary was when I went for a field day at Loyola High School. Some of the seminary football players were there for the athletic outing. I was very impressed by these athletes. I thought if I could go to the seminary and still be able to continue my football career, so be it!

I'll never forget my first day at the seminary. I felt a little strange, but the seminarians seemed to be a regular bunch of guys. Father Marshall Wynne, the principal, stood up front. "I have some bad news for all of you who are athletes and are interested in football," he announced. "Because of the many injuries we had last year we've decided there will be no competitive football this coming year."

My world collapsed. *My God*, I thought. *This is it.* Very upset and disillusioned, I left for home.

When I arrived there I saw my father. "The seminary canceled out football and now I can't play there," I said.

All he said was, "Son, we didn't send you to the seminary. If you don't like it, get the hell out. Don't be moaning around this house."

Jeez, I got so mad that I went into my bedroom and smashed my fist against the wall. I was really upset. But I guess my dad knew how to handle me at that time. He made me so angry that I forgot about not being able to play football. That's the way the cookie crumbled. I entered the seminary without being able to play, w h i c h  w a s  a great disappointment to me.

The classes were difficult and the administration decided that I'd better drop back a year to catch up. I began again the following year.

Our first night I remember playing pick-up basketball in the gymnasium. I didn't know any of the fellows, but I recall Emmett McCarthy, Dick Murray, Russell Karl, and some others were playing two-on-two, three-on-three basketball, with a lot of elbows being thrown and hips flung out. I got a little irritated. One guy in particular, Emmett McCarthy, bugged me. We finished playing, went into the locker room, showered up, and everyone cleared out except McCarthy and me.

As we exchanged words, we got angrier at each other. Suddenly there were fisticuffs and some blows struck, but just as quickly as it started, we solved it, shook hands, and went on our ways. Strangely, that was the beginning of a friendship that has lasted to the present. We have been firm friends ever since.

I found the seminary difficult. I never liked it. The studies were extremely challenging. I was especially afraid of learning Latin so I bought a little table for my bedroom at home, a room which I shared with my brother John. I got the table for about five bucks and added a chair from the kitchen. I had made up my mind that I had to learn how to study, so every night after dinner I would isolate myself in my room, determined to see whether or not I could grasp Latin, Greek, English, and all of the other subjects. I was really struggling. I particularly remember Friday nights as it was when I used to pitch softball in various parks. The guys would come over and say, "Jim, we need you to pitch tonight at Slauson playground, or Manchester playground, or Harvard ball field." What a struggle it would be not to go out with them! Of course my brother played end at Cathedral at the time, and he was in and out of the house all the time.

I found it extremely hard to be so isolated; however, I hung in, determined to see this thing through. It was 1932, the year of the great earthquake. I can still recall studying in my room at about seven o'clock at night when that big earthquake hit, damaging a lot of Long Beach. My father opened my door and said, "Now, don't panic! This is an earthquake so just relax and get under the bed." He stood in the doorway between my room and the hall. That was one of the greatest earthquakes we've ever had in this area.

Although I never liked the seminary, I did begin, through a lot of effort and study, to grasp Latin, then English and Greek. I somehow got through mathematics, too. The real difficulty was going to and from home on the streetcar. It was really boring. Also, I did janitorial work after school for one year to help pay the tuition. I couldn't wait for the weekends so I wouldn't have to go to school. We played ball on the seminary asphalt, but I missed the other athletics so much. To make up for that I used to play a little semi-pro football and baseball. I also played for the St. Columbkille Parish ball club and with Holy Cross's Parish team. That satisfied some of my desire to compete.

The seminarians all lived in the area—Emmett McCarthy, Dick Murray, Phil Grill, Pat Burke, and some of the others. Whenever we had any free time, we'd make it a point to go to the snow and ski or ice skate. During the summer we all tried to make a few bucks working at various jobs. We worked for the railroad, or movie studios, or at migratory fruit picking. Sometimes we also worked for Bache property maintenance, doing controlled brush burning within the Hollywood Hills.

There was always something for us to do in our free time. We would meet and enjoy ourselves by going to the show or just playing pool or cards. On days off we would meet at 17th Street in Hermosa Beach and spend time body surfing and having lots of fun. We also skied and fished. That's often when the question of whether or not we would make it came up.

This was a good group of fellows that I went around with. They were about as talented as I was, which wasn't the greatest, but we liked our sports. Most of them were brighter than I, but we enjoyed being together.

Although we all had attractive sisters, we made it a point not to date. We wanted to see if we could handle the lack of feminine companionship. If a fellow felt he couldn't handle living without the daily friendship and ultimately love of a girl, he might as well check out. Our camaraderie helped us to meet the challenge of living celibately. Of the original seven guys who got together and strove not to date unless it was a real necessity, six of us were ordained.

When I was going into my fifth year at seminary we put on a student play for parents and friends. Our director, Dr. Peatfield, decided we needed a makeup crew. He had an RKO Pictures contact that was going to get makeup artists to come out to our cast. Unfortunately, a strike occurred among the makeup artists that had been procured by Hermes Pan, a choreographer at RKO. When they could not participate, out of the goodness of his own heart, he came with some of his dancers to make up our cast members. It was the first time he had ever met seminarians.

I was dead set against having any makeup put on, even for the dress rehearsal. I did say, however, that I would allow it to be applied on the actual play night.

Hermes and some of his dancers took good care of us. At the end of the play he invited our whole cast to tour the RKO lot. He was a recent Catholic convert, and he wanted to show the fellows a good time. I thanked him but politely refused, telling him I couldn't make it because I had a baseball game to play and that was more important. He later phoned me, however, and said, "Look, I know you couldn't come to the studio, but I'd like to take you through if you don't mind."

It was awfully nice of him to invite me, especially, to take a tour. I thought, *well, why not*? So, he showed me around RKO. He was very kind, and I enjoyed it, but the studio didn't exactly turn me on.

After I thanked him, we began to talk some more. He was very interested in the church and tremendously curious about the life of a priest, particularly the priesthood vocation. "Would you like to come to my house and meet my parents?" I asked him. "We live over on Gage Avenue in South Central Los Angeles."

"I'd love to."

(Hermes was only about four or five years older than I was. He had had a hard time in his early career as a dance director, but since then he had become quite successful as Fred Astaire's choreographer and was living in a beautiful home in Studio City.)

He drove up to our house in his big Cadillac and met my mother, father, and my sister, Mary. They were simple people but genuine. He seemed to like my family and the way they lived and became very close to my parents.

I gradually introduced him to the other seminarians: McCarthy, Murray, Karl, Holcombe, and some others whom he really liked. As a choreographer, Hermes was very much a genius in his own right; however, the studios didn't satisfy his love for the church and its apostolate. Whether we were out skiing, at the beach, or at home, he loved to spend time talking with us about theology and philosophy. He was a wonderful man, and I liked him very much. He became a good friend to me and all of the seminarians.

One night a group of us decided we would go out to Ocean Park. We were all having a great time checking out the fun house. Suddenly I saw Hermes standing before the mirrors—those strange ones that create different shapes. He went inside a barrel that rolled around and as he was walking through, I noticed him doing all sorts of gyrations, making all kinds of pantomimes. I'll be darned if that night he didn't create what is called the "fun house number" for a movie featuring Fred Astaire. Hermes had the fun house duplicated at the studio with Fred Astaire playing the role of the man dancing through the various barrels and pantomiming in front of the strange mirrors. The number was a smashing success, winning Hermes Pan the Academy Award for best dance direction.

At that time I was trying to make a few bucks to get through the seminary and pay my bills. Jobs were very difficult to come by. I had worked for Bache Property Maintenance, cleaning the sides of hills and burning big areas of dried brush around Hollywood. It was hard, dangerous, and difficult work. Finally, jobs became so difficult to find that Louie Kotch, Dick Murray, Pat Burke, and I went to Little Rock, California, where we picked and boxed pears for the ranchers.

The first night out we didn't have a tent, just a blanket and a few cooking utensils. It rained all night. The rest of the time was beautiful, however. We slept on blankets spread over piles of sagebrush, cooked our breakfast, and occasionally got together some money in order to eat dinner at a restaurant in Little Rock. (We made only thirty-five cents an hour.) We retired at about eight o'clock at night, sleeping alongside a little fire. The sun would awaken us at five o'clock in the morning. Sometimes we worked in 110-120 degree heat, but we needed the money.

Although it was challenging work, meeting the migratory fruit pickers and their families was great! They were from Oklahoma, Texas, etc., driven from their own parched land. At night we would go to their camps and they would bring out a jug of wine. Then we would sit around and sing, just having a great time with them. I really loved those people. At times they'd have their babies in some storefront space where the younger kids would try to keep the flies off the infants. There might be eight or ten babies lying in one bed, sometimes with flies hovering and lighting on them. I felt kind of sick about it, but that's the way they lived. The more kids they had, the more kids there were to later pick and box Bartlett pears.

There were also lots of religious fundamentalists. Sometimes we got into really heated arguments about God and what He demanded. Whenever there was any kind of music and dancing, the fundamentalists would say dancing was evil and all these things could possibly lead to sin. That's when my friends and I would take a firm stand. We had some good arguments with them. This was a lot of fun, and it kept us occupied.

I remember when Louie Kotch and I had a very important ballgame to play in Culver City. Peanuts Lowry was a big star for the St. Augustine's team, and we were going for some kind of a championship. We had to bum a ride there.

It was raining when we left Little Rock and some guy picked us up. He was in a hurry to get to St. Mary's Hospital in Long Beach as his wife was having a baby. It was terrifying! The roads were slick, and he was driving that car over seventy miles an hour. I pulled out my rosary from my pocket and said to the Blessed Mother, "If anything happens, I hope it won't be fatal and we won't have an accident."

Once we hit the railroad grade and the car left the road. It flew about forty feet before it touched down again, into a dangerous skid.

*This guy is going to get us killed*, I thought. I kept praying that whatever happened, we wouldn't be killed.

He lost control of the automobile when coming into Los Angeles. I braced my feet against the dashboard just before we smashed into a brick building. When the car came to a halt, it was pretty well demolished, almost totaled. There was an awesome stillness. I saw the driver slumped over the wheel.

Fortunately, we all survived. Lou Kotch had a bruised shoulder, the driver a sore neck, and me a bruised right hip, but our Blessed Mother had been with us.

We hadn't gotten home yet so we still had to bum a ride the rest of the way. I will never forget how happy I was when a guy picked us up in his Model T. We rode about twenty miles per hour down the street till I got to my house and Louie Kotch got to his. I didn't tell my folks about the accident because it wouldn't have done any good anyway. After all that, we eventually got out to Culver City to play in the ballgame against St. Augustine's only to get rained out in the third inning. Then we had to bum our way back to Little Rock.

I'll never forget that weekend the Blessed Mother prevailed. Thank God we came out of it without losing our lives or being tremendously hurt.

I worked three or four summers in Little Rock; they were just great. I got to know the migrants, the fruit growers, and to enjoy the beauty of the desert, plus learn about Bartlett pears. When that work came to an end, Hermes said, "I might be able to get you a job in the studios."

"I'll be glad to get anything," I replied.

I was about twenty or twenty-one years old when Hermes brought me to meet Sid Rogell and Dave Garber, respectively the manager and superintendent of RKO Pictures. After I told them I needed a job, they talked to me for a while. "Where would you like to start?" they finally asked.

"Wherever I can," I responded. "By the way, I won't be staying permanently because I intend to quit at the end of the summer."

"What? You want us to hire you, and you're only going to stay for three or four months and then quit? There is no future in that for us or for you. We want to hire someone who might have a future with us."

"Well, no," I said, "I want to leave at summer's end to become a Catholic priest."

"What!"

These two Jewish gentlemen then said, "We gotta help this young man get a job, especially if he wants to become a priest."

They contacted the maintenance department to see if a temporary job was available. (An Irishman named Mike Brady headed up that department.) "Mike, do you have any jobs in the maintenance department?"

"No, we're filled," he replied.

"Well, make some work for this young man here."

"Hell, I don't know what I can do."

"Don't say 'hell!' This man is going to be a priest."

Anyway I got the job.

I remember going into Mike's office. He had a picture of a rather sexy girl on the wall over his desk. He looked at it and said, "Oh Jesus, I shouldn't have that up for you to look at if you are going to be a priest."

I'll never forget coming in the next morning. The picture was down, and there was a watercolor of some flowers in its place. Obviously they had some respect for who I was and for what I was studying.

I loved doing maintenance work because working from set to set enabled me to see a lot of the actors perform. I'll never forget when George Gershwin died and this announcement came in over the loud speakers: "Let's have one minute of silence for George Gershwin, the great musician and composer." Everything shut down. The actors, directors, camera crews, etc., stood or sat in silence. It must have been the longest minute of their lives because they weren't used to silence. It was a long minute for me, too.

I used to enjoy watching John Barrymore perform. At that time his memory was poor. He, Jack Oakie, and Herbert Marshall were there, along with Lupe Velez and Gary Cooper. Gary and Lupe were kind of running around with each other then. She had a little Chihuahua dog that she really loved.

It was about that time that I met Fred Astaire. I was standing on top of a rubbish heap we were getting ready to put into disposal trucks when Hermes appeared, walking down the studio's Broadway Street with Fred Astaire. "Hey, Jim," Hermes said. "I want you to meet Mr. Astaire."

He was the central figure on the lot, its biggest star. I came down off the garbage bin and said, "Wait a minute, Mr. Astaire. My hand is dirty. I don't want to shake your hand."

"Look, my hand is clean, and yours is dirty; let's mesh," he responded.

We shook hands. I liked him, and for some reason it was mutual. That was the beginning of a friendship that lasted until I buried Fred when he died some years ago.

Whether at RKO or 20th Century Fox, I had some great times at the studios. I was able to observe Clark Gable and meet him later. Also, I was there when Lucille Ball was just a showgirl. Producer George Abbott had come out from New York to do a musical film with a little Cuban guy named Desi Arnaz. (Arnaz wore a distinguishing leather jacket.) It was there that he met Lucille Ball. The two of them were later married, and, of course, Desilu Productions resulted from that union.

I also recall Maureen O'Hara and Charles Laughton making that great film, *The Hunchback of Notre Dame*. I was there to observe them and see the make believe in their lives.

At that time two of the studio's leading young stars, Judy Garland and Mickey Rooney, were making films together. I remember thinking, *My gosh, they're about my age. They are so successful and making so much money, how in the world will they be able to handle all of this success?*

Now we know that as the years went on their success became

very difficult. Judy died a tragic death; Mickey tried to get his act together, but he had a number of marriages and many tough experiences. Success is very difficult to handle, especially for the young.

In later years I graduated from working in the maintenance department to working with Hermes in the choreographic department at 20<sup>th</sup> Century Fox. I interviewed showgirls, assisted Hermes around his office, and looked at films turned in by prospective dance teams. I got to meet a lot of dancers, both men and women. They were wonderful people.

One dance team from New York was called "Poppa and Estrella." They were a bomb! Hermes and I coined a phrase that if a thing was no good it was a "Poppa."

That was the first time I came in contact with homosexuality because some of the guys were gay. They were all in the closet then. I found them to be nice fellows—very much confused at times—but there was camaraderie among both straight and gay dancers.

Hermes himself was extremely talented and so good to his dancers. He led a good, solid Catholic Christian life. Everyone admired him because there was no hanky-panky taking place around him. He wanted his set to be decent and honorable and made sure the girls were treated with respect.

One of the dancers who did the lifts got extra pay for his work. He looked like a truck driver, but actually he was gay. The paper reported an incident stating that the police had caught him engaged in an indecent act with another male. I happened to be with Hermes when this man came to the office and asked, "Did you read the article in the paper about my moral failure?"

"I did," Hermes replied.

"I guess that there is no need for me to compete for one of the dance roles in this new film you are doing."

"The audition will be at one o'clock tomorrow," Hermes replied. "I want you to report there like everyone else. If you have the necessary talent, I will hire you regardless of what you did or what was in the papers."

"Mr. Pan, it sure is nice of you to do that."

"Scripture says that Christ told the sinful woman, 'Let he who is without sin cast the first stone,' so I'm not casting any stones. If your tryout is good, I will hire you."

And I believe Hermes did hire him for that film. That made a profound impact on me. Hermes always had enormous respect for the dancers' abilities and professionalism; they had a tremendous respect for him, too.

I used to watch Hermes prepare his dance routines. Fred Astaire would come to Hermes' office to discuss ideas and steps and then later on they would meet on the set with about sixty dancers and a piano player named Hal Bourne. Oftentimes Hermes seemed to have put little thought into what he was going to do. He never seemed worried or anxious. Beforehand, he'd be in his office playing gin rummy with Mrs. Kenny Williams and another associate, Angie Blue, a dance director, and me. When rehearsal time came, Hermes would leave for the set and when he walked onto it, all of the dancers would be watching him. He had this way of standing and putting his right hand behind his left ear, seeming lost in thought. Then he would say to Hal Bourne, "Give me this kind of a rhythm and beat." Bourne would start playing the piano and Hermes, the genius at work, would start improvising. All of a sudden, the dance began to develop!

Next Fred would come on the set, and the two of them would kibitz and work routines together—two great masters at work. Ginger Rogers would arrive and Hermes would work some steps for her into the routine. She was a magnificent partner for Fred. I'd be in and out, just observing all these things and helping out any way I could, even bringing in cigarettes and cakes. I was a great flunky.

At times I was able to teach catechism classes to actress June Haver on her set. I helped her through the Baltimore Catechism. Later on she became a Catholic.

Knowing I was about to become a priest, a lot of the guys, like the cameramen, and gals would come along, just to chat and confide.

Without realizing it, I was able to do a lot of apostolic work by talking to them about Christ and the church, and why it is important to be morally good.

One time I talked to Tyrone Power, a superbly handsome, wonderful actor who died prematurely. He was such a perfect gentleman. I also had conversations with Cesar Romero, who was a close friend of Tyrone's. They were starring in the film *Captain from Castile,* which was made in the early forties.

I used to see Clark Gable quite a bit. Here was a man who had charisma and charm that absolutely caught the attention of both men and women. I have never encountered anyone else with the charisma that he had. Clark oozed manliness and personality.

One night, Hermes, myself, Clark Gable, and his wife Sylvia Ashley were guests for dinner at the Astaire's ranch in Chatsworth in the San Fernando Valley. Fred, his wife, Phyllis, and Clark were unassuming people and so down to earth. Clark was a good conversationalist, especially regarding hunting, fishing, film, and life in general. It was nice talking with him.

One Sunday Hermes said to me, "By the way, Lucille Ball and Desi Arnaz have put together a pilot program for TV. They would like me to come out and critique it. Do you want to come along, too?"

"Sure, I'll tag along."

So, we went out to their home in Chatsworth. Present were Lucille Ball, Desi Arnaz, Hermes, and myself, plus June Haver and a showgirl who was Lucille Ball's sister. (She was with her husband.) They put on this original pilot of Desilu, the first one they had done.

Hermes thought it was quite good. "What do you think?" he asked.

"Oh, I don't know," I said. "I don't think it is so hot."

Was I wrong! This pilot became the source of the Desilu series. Of course, it turned out to be a jackpot. Desilu Productions later took over the studios at RKO, and Lucille Ball and Desi Arnaz were superstars. That shows what a judge of talent I was!

I enjoyed working with some of the other actors such as John Erickson and Ricardo Montalban. No matter how great the actors were they needed to reinforce their self-esteem. Even Fred Astaire worried about the success of each of his films. As a contractor or an engineer arrives at his middle years, he gets better and better, his skills more honed; but as far as the actors were concerned, they were the talent *and* the product. They were always critiquing themselves and worrying about the future. They did not want their latest picture to be a bomb.

Those days I spent in the studios were really instrumental in helping my vocation to the priesthood. Every time I left at the end of the summer I was always more determined to become a priest. I saw so much of the superficial atmosphere and passing glamour of the studio life and its lack of reality.

The seminary did not know I was working with dancers. One time someone asked my mother, "Why do you allow your son to be with all those beautiful showgirls? He shouldn't be out there if he is going to be a priest."

Characteristic of my mother, she said, "If he can't handle all those beautiful women now, he shouldn't become a priest."

*Those*, I thought, *were really wise words.*


When I was working at the RKO, part of my job as a janitor was cleaning some of the projection rooms, the halls, the toilets, and the offices. I told the boss that I reported to work at seven o'clock p.m. and only worked till two a.m., that I didn't need eight hours to get the job done."

"Oh, you don't?" he said.

"Yes. If I do it right, can I take an hour to sit around and read and eat my lunch or do as I choose?"

"Well, let's find out if you can do it," he responded. After that, he came around and checked my work by putting his wet finger in the Venetian blinds to look for dust. He also inspected the toilets, carpeted halls, and wastepaper baskets. Finally he said to me, "Hey, kid, you can do it." I was allowed a leisurely hour off.

During my time at the studio, I had a chance to observe Orson Welles making the classic film *Citizen Kane*. Welles was a very young man, in fact very slim, and he would be at the studio up until one or two o'clock in the morning. He seemed to live in the projection room editing, working on, and observing footage. Of course, the final result was that magnificent film.

I used to leave the studio about two a.m. and walk down to Western Avenue to grab a streetcar that would take me to Figueroa Boulevard and Gage. Then I would walk about a mile and a half to get home, arriving about three a.m. My mother always had a sandwich and a glass of milk ready for me. I would eat and go to bed, wake up the next morning about ten or eleven o'clock, eat breakfast, and then bum a ride down to the beach. I would surf at Hermosa Beach at 17th Avenue and then again bum a ride home, returning about four p.m. My mother would have dinner for me at five, and then I would take a streetcar to the studio. That was my routine during the summertime.

I was making thirty-five cents an hour at the studio. It also gave me an opportunity to have some fun. A lot of things happened while I was there. For example, as janitor I used to clean the offices of Garson Kanin and a number of other producers and directors, as well as the dressing rooms of Fred Astaire and Ginger Rogers. As I got to know Fred and Phyllis Astaire very well, they had me and Hermes Pan to dinner at their home. At the table that night were two other guests, Alfred Gwynn Vanderbilt and his wife. I was twenty-three years of age and wore the only suit I owned—a black one—along with a white shirt and a red tie.

"By the way, Mr. O'Callaghan, what do you do?" Mr. Vanderbilt asked.

"I'm a janitor."

"What do you mean you are a janitor?"

"I clean Fred's dressing room at the studio." I looked at Fred. "As a matter of fact, Fred, while we are on the subject, I've told you again and again to put those empty Heineken beer bottles into the wastepaper basket, not on the floor, because you double my work."

"You're always on my back, Jim," he said.

"Well, do it."

"You are putting me on," Mr. Vanderbilt said.

"No, I'm not. I *am* Fred's janitor."

We kind of left him hanging with that and never let him know the difference.

I always had a wonderful time with the Astaires. His wife Phyllis was a reserved person, very devoted to Fred. When she first came to Hollywood, she was reluctant to have many entertainment industry people at their home. Some of those who came were Randolph Scott, Sam Goldwyn, and a few other quieter ones.

The Astaire's children were often around. Usually their daughter would eat in the company of her governess, but Fred, Jr., was there, as well as Peter, her son by her first marriage. I got to know them very well.

Hermes and I were invited to dinner frequently, and we had great discussions as Phyllis was interested in religion and in discussing topics of moral implication. Often Fred would nod off, and she would kid him for always falling asleep.

Phyllis was very close to Hermes, and he was very close to the Astaires. Sometimes the four of us would go up to Hermes's house and he would cook us dinner.

Hermes was a gourmet cook. In the course of the dinner, Fred might stand up and just do a spontaneous dance which was utterly out of this world. Hermes would also go through some steps. To see those two talented artists in action was a great joy. They were such gentlemen and so artistic.

Fred was very much interested in the Dodgers, the L.A. Rams, and sports in general. In his own way, Fred would bring up something about sports, but Hermes didn't know too much or care much about them. Neither did Phyllis. We used to kid each other about that.

Sometimes we would discuss radio and television. "I will never go on television," Fred vowed. Hermes and I had the last laugh on him because he did tremendous work in television later on and won many awards. *Astaire and Me* was a classic.

Fred was a very abstemious person. As soon as he arrived at Hermes' home he would have a glass of scotch and maybe one more at the most. He only smoked two or three cigarettes a day. It was obvious he was always under control.

He kept a set of drums in a room just off his bedroom. Sometimes we'd go in there and watch him play. With his great sense of rhythm, he was utterly magnificent. Of course, he contributed much to music and to the beat.

He also had a pool table. He was a real pool shark and a bit of a hustler. Years later I would come down from Long Beach to have dinner and Fred would announce, "Let's play some pool." I wasn't in his league at all, but Fred would challenge me: "I'll give you seventeen points to reach twenty-one and I'll start from scratch." I could not beat him as he was so skilled and fierce a competitor.

After dinner I had to make the long drive back to Long Beach. Then I would get up at five in the morning to celebrate the six-thirty a.m. Mass.


I remember one night Fred asked if I would come to the TV studio to see *An Evening with Fred Astaire,* which was performed live. His son, Fred, Jr., was the assistant producer. I was sitting next to him and after it was over I said, "Congratulations. It looks like your production is going to win a lot of awards. It's great!"

"You know, Father Jim, you will never see my name on one of these productions again," he replied. "I don't belong up there. I'm just hanging on my father's coattails. I don't have that talent or ability so, as of tonight, this is it."

I admired Fred, Jr., for that. He was a solid young guy, the son of a most successful and famous father, and it was very tough for him. Later he went to Paso Robles where he bought a ranch, built a home, and raised cattle and horses. He led a happy life. I always liked him because he was a very humble man, in so many ways like his father.

Once I went to New York with Hermes. We met up with Fred and Phyllis. Despite being a legend in the public eye, he was such a shy person that as we walked the streets of New York, he would push up his coat collar around his ears and pull his hat down over his face so that he would not be recognized. Yet everyone still recognized the Astaire walk and his silhouette.

We were sitting down in a restaurant having dinner one night, and Fred was slumped down in his chair so that he wouldn't be recognized. There was a band playing, and all of a sudden we heard one Astaire tune after another. Quickly the spotlight was on him as he really tried to hide by sinking even lower into his chair. In many ways he was a self-effacing person.

I also recall being in one of the stylish restaurants in Beverly Hills one night with his sister Adele, Phyllis, Fred, and Hermes. Many other show people—actors, actresses, starlets were there also—but as soon as Fred walked into that chic restaurant, an awesome stillness filled the place because they all recognized the talent and the genius of this humble man.

Fred loved horses. He and Phyllis owned a horse ranch. I think one of the happiest moments in his life was when his horse, Triplicate, won the Hollywood Gold Cup.

Fred had asked me if I could join him for the race but I said, "No, I'm not allowed to go to horse races." (At that time it was forbidden for priests in our archdiocese to go to the track.) "Fred, I can't go," I repeated.

"If I win, can you join me for dinner at Romanoff's?"

"Well, I'll ask my pastor."

I'll be darned if his horse didn't win the Gold Cup!

I asked my pastor if I could go, but he was not too happy about it. Monsignor Bernard J. Dolan was a tough Irish pastor, but he finally let me. I'll never forget going into the restaurant and seeing Fred being interviewed by Vincent X. Flaherty, the sportswriter. Fred had $100 bills stacked in his hat band and coat pockets. He was completely overjoyed because his horse had won.

Although Phyllis had been one of the Socialite 400 [sic], she was dropped from the group because she had married an actor. Still, she was versatile, the type of woman who could be as common as clay, solicitous to everyone, yet sharp as a tack, sophisticated, and altogether just a lovely person. (She was from a very wealthy family in New York, the Bulls.)

Phyllis seemed very fragile in appearance, but I had been out at the Astaire ranch in the San Fernando Valley where I actually saw her shoveling horse manure, fixing fences, taking care of the horses, and carrying a shotgun as she hunted dove. She was a tough little lady, and, at the same time, as gentle as one could possibly want.


I remember one night when Hermes, Fred, and Nelson Riddle were at my place for dinner, talking about the beat of the bossa nova. Fred said there was a half beat in there somewhere that they did not pick up, but Nelson Riddle, who was educated in music, and Hermes, who had a lot of good vibes and common sense in that area, disagreed. "You guys are wrong!" Fred said. "There is a half beat in there that you are missing."

Of course, I knew nothing. I couldn't tell if there was one beat or two beats. But I'll never forget the morning after our dinner Nelson Riddle called. "Do you have Fred's private phone number?" he asked.

"Yes."

"Could you give it to me? Fred was right. There was a half beat in there that I missed."

This was just another incident showing the talent and genius of Fred Astaire. He was absolutely outstanding in his love and understanding of music.


One of the funniest stories regarding Hermes was the time he had received a call from Cole Porter in New York, asking him to come visit to discuss dancing in the show Cole was about to produce on

Broadway. Hermes flew back to New York and met with Cole in his apartment. Cole was a very fastidious man and wanted to take Hermes out to a wonderful dinner where they could also discuss the possibility of Hermes choreographing the play. The restaurant, chosen some days ahead, was the Pavionne, and Porter had a menu meticulously planned with various courses and the proper wines.

They met first in Cole Porter's apartment. Hermes said it was very beautifully decorated. They had a few drinks, discussed the play, and then went out to the Pavionne, a magnificent restaurant with all the waiters hovering over them. Cole was the perfect host. During the entremets and soup, Hermes realized that it was Friday. (In those days Catholics did not eat meat on Friday.)

Hermes was really worried about this because Cole had ordered a specially prepared chicken dinner for the entree. So, Hermes figured a way to solve the problem without discussing it or saying anything to Cole. The chicken was served along with the vegetables. As they were conversing, Hermes would flip a piece of chicken off his plate into the napkin on his lap. He kept doing this throughout the course of the meal. Finally, all the chicken was in his lap.

The waiters came, took up the soiled dishes, and cleaned the table. Then they brought out dessert and coffee. Following coffee and an after dinner drink, Cole said, "Well, I guess we'll go back now and continue our discussion at my apartment." As they were getting up to leave the restaurant, Hermes forgot all about the chicken in his lap. He shook out the napkin like a bullfighter flourishes his cape. The chicken flew all over the red carpeted restaurant floor!

Cole was startled, but said nothing. Likewise, Hermes kept quiet; he thought the best thing to do was just to go on with the charade.

Fred Astaire telephoned me a couple of days later. "Jim, something strange happened. Cole Porter called me and said, 'You know your friend Hermes is an awfully talented man. I really like him, and I'd like to have him do the show for me, but is he a little weird?'"

"Why?" Fred asked.

"Well, we had a great time in my apartment and then went out to dinner at the Pavionne. We discussed everything, and were enjoying ourselves, but for some reason or other he kept flicking the chicken off his plate into his napkin on his lap. Then, at the end of our wonderful meal, with a flourish he stood, shook the napkin, and the chicken went all over the floor. What goes with this guy?"

"Actually he's a Catholic who didn't want to eat meat on Friday," Fred explained. "I guess he thought that was the best way he could handle it without disturbing you since you went to such extremes planning this wonderful meal."

That's the kind of man Hermes was. He lived his faith and this was an example of it.

When I was a theologian at St. John's Seminary, Hermes's mother became very ill, and I visited her. (She always called him "Snooks," which is an old southern nickname.) "You know he is a very sensitive person. When I am gone would you look after him?" she asked. "He needs someone he can trust and who will care for him."

"I'll do what I can," I reassured her, "although I don't think he needs me."

Her death was a devastating blow to Hermes. They had been living in Encino in a beautiful Spanish home amidst orange trees, with a swimming pool and a badminton court. After she died, Hermes said, "I will not live in that house again. I don't want to go back."

I didn't know what to do. At that time, I was in the seminary. I talked to my mother and father, who still had my little quarters consisting of a bedroom and a half bath in the back of their house. They said he could come there and stay until he got over his grief and obtained another home.

Hermes was devastated at the funeral. He did not even want to go to the cemetery. Needing a little comfort, he did choose to live at our house at 229 East Gage Avenue in Los Angeles. Our home was a very simple place compared to his in Encino.

He lived with my parents and my sister Mary for about a year, until his home was built in Studio City. My mother fed him breakfast and prepared other meals for him whenever he was there. Sometimes people would call him on our house phone— Fred Astaire, Louella Parsons, Joan Caulfield, Kenny Williams—or some of his other friends from the studio or family members. It meant nothing to my mother. She simply said, "Mr. Astaire (or whoever it might have been) is on the phone."

Hermes felt very comfortable at our home. It was beautiful to see the close relationship between Hermes and my father, who was a difficult man to know as a parent. He really liked Hermes. They would go off and have a beer at Covonovich's bar on San Pedro Street or go to Joe's poolroom. Hermes loved being with our family.

During Christmas vacation, which I spent at home, Hermes would tell me, "On Christmas Eve I will be giving a party in my bungalow at the studio for the dancers, some of the actors, and the chorus girls. No matter what, come and pick me up and bring me home. That night I'll go with you to the Midnight Mass at the Little Sisters of the Poor." He had a great devotion to these sisters as he had worked for them when he first came to Los Angeles and had no work or funds.

I remember going out one particular Christmas Eve. It was always the same old story at parties, where I had to be the bad guy. As soon as he got a few belts, the dancers would say, "Oh don't take him! Don't take him away!"

Then Hermes would say, "Don't take me; I'm happy right where I am."

"Now Hermes, you told me I had to get you out of here." And I *did* have to get him out of there.

This was a difficult problem. I remember once driving him home when he was pretty well under the influence, and my mother gave him a really big straight whiskey when she met him at the front door. "Oh, Mom, for the love of God, he doesn't need this right now," I said. But that's the way it was.

After living with my parents for a year, he came to me simply devastated. Apparently he had gone to my mother, handed her a check for the year, and she had said, "Get out! We took you in as a friend, and you are treating us as though you were a boarder! Now get out!"

"Well, Hermes," I said, "you really blew that one because you know she didn't take you in for money."

"What can I do?"

"I don't know. She likes green. Maybe you could get her a green coat or something and bring it as a peace offering."

He got her a little green coat, and, thank God, she accepted it. Peace was restored, but he learned a big lesson. She liked Hermes for himself, not for what he represented or what he could give. This is yet another example of the great influence she was in our lives.

Hermes began to become very comfortable with the seminarians—my classmates McCarthy, Murray, Karl, and Phil Grill. We had a lot of great times together. Hermes loved to discuss theology and philosophy. He would have been an outstanding professor, especially in philosophy, because he had a keen Greek philosophical mind. He could discern, he had great retention, and he read extensively. After skating or skiing at Big Bear, we'd sit around the fire and discuss religion and philosophy until maybe one or two o'clock in the morning. We just had a ball. He enjoyed every bit of that because it was so different from the life of the studio—the tinsel, and the superficiality. Discussions were lively and challenging. He exerted a great influence on us young seminarians, and we in turn were a tremendous influence on him.

Once I went to Europe with Hermes. Since practically all I knew was sports and their memorabilia, I thought I might be able to learn something about art. I learned a lot from him as we toured France, Spain, and Italy. He would always frame a village square in France, or a street scene in Italy, or perhaps a beautiful plaza in Spain, and say, "Look at the beauty there."

We also went looking for paintings in galleries, shops, etc. I began to develop an appreciation of art. I had no talent, but I began to appreciate the paintings and art forms.

We drove through the countryside taking in the scenery from lakes, vineyards, village squares, and churches. I learned a great deal just by being with him and sharing in his wonderful appreciation of art, nature, and music. Otherwise, I would have had little appreciation for them.

Meanwhile, I picked up a few paintings along the way. In Italy, we went to the top of a building in Rome where there was a gallery that featured works by artist Ivan Moska. Hermes gave me one titled, "The Fly." It cost fifty dollars. I picked it because it is a palette knife painting showing a black spider advancing toward a red fly caught in its web.

That painting has always hung in my home. It tells me that the spider is the devil and he is always trying to entrap me—the fly. Now it is recognized as a fine painting and much more valuable.

As for dinners, we would select a three- or four-star restaurant one night and then a more reasonable family restaurant the next. We enjoyed the contrast.

We also made a trip to Acapulco, Mexico. It gave me an appreciation of Spanish art and literature.

Hermes and I talked about so many things. He was not an educated man in the sense of having gone to college, but he had a tremendous appreciation of life, travel, reading, and personal experiences. His library was characteristic of a priest or a philosopher. People were surprised by the theological books he possessed and which he read and understood.

One day Fred and Phyllis Astaire called to ask if Hermes and I would meet them at Romanoff's. They wanted us to join them for dinner with a friend of Lord and Lady Cavendish, a young flyer who was an ace in World War II. I believe his name was Colonel Gus Daymond, or Major Gus Daymond. This flyboy had it all together. His image had been on the cover of *Life* magazine with some other war heroes.

Gus was a super hero. He was Mr. Big, with a waxed mustache, riding crop, boots, officer's pants, and all that lettuce on his lapel. He had attended Cal Tech and was bright, young, and very handsome. I thought *Man, this guy has the whole world under control.*

Gus brought a starlet along to dinner. We had a discussion about Lord and Lady Cavendish, whom he had come to know well when he was flying fighter planes in England. During the course of the meal, the question of a miracle came up, and Gus said, "Let's not be ludicrous. There is no such thing. As a matter of fact, regarding good and evil, the only thing I think is sinful at all is stealing; nothing else is a sin."

Hermes handled that very well. (At that time he was conducting classes in his home to which he invited film people—especially dancers and actors—for a series of lectures on the Catholic Church. Father Eugene Burke, CSP, Father John Cremmins, and I would conduct the classes at different times.) Hermes said to Gus, "Why don't you come some night and participate in our inquiry class? Maybe you will learn something."

He accepted the invitation and arrived with a starlet as his date. He got hooked, and after that he came often. Finally Hermes said to me, "Gus would like to take instruction on a regular basis."

I replied, "I'm in Long Beach and it's way too far for him to come. Maybe I can arrange with Father John Cremmins at St. Charles in North Hollywood to instruct Gus."

Gus did take his instructions. In the meantime, the film gossip columns would be stating that the war hero Gus Daymond had been with this starlet or that starlet. He was much featured and people liked to be around him because of his war fame. Within a matter of months Gus was received into the Catholic Church as a convert. After his conversion he came to me and said, "Father Jim, every time I am in my bed in North Hollywood and I hear the bells of the church ringing in the morning, I think *I should be there to receive my Lord in the Eucharist*." So, Gus would get up and go to Mass.

After his conversion, I lost track of him. Amazingly, a couple of years ago I received a letter from him from San Diego. "Do you remember me? This is Gus Daymond. I am retired now and financially well off. I have done very well in aeronautics.

When I heard from a priest in the Laguna area that you were at St. John Vianney, I thought I would contact you. Remember that little book you gave me years ago? Well, I read it every day. I also go to daily Mass. I am very much at peace and happy with my Catholic faith." He then asked, "How is Hermes? If you talk to him, arrange for us to get together and have dinner."

I phoned Hermes that night. "Who do you think I heard from?"

"Who?"

"Gus Daymond."

"What!"

"Yes."

"Give me his number so I can call, and let's get together for dinner."

"Absolutely."

We set up a date. That phone call turned out to be our last conversation. Hermes was found dead in his chair the next morning. Isn't it amazing that contact with Daymond had me call Hermes just then? I am grateful that we talked just before he died. God works in strange ways.

I spent a total of five years at the junior seminary as I had to repeat one. I never cared much for it, and it was a great relief to graduate. I'll never forget when I asked my Dad, "Are you coming to my graduation?"

At the time, he was working the graveyard shift as a stationary engineer for General Petroleum Corporation. He was very dedicated, and it was difficult for him to get time off. I remember him saying, "I'm busy at work; and after all, I see you every day."

I thought that was rather amusing. Indeed he didn't go to the graduation, but it didn't bother me.

In those days we didn't need to be reassured that we were loved. Did our parents love us? We took it for granted. We knew they did. They would correct, discipline, or do whatever was necessary, but the question of whether or not they loved us never came to our minds. We didn't worry about self-esteem. My father always made it very clear to me, "You are an O'Callaghan, and automatically, even though you have no money, you have class. Take care of that name." I was always proud of being an O'Callaghan and felt I had class.

It was a happy day to leave the junior seminary.


For my final two years I went up to St. Patrick's Seminary in Menlo Park, CA. An old brick building three stories high, it was the major seminary for the archdiocese of San Francisco, preparing seminarians from Oakland, San Francisco, Vallejo, Menlo Park, and Sacramento.

It was my first time being away from home for an extended time. When I first got there, it rained for a great number of days. It was dismal.

The school was run by the Sulpician Fathers. This was a wonderful but old-fashioned seminary, steeped in tradition. I was very homesick for the first couple of weeks but hung in. I was really surprised by my homesickness. I would not unpack my bags for the first five or six days. The constant wet weather didn't help. A theologian friend, Ed Wade, helped me through it.

As seminarians, we worked various jobs on vacations but recreated together. We had lots of fun. We tried to keep the recreation separate from the company of the young ladies. I think it was a good discipline. At times one of our seminary buddies would say, "Well guys, good-bye. I met this girl during vacation, and, man oh man, this is it."

We'd say, "Well, that's that." If they were drawn to marriage and called to that vocation rather than the priesthood, then we felt that is where they belonged

There was a great mix of men. The seminary was divided into two sections: One section was for the philosophers, and the other was for the theologians. There was a real line of demarcation. As philosophers we did not socialize with the theologians. One remained in his own section of the large grounds and buildings that comprised about forty acres. There was plenty of space to function in. The seminary consisted of old wooden buildings for both philosophers and theologians, and each student had his own room. The rules were very strict. We were not allowed to enter any other student's room unless absolutely necessary. No smoking was allowed in the building because it was a wooden structure.

We wore our cassocks and collars for classes and recreation at all times. The only time we were allowed to remove our cassocks was when we were in our rooms, taking field trips, or playing athletic games. It was a crowded seminary then, with a wonderful bunch of students.

There was a tremendous spirit of rivalry between the San Francisco and Los Angeles seminarians. We constantly played basketball, football, baseball, and handball games. We always referred to San Francisco as "Frisco," and that really fried the San Francisco students! They would tell us, "You should say 'San Francisco'." We called ourselves "L.A." The basketball and football games that took place between the San Francisco students and the L.A. students were tough, challenging, and sometimes pretty bloody. Later the faculty had to cut out some of the contests because of the enormous rivalry.

The seminary was very strict. Except for a few times during the year, we were not allowed to leave the seminary. We had permission to go home for Christmas and Easter; other times what we had was called an "eight to eight." We could leave the seminary at eight o'clock in the morning, but we had to be back at eight o'clock at night. On our day off, we were allowed to take hikes or recreate in other ways. Sometimes we would dash up to San Francisco to try to take in a show or a ballgame.


After I had been there a few weeks, somebody asked me, "You want to play ball this afternoon?"

"Yes."

"What position do you want to play?"

"I'll take third base."

I didn't realize what was happening, but the baseball field was near some trees. The wise seminarians had contacted a caterer in Menlo Park for milk shakes. "Third base" meant strawberry ice cream. "First base" might stand for plum or peach. After we placed the order, the local ice cream parlor would park its truck next to the trees. Then we would walk over there to pick up our order. For some reason, it always tasted better that way.

The meals at the seminary were eaten in silence. A lector read from Scripture and the fathers of the church during the meals. The dessert we always called "mysterium" because no one knew what the dessert was or what it was made of. Our meals were very regular and disciplined.

I admired the Sulpician priests because they attended every religious ceremony we had. They got up early in the morning to pray with us. They were also at the benedictions and the holy hours. There was a tremendous reverence and spirituality among the Sulpician fathers. I was assigned a spiritual director, Father Redon, a very saintly man.

When I first went to see him, he just didn't seem to me to be the type of man I would pick for a spiritual director. He was very thin, almost emaciated, and wearing small wire glasses. As I sat down before him I thought to myself, "My God, what am I doing with this man?" After all, I was a brash, rough-hewn type of guy. He looked at me quietly, his piercing eyes appraising me through his glasses. He said to me in his French accent, "Has Jesus been good to you?"

I thought, *My God, what is this Jesus has been good to me?* I realized as I looked at this priest that he really penetrated me so that he seemed to read my soul.

He was a magnificent spiritual director. He had a great way of discerning spirits. He would tell one seminarian, "You don't belong here; get out!" He would tell another seminarian, "Hey, don't leave! You belong here; God wants you to be a priest."

He was very ascetical. When he said Mass, he almost seemed to levitate from the altar. For two years, I was blessed to have Father Redon as my spiritual director. He really tried, in his unique way, to work with me.

We also had a Father Grotto, who was kind of pompous, but a

talented man and a great choir director. Our choir was made up of some eighty seminarians, a magnificent choral group. One day he said to them, "There is something wrong with this choir! There is a voice that's causing problems. I'm going to audition each one of you alone until I find out who this person is."

We each took turns. When I got there, he tested my voice, and then he said, "You are the one! You are out!" I was put out of the wonderful choir at St. Patrick's Seminary! As a matter of fact I have never regained any confidence since then, and I lost all my self-esteem. I'll never forget being put out of Father Grotto's choir, and what's more I was never allowed back in again!

Each professor received a name from us. As we were with them all the time, we really got to know them. We named the rector "Beppo." He was a little guy; about five foot four, with a prominent bulbous nose. In the morning, before he gave spiritual direction, he laid a bandana handkerchief on his desk that was on a raised platform in the prayer hall. Next he took a snuff box out of his cassock pocket and placed it on the cloth. Occasionally he would snuff it behind the bandana. We wouldn't even dare crack a smile because our professors had our destiny in their hands.

We saw a lot of wonderful guys leave, and it was tough on all of us. But a great number stayed. It was challenging, but many of the best opted for priesthood.

After a number of years, suddenly we were facing ordination, an event that was hard to believe. I never thought I would make it. During the whole summer I said, "My God, I'm actually making it."

I was ordained by Archbishop John J. Cantwell on April 27, 1943. I didn't get a big high out of this. I was too nervous. It was just something I had to go through. I think the only thrill that I had at the ceremony was after we were ordained to the priesthood and our parents and friends came to receive our priestly blessings for the first time. I will never forget my father and mother coming up and kneeling at the rail to receive my first priestly blessing, seeing my father's big, rough, calloused hands. He had on a shirt and tie, and he looked so dignified. My mother was wearing her hat, the green coat (from Hermes), and a lovely dress. She knelt by his side. I saw those two people, and I thought, "My God." As I went to give them my priestly blessing, I felt that I should get down on my knees and ask for their blessing. Without them I could not have made it. That to me was the most moving feature of my ordination on that day.

Next my sister Mary, Hermes, and many others approached and I gave them my blessing. Although some other relatives were there, too, my brother, who was in the naval service at boot camp, was unable to attend. I certainly missed him.

We held a reception at our home on 229 East 63rd Street, Los Angeles. This is because we couldn't afford a hall. However, we had a ball there, partially closing off the street and having food and drinks out on the front lawn and whiskey in the back bedroom. The festivities went on all day and into the night. People came from everywhere—the guys I played ball with, seminarians, ex-seminarians, some of my brother's friends, the studio people, and all the people I had worked with over the years. They were so very proud that one of their friends had actually made it to the priesthood. Most surprising was that out of our entire group it was me. For me to make it was an amazing thing.

My mother took me aside at one point during the reception and said, "You no longer belong to your father and me. Now you belong to the Church. Your father and I will never interfere with your life. Be a good priest; be at the service of the people, and if you want to come and see us you can, but we will never interfere in your priestly life because you belong to the Church, Father Jim." She was so right and always on target.


Months before the ordination Hermes Pan had said, "I'd like to give you your chalice."

A priest's chalice is like a man's wedding ring. It's very important for the priest. I wanted one with a little Celtic design.

The chalice he had made had a node with a Celtic design carved in it. It came out simple and beautiful. I really love this chalice, and thank God I have been able to use it now for fifty-nine years. On the interior bottom of that chalice Hermes had inscribed something that really touched my heart:

> *Behold the precious blood flowing from the wounds of Christ, taking away the sins of the world. May it protect you, preserve you, and guide you lest you ever separate yourself from me." Hermes to Jim, May, 1943.*

When I buried Hermes a few years ago at Good Shepherd Parish in Beverly Hills, many studio people were there, including actors, producers, writers, and dancers, along with his own family and other mutual friends and admirers. During the course of the eulogy I said, "You see that chalice sitting there upon the altar? That was given to me by Hermes Pan way back in 1943. I have celebrated thousands of Masses using that chalice in which the wine in that chalice and the bread on the patin are changed into the precious body and blood of Jesus Christ." I continued, "Now to think in this funeral Mass, I'm offering up the precious body and blood in the very chalice he gave to me. May Hermes Pan rest in peace."

The chalice is very dear to me. It bespeaks my priesthood. It seems like an extension of my hands. Frequently priests leave their chalices to someone special. I was going to leave mine to a great friend, Frank McKay, a Maryknoller who has since died. Recently Father Joe Shea, my former associate and great friend, came to me and said, "Hey, Jim, I want to ask you something."

"What's that, Joe?"

"About your chalice…"

"Yeah, what about it?"

"I wish you would give me that chalice when you die."

"Yeah, Joe, I'll give it to you, but don't be breathing down my neck waiting for it to happen. You will have to wait for it!"

I am very happy to say that the chalice that means so much to me, will go into the hands of one Father Joe Shea, a wonderful priest, upon my demise. The chalice could not go to more priestly hands.

These are tremendous memories that I have. And after a couple of weeks of vacation following my ordination, our first assignments came out. Lo and behold I was assigned to none other than Bernard J. Dolan, a tough icon in the archdiocese, in the parish of St. Anthony's in Long Beach.

Thus began a real saga in my life.

# PART TWO:
## LIVING OUT THE PRIESTHOOD

# THE FIRST PARISH

I received my first assignment in 1943. Father Frank Roughan, who was the associate at my home parish, St. Columbkille, drove me over to St. Anthony's Parish in Long Beach, California. I arrived with a couple of suitcases filled with clothes and a few books.

We rang the front doorbell and were met by Monsignor Bernard J. Dolan himself. He was a gruff, tough Irishman, a former chancellor of the archdiocese and a member of the Archbishops' Council. Monsignor had worked very closely with Archbishop Cantwell.

"I'm your new assistant, Jim O'Callaghan," I announced. ("Assistant" was what they called us in those days.)

"Yeah, I know. I have been expecting you."

A dominant and feared person in the archdiocese, he had this way of glancing sideways at people. The times I did look directly into his piercing blue eyes, I knew he meant what he said, just like my father. I have only met three infallible men in my life: the Pope, my father, and Monsignor Dolan.

After a few pleasantries, he announced, "Tomorrow morning, Father, the first thing you do is go over to the girls' high school and teach the seniors religion at 8:45. Then at 9:45 you go to the boys' high school and teach religion."

"Well, Monsignor," I said. "I have never taught. I wouldn't know how to teach. I was just ordained."

He replied, "You mean to tell me you don't think you can go and teach those classes?"

"I've never taught," I repeated.

"Are your bags unpacked yet?"

"No."

"Well, if you don't get in those classrooms and teach, I suggest you don't unpack. The red car runs right down Atlantic Boulevard to Los Angeles. You can get on that red car and report to Archbishop Cantwell tomorrow morning and tell him you are not fit for this parish."

"Yes, sir."

I immediately left and went over to the brothers' home, across the street from St. Anthony's Church. There I met a Brother Stanilaus, a wonderful, well respected veteran brother. I told him, "Monsignor Dolan has assigned me to teach senior religion in both the girls' and boys' high schools. I've never done that. I'm just a newly ordained priest. How do I teach?"

"Can you maintain discipline?" he inquired.

At that time I was 190 pounds. "That, I can do."

"Well, if you can maintain discipline you will be able to teach," he declared. "Just prepare for each class, keep ahead of the kids, and don't try to outfox or fool them."

"Thank you, Brother."

I reported back to monsignor: "I'll be in the classrooms tomorrow morning." Foolishly, I added, "Boy, I hope it's busy around here because I really want to do a lot of work."

"One other thing I want you to know, Father," he instructed me. "You are here to minister to the people; they are not to minister unto you. You are on duty at all times, except for your day off. So be here and work hard and we'll all get along together."

That was how we started.


It was a rather unique parish. The church was located across the street from a large convent, on the corner of 6th and Olive Streets in Long Beach.

We had four priests, twenty-seven Immaculate Heart nuns, and nineteen Holy Cross brothers. The brothers were from Notre Dame University and St. Mary's College in Texas. Our high schools had six hundred girls and about seven hundred boys; our grammar school had about six hundred students. Most of the classes were taught by religious brothers and sisters, while we priests participated by teaching both in the boys' and girls' high schools. When we could, we also taught in the grammar school. It was an excellent, incredible Catholic institution with a stimulating atmosphere that produced a tremendous *esprit de corps.*

Of course, the power behind it all was Monsignor Dolan. Even though he had one principal for the girls' high school and another one for the boys' high school, he was in charge. It was a tremendous block of schools that produced marvelous young men and women over the years. Many future marriages took place between the boys and girls who had attended our school.

One year we had six priests ordained from the senior class. Among them was Archbishop William Levada of San Francisco, Bishop George Niederauer of Salt Lake City, Monsignor Anthony Leuer, Monsignor John Fitzgerald, and Father George O'Brien. A number of other young men also were ordained in future years. We had vocations to the Oblates, the Jesuits, Franciscans, Claritans, and other religious orders.

Unbelievably, from every senior class of the girls' high school, there would normally be nine or ten young ladies who entered religious life. The Immaculate Heart community received most of these aspirants.

We had 6:30 Mass at the sisters' convent, the church, and the brothers' home every morning. I celebrated Mass for either the brothers or sisters in their respective chapels; Monsignor Dolan always said his in the church. We started the day early, and we worked all day, until late at night. The parish presented a great opportunity for camaraderie and varied ministries. What a great place to begin my priesthood! I had the opportunity to work with high school students, take census throughout the parish, and administer the sacraments. Monsignor wanted us on our feet at all times.

I very much enjoyed the camaraderie of the sisters and brothers. I often envied the brothers because their only duties were to teach the high school boys, prepare their classes, and be the outstanding gentlemen religious they were. Sometimes I thought they were lucky because they didn't have to do all the pastoral work that we priests had in addition to teaching in the high school.

The brothers had a small, convenient little chapel. I would literally sneak into there after I finished my second class in the high school and spend some time before the Blessed Sacrament.

Then I had to report to the center and begin my pastoral duties. Monsignor Bernard Dolan said there was no such thing as idle time. A room was only a place to hang your hat. (We wore hats in those days!) How often he would lose his and borrow mine — we both had big heads. Then, of course, he lost mine.

It was hard to get a nap and find some leisure time because I was either in the parlor counseling or catechizing, or on the street taking census, meeting with people, or in the school. I was always on the run. It was a very busy parish, quite consuming, but I loved every minute that I was there.


The senior assistant, Father Mike Lawlor, who was a wonderful Irish priest, took me on my very first sick call. "Would you like to go out to see how we take care of the sick, especially when they are critical?"

We soon arrived at the home of a well-known couple, Officer Logan and his wife, who was dying of cancer. They had quite a large family. Father Lawlor was compassionate, kind, and caring. I learned a lot as I saw him minister to her.

Mike also had a wonderful sense of humor. I loved him because he was an Irishman with a soft heart. At times I could play him like an instrument. For example, if I knew that Mike was getting uptight, I would say, "You know, Mike, you are not looking good. You need a rest. Get out! You should play some golf and enjoy yourself."

"By God, Jim," he'd say. "You know, I haven't been feeling well." And off he would go. I would cover for him, and at other times he for me.

Sometimes when I wanted him to cover for me and he had other plans, I'd say, "Mike, it looks like you should stay in. You might catch a cold. It seems to me like you are worn out."

"You know, Jim, I'll stay in."

This wonderful fellow whom people loved so much later became pastor of St. Cyril's in the San Fernando Valley. He died prematurely, but he left a wonderful, wonderful tradition of a loving priesthood. People still speak of his warm and compassionate ways.

Monsignor Dan Sullivan was the other associate with me. His great expertise in finances—he had been in the business world before he came into the priesthood—made him very helpful to Monsignor Dolan. Dan was a very competent priest who, along with parish works, could manage the business and finance of the church. He did not teach in the high school as he was more involved in rectory affairs.

Dan was a good influence in my early years. Later on I had the pleasure of living with him when I was chaplain of the Newman Club at Los Angeles City College and he was pastor of Good Shepherd Parish in Beverly Hills. I don't think Dan and I ever exchanged a cross word. He was always such a wonderful, charming, gentle, and capable priest.

St. Anthony's gave me an opportunity to work with the youth in our grammar and high schools. I also met a lot of elderly people. Many were retired farmers from Iowa. People used to joke that if you walked down any street in Long Beach and held up your finger, there would soon be a horseshoe around it!

I learned so much from ministering to the people. One day I was visiting homes on Golden Avenue, taking census by ringing doorbells, when I came across a little house which had a broken-down picket fence in front. The house was rather dilapidated. I walked up onto the little creaky front porch and spoke through the screen: "Are there any Catholics living here?"

A voice cried out, "So what!"

Another voice from deeper inside the house responded, "You shouldn't talk to a priest like that."

"Do you mind if I come in?" I asked.

"Suit yourself," she replied.

So I entered and saw an extremely sick young lady lying on a couch in the living room. She was very emaciated and quite hostile.

We sat and talked, but I got nowhere. Her mother kept interfering, saying that the girl should have more respect for a priest. I finally said, "Please, lady, leave her alone with me."

After speaking with her for a while, I found out she was a fallen-away Catholic. Then I said, "Well, I guess I'll leave. Do you mind if I come back?" As I went out the door, I remarked, "I want to come back because I want to help you."

She shrugged. "Suit yourself."

Over a period of weeks I came back to see her regularly. At the young age of thirty-four, she was dying of leukemia. It turned out that she had been a bar hostess on Beacon Street in San Pedro. She was soured on life, very unhappy. She felt life had shortchanged her because she was dying so young.

I had noticed that there were always a lot of people, such as longshoremen, bar hostesses, dock workers—and no doubt a few prostitutes—ministering and caring for her. They brought her groceries, soup, fruit, and flowers. There were also other caretakers, young ladies who would administer a shot of morphine to ease her pain. One was a nurse. I was really impressed by the devotion they all had for this young woman.

After two weeks she began to look forward to my visits. I talked to her about life…where she came from as a child, her prayer life, and why she had abandoned her faith. Ultimately, I got her reconciled to the church and began to instruct her in the Baltimore Catechism. Slowly but surely I prepared her for her First Confession.

I have never seen anyone become holier or more resigned. I talked with her about suffering, and in time she made her confession, received Holy Communion, and accepted the Anointing of the Sick and Apostolic Blessing. She now was going to confession and receiving the Eucharist regularly. She was very close to God.

She was so fragile that her body seemed almost transparent. Eventually she got so weak that she could hardly move her head. I got a decade of the Rosary to put around her wrist and taught her how to say the Rosary. She did this every day. I had never seen such a beautiful change in a person over a period of weeks. She died a peaceful death. All the while people kept a comforting circle around her, watching and caring for her. Anyone that was loved so much by the average person certainly had to be full of love herself.

I buried her from a little church near Beacon Street. (The church would later be a mission assigned to the new church, Mary Star of the Sea.) On the day of the funeral, the little church was jammed packed with people from Beacon Street and the surrounding areas. It was one glorious funeral. That little lady certainly went to her God. She was an enormous inspiration to me as a young priest.

My faith was constantly affirmed by having the privilege of assisting and enabling people to enter into the kingdom of heaven and also to return back into the bosom of Mother Church. (This is what we used to say back in the 1940s and 1950s.)


I recall another incident on a Fourth of July holiday. I had returned from San Pedro and was alone in the St. Anthony's Rectory when the doorbell rang. I opened the door to find a grimy-looking man in his mid-50s. He was thin, unshaven, watery-eyed, and his clothes were baggy and soiled. He stood staring at me, unsteady on his feet and reeking of alcohol.

Breaking the silence, I asked, "What can I do for you, sir?"

Hesitantly, he thrust into my hand a piece of torn wrapping paper on which he had written, "I have just had my tongue amputated because of cancer. I am terribly distressed. I don't really know my God, and I wonder if you could teach me about the Lord and the Catholic Church. I need help."

His note certainly got my attention, but I realized he was in no condition for catechism at that time. "Come on in," I said, "and I'll give you one of my cards."

"*If you ever need me,*" I wrote on the back, "*get this card to me and I will find you.*" Then, caught up in my parochial ministry, I soon forgot the incident.

A few months later, a nurse came to the St. Anthony's Rectory and presented me with the card I had given the man that day. It was now soiled, bent, and torn. On the back, however, was a note. "*Father,*" he had written, "*I need you now! I am a patient in the Harriman Jones Clinic on the second floor.*" He had also written his name and room number.

I immediately drove there and was escorted to his room by a nurse. Just before we entered, she stopped. "Can you handle cancer that is very disfiguring?" she asked.

"What do you mean?"

"In all my years of taking care of cancer patients," she responded, "this man's cancer is the most repulsive I can ever recall."

As she pushed open the door, a terrible odor rushed out of the room. Seated in an armchair, facing the window, was the most frighteningly deformed person I had ever observed. The cancer had been cruel. His head had doubled in size. One ear was gone, as was his right eye. The top right side of his head had a potato-like growth; his lower lip and jaw were gone. As I looked, I became rather dizzy. "Oh my God," I blurted. "Will you help me? I can hardly bear looking at you."

The man gazed at me with his one functioning eye and nodded.

I took a deep breath and approached him. With a pad and pencil he wrote, "Will you teach me? I want to be a Catholic."

I realized that God had left him with one good eye and ear. He could see, listen and write; therefore, I could certainly teach him the truths of the Catholic faith.

Later, as I said good-bye, I assured him I would instruct him. "I'll be back," I said. On my way out, I checked about his condition at the nurses' desk. They said he could live for a number of weeks. Still, I asked them to promptly alert me of any change.

We began brief but formal lessons two or three times a week. What a student he was! He wanted answers, even challenged me on certain points of faith. Within a matter of a few visits, I no longer saw a hideous man. Instead, I saw a beautiful human being. I actually began to look forward to our visits. Indeed, he'd become a tremendous source of grace for me as well as an enormous affirmation of my priesthood.

His progress was great, but one afternoon I came at our regular meeting time only to discover the blinds drawn and the lights out. I saw the silhouette of my friend against the sunlit window, standing with his big heavy head resting on the sill, arms hanging at his side. It was a sight of utter depression and hopelessness. I knew no words could help, so I turned and walked out.

My friend was unaware that I'd been there, but the Holy Spirit works in strange ways. For some reason, the thought came to me that what he needed was a crucifix. I got in my car and drove to a nearby religious goods' store where I found a beautiful, small wooden crucifix. I purchased it and drove back to the hospital.

Upon returning to his room, I found my friend in the exact same position as before. This time, though, I turned on the lights and opened the blinds. I took him in my arms and sat with him in his chair. Still, he looked at me in absolute despondency. Seeing him suffering so terribly, I was filled with overwhelming compassion, but I felt helpless. So I took the crucifix out of my coat pocket and placed it in his hands.

He looked at the crucified Christ intently with his one eye. Suddenly, a tear formed, rolled down his cheek, and fell off his upper lip. His face seemed to light up. Then, taking his pad and pencil in hand, he wrote, "I understand, Father O. I can unite my suffering with the suffering of Christ for the good of souls, like St. Paul tells us, to make up for His suffering. This really makes sense to me."

Shortly after, I received him into the church. Sustained by the sacraments, he eagerly awaited his personal meeting with Christ, and though he was physically unable to receive the Eucharist, he made many spiritual communions. I could see the change; he was at peace.

As expected, I soon received an early morning phone call from Harriman Jones Clinic informing me of his passing. I went to the hospital, blessed his body, and prayed over him. At last, his journey was over.

Later, it dawned on me what a gift I'd received. Truly, this man had left an indelible mark on my priesthood. It is consoling to know that Christ used me a little bit in that beautiful conversion.[1]

When I first came to Long Beach our football teams were average. We had neither the material nor the coaching to really compete in the top level of high schools so one day Monsignor Dolan said to me, "We gotta get a better team. We gotta win."

"You can't win without horses," I replied. "You need ballplayers. You gotta have good coaching. If we get good coaching and ballplayers, we can win ballgames."

He didn't understand the amount of work that went into this when he ordered, "I want you to do something about it."

It was an awful burden to put on me. Although I loved athletics, I had parish work to do, plus teaching in the high school. I also was involved in coaching the grammar school basketball team and working with them on both baseball and touch football. However, any work that I did at the grammar school looked to Monsignor like I was just having fun, even though it really was hard work. Finally I said, "Well, okay, I'll see what I can do."

I started scouting around. I heard of a coach in Illinois named Ennio Arboit, who had been acclaimed as High School Coach of the Year. We got him to come to Long Beach and work with Jacques Grenier, our head coach. Then I began to go out recruiting ballplayers. I spent a lot of my spare time visiting grammar and junior high schools, checking out talented athletes that were playing sports in the seventh and eighth grades.

---

[1] Reprinted from Catholic Digest, 2115 Summit Ave., St. Paul, Minn. 55105, Dec. 1996. (Copyright symbol) 1996 by the University of St. Thomas.

Sister Leonella of the Immaculate Heart Sisters and I put on a grammar school basketball tournament involving twenty-four to twenty-eight teams. We worked very hard to put this together. During the ten days of pre-tournament, I visited twenty-five or twenty-six schools and talked to students in the fifth, sixth, seventh, and eighth grades, but sometimes even the first grade. I pepped them up about our tournament. We had prizes for the best cheerleaders, best rooting section, and the most spirit.

I would practically break my back trying to get things going. We put together a program with ads, pictures of all the teams, and an announcement that the tournament would be held at St. Anthony's gymnasium in Long Beach. During all this I was still coaching St. Anthony's grammar school basketball team. (As a parish priest I was really working, but then again all the priests were consistently busy, too. We loved what we were doing, were enthusiastic, and had great times together at meals and after school.)

As many as seven thousand people attended the tournament. Once it ended, we were able to follow up on lots of athletes. We had given all-stars to maybe fifteen ballplayers. Among them, we had eight or more "blue chippers" at the grammar school level. Some of these kids came from Maywood, Compton, Wilmington, Banning, Norwalk, and, naturally, Long Beach. We enrolled these athletes into the high school and began to develop very good talent.

That's when Monsignor said he wanted me to coach. I retorted, "Oh, come on," but his word was law, and I had no choice. It was not that I didn't want to, but again, it was a matter of time. During my first season as a B coach we won none, lost eight, but it was perhaps one of the best coaching jobs I ever did because the morale never went down, and these kids were tigers by the end of the season.

The next year, naturally we did better. Our winning continued so that we finally won it all. Later on, Walt Osgood (who eventually got a scholarship for football and baseball at Notre Dame), was the captain of our B team. We went undefeated that year.

When I turned o v e r our ballplayers to Jacques Grenier and his assistant, Jack Bouchard, we began to win league titles.

In 1949, we finally won against Santa Barbara in the big CIF championship of Southern California, held in the Los Angeles Coliseum. At that time, Eddie Matthews was playing fullback for Santa Barbara, and a great passer called Punky Bowman was quarterback. We also had Johnny Olszewski, Billy Mays, Dean O'Hare, Johnny Peterson, Jack Senske, Danny Carroll, and others on our team. They were great ballplayers. Altogether in weight, our line was 176 pounds, backfield 165, but we won it all.

One of the greatest moments of my life was when we won that championship. Monsignor Dolan was beside himself. Johnny Olszewski, our captain and fullback, was player of the year. He set a record of touchdowns scored that particular year. (Years later, I buried John in December, 1966. He had died at the age of sixty.)

I met some tremendous kids. From that CIF Championship Team of '49, five players went on a package deal to the University of California, Berkeley, and at one time in the Rose Bowl they all played at the same time in the same game. It's amazing that one little high school produced so much talent.


I thoroughly enjoyed all of this. Although it was time consuming, it gave us a wonderful opportunity to be with the boys and to work with their fans. I had some tremendous experiences with the guys.

Every day during practice, Monsignor Dolan would come out on the field, even in the cold weather, and check out the varsity. Then he would check on the B team to see how we were doing; all the guys loved Monsignor Dolan. They were delighted to see him out there, as well as a number of other priests that stopped by.

I very much believed in conditioning. I used to run the tails off our guys. At the end of practice I'd have wind sprints, with tackles, guards, ends, and backs vying against each other until no one let up. Many times the guys would mumble "SOB" under their breath as they passed by me on their way to the dressing room. They didn't mean it for me as a priest, but as a coach, because I wanted to get them in top condition. The other team might have better talent, but they would never tire out our boys.

I remember a special incident one season.

We were going to play Cathedral High School for the possible league championship. I had a captain named Raymond Arroyo, a wonderful young boy from Wilmington who later went to Notre Dame on a scholarship. (The scholarship was a scholastic one, not an athletic one since he wasn't big enough for top collegiate football, being only 175 pounds.) That year, he was third string All CIF Halfback, named as such by the Southern California Athletic Federation.

I worked the kids hard. Before one game, I was concerned about our team's conditioning. Cathedral High's coach, Brother Maris, was a marvelous student of the game. He also had a great ball club. They had a very speedy back, one of the fastest in Southern California at the B level. This fact bothered me.

One day as we started practice, Captain Arroyo said to me, "Father, the squad requested me, as captain, to speak to you."

"What is it, Raymond?"

"They tell me, and I agree, that you are working us too hard. We're tired of you drilling us and making us sprint before and after practice."

"What do you suggest?" I asked.

"We want you to cut out some of these wind sprints and drills."

So I ordered the managers, "Assemble the squad."

When the squad gathered around me–about fifty-five of them–I told the guys, "I heard your request through Captain Arroyo. Here is what I want you to do: Bring the managers out."

After they got there, I said, "Now, I want you managers to go and stand by the locker room doors. And fellas, to start out this practice, I want you to do five laps. Any man that doesn't want to do these five laps can head to the dressing room and turn in his uniform. You will have had it!"

They were furious, just fried, but not one player turned in his uniform; they did the laps. It was a tough practice.

Finally, we played the game at Cathedral High School. The score was tied deep into the fourth quarter, with just three or four minutes left. Then this very flashy back from Cathedral broke loose from their twenty-yard line and went streaking for a touchdown. Raymond Arroyo–who was not as fast as this back but could carry his uniform better because he was a bigger boy–started after him. He nailed him around our four-yard line. We held and then came right back to score in the closing minute and to win the title.

As we were going into the dressing room, victorious before the whole squad, Raymond Arroyo turned to me with a big smile on his face and a thumb up in the air. "Thank you! Thank you! Thank you!"

So many wonderful things happened during my coaching years. One team captain, Joe Amalfitano (who later became third base coach for the Los Angeles Dodgers and before that had been the Chicago Cubs manager) was the quarterback.

After Jacques Grenier left, he was succeeded by Ennio Arboit. His assistant, Jack Bouchard, came from Loyola High School. For a while we had a high caliber of young men. My job was to oversee the B players that I had recruited and to train them the first two years. I was helped by Jack Errion, Dick McDonough, and Elmer Layden's brother, Clarence, all of whom also lived in Long Beach. Don Lee was another coach I worked with for a while. I had a really wonderful experience working with all of those coaches.

I had a team rule that anybody who was smoking or drinking would be suspended. Another well-known prohibition was that none of our boys could go down to the Pike in Long Beach. That was declared off limits for our students and we meant it.

One day some of our B team broke this "anti-Pike" rule. As luck sometimes has it, they were caught.

They knew this meant an automatic suspension for its violation. I had just offered morning Mass for these boys before their later game when I got a phone call from an officer Logan. "I have seven of your boys down here having breakfast," he said. "I know they are not permitted in this area. I will bring them up to you."

After he drove them to school in a station wagon, I asked them, "Why did you go off limits?"

"We went to the Mass you offered, and we had communion," Joe Amalfitano answered. "Then we went down to get breakfast. We did nothing wrong."

"You did," I replied. "You went down on the Pike and that's off limits, so you have earned an automatic suspension. None of you seven can play in the game today."

I thought it was the right decision even though it meant we would lose five first stringers and two subs from the roster. It was a tough blow for me and the team.

Years later I was out one night for dinner with Joe and some of his friends. Among them was Mike Morgan, a former Yankee pitcher, and John McNamara, former manager of the Los Angeles Angels. We were talking about football, and Joe mentioned, "You know, Father was my coach in high school football. I played quarterback for him."

"We didn't know you played quarterback, Joe!" someone said. "Oh, yeah," he replied. "As a matter of fact, one day Father O suspended us because we were down at the Pike and it was forbidden for our students to go there. That really taught me a lesson. I realized that through my own foolishness and the thoughtlessness of the other guys, we penalized the whole ball club. We lost the game by six points. I took this lesson throughout my life."

"Well, you never knew what it meant to me, Joe." I said. "It was very difficult for me to jeopardize, as well as possibly lose that game. But the rule was broken, and hopefully you all learned. That's what counted."

It was always a delight working with the football players, and I think Monsignor Dolan showed wisdom in having me coach. One time I asked him, "Why do you want me out there coaching? I wasn't ordained to coach football."

"It's good for the boys to see a priest out there, and it is also good for vocations to religious life."

He was actually very right about that.

I remember one incident: the only time that I ever slapped a boy in my entire life. Jim Smith (we will call him) was playing center on the varsity football team, and he had a younger brother, Richard, who was quarterback on the B team. The older Smith was stupid and dishonest enough to find a credit card and use it to purchase tires and gasoline. He got caught. Naturally, he was suspended from the team.

I remember his father and younger brother coming out onto the field with him while I was coaching. They had interrupted me during practice–something I never tolerated. "Will you help get my son back on the varsity team?" the father asked. "After all, the poor kid made a mistake."

"The poor kid nothing," I said. I couldn't believe the father was sympathetic to a kid who would use a found credit card to purchase items. I was very upset.

Smith was standing there submissively with his brother nearby feeling sorry for him, but the father's attitude bugged me. Suddenly I reached out and slapped Smith across the face, the only time I have ever struck a youngster in my entire life. I said, "You were guilty of stealing. You are a scandal to your family, you are a scandal to the school, and you are a disgrace to the football team! Before God, what you did was a sin and could be very serious. I don't want you on this field! All three of you get up in the stands! I hope you learn a lesson from this and never do a thing like this again!"

They retreated up to the stands. I was really upset, especially since I had been confronted by them on the sidelines.

Two or three days later I was crossing from the school to the church when young Smith stepped out from the side door of St. Anthony Church. "Father O, can I talk with you?"

"Sure, Smith."

"I want to thank you, Father, for what you did to me. That slap across the face made me realize I had disgraced my family, the school, the football team, and I certainly was guilty of sin. I want to thank you for what you did."

It was really worthwhile to find the young man repentant and asking forgiveness.

Smith went on to play varsity football, and he turned out to be a fine young man. He later attended college.

When kids get into trouble, I think if they are challenged and corrected properly, and made responsible for their actions, they will later succeed in life.

Teaching in a high school was really a neat experience, even though I never wanted to be a teacher. I had thought to myself, I'll join the diocesan priesthood because I don't want to teach; however, I ended up teaching for about the first thirteen-and-a-half years of my life as a priest. Then, as chaplain in the Newman Club at Los Angeles City College, I was teaching again. Later on I taught ethics at St. Vincent's College of Nursing in Los Angeles. So whether I liked it or not, I was teaching, but I must say I did enjoy it.

I will never forget Ronald Rivers, a very bright young man in our senior religion class at St. Anthony's. (He later became a doctor.) When students in the class spoke without permission, I had a policy of correcting them. No one can teach without quiet and discipline. I recall one day Rivers was messing around in class, and I publicly criticized him for his behavior.

"How dare you?" he said after class. "You embarrassed me before my peers. You shouldn't have done that publicly."

"Well," I said, "that's just too bad. You were out of line, and we should have order in this classroom. So you may better understand that, I'll have you write a paper on fraternal correction–what it is to correct and why one should be corrected. Get that to me in a few days."

When I received the paper from him, it was a story of a big black frog that lived in a pond and sat on a large toadstool near the water's edge. He lorded over all the other frogs by croaking and splashing around. This big black frog was the king of the pond. However, this big frog was going to get his comeuppance.

As I read it over, I began to think, *Golly this big black frog has to do with me. But I have to be careful for this Rivers is a very bright boy*. So I asked, "Ronald, what about this paper?"

He responded, "Oh…that should have gone to my English class."

Because he was so clever I couldn't say he was lying, but I knew he had deliberately placed it on my desk. "Take that paper, and give it to your English teacher," I said. "I want you to write me a 350-word paper on fraternal constructive correction."

A few days later I got a paper back entitled, "Paternal Constructive Correction or How to Correct a Priest."

Man, was it descriptive! "What is this?" I asked.

"Oh…I thought you wanted to know how I am supposed to correct a priest."

This guy really raised my dander. Knowing he was quite talented and spirited, an upfront young man, I thought, *I'll have to be careful how I handle him.*

"I'll tell you what you must do, Ronald." I said. "I want you to go to Mass every morning for a month, receive the Eucharist, and maybe you can talk to the Lord about getting your act together. You must realize when I give you a penance; it should be fulfilled in a spirit of charity and understanding."

"Whatever you say," he replied.

After about ten days he came to me upon the advice of his father. "I want you to know that that big black frog I wrote about—it was *you*! And that paper about correcting a priest–I knew it was supposed to be about how to correct our brothers; however, I wanted to turn it around and correct you, a priest."

"Ronald, I'm glad you learned that much. All is forgiven; just finish your penance."

Because the Eucharist and the Mass kind of softened him up; the situation turned out well. Later, after his graduation, I was quite happy to see him again. He became an outstanding leader, college student, and doctor.


One has to be careful about handling students so as not to get a potentially good young student started out on the wrong foot.

One day after the kids had come into Latin class, I noticed this big guy, about 220 pounds, at the end of the room. I estimated he was only a sophomore or junior.

We had about sixty guys there so I said, "You on the end down there. You're a big guy. If you are smart, you'll keep your mouth shut, and we'll do well, but if you're dumb, you better keep your mouth shut, or you will never make it at all. So be smart."

That young man turned out to be Ernie Cheatham, Jr., a great student who later became an outstanding football player for the Philadelphia Eagles. He went on to become a high-ranked general in the Marine Corps with a remarkable record. He is now retired.

Many of these youngsters had enormous potential. It was so great to follow them as they grew up and to meet them as they came back. It became ever clearer to me that if I treated them fairly, they would respect me. The one virtue they all appreciated was justice. Students want and respect justice. Treat everybody the same. It's easy to be merciful to one but not to another. That does not wash—justice treats everyone the same.

In between coaching and teaching, I went to the hospital on a sick call. I was rubbing the inside of my elbow while walking down to the first floor.

"Why are you rubbing your elbow?" asked my friend, Sister Alphonse. (She was a great nurse and supervisor.)

"I have kind of a swelling that has been bothering me for the last few weeks."

"Let me see that." After she had looked at it, she said, "You better have a doctor check that out; it's a lymph node."

It so happened that the chief of staff was coming down the hall at that time. "Doctor," she called, "look at this."

After looking at it the doctor said, "You better have that checked out right away. As a matter of fact, go up to the emergency right now and let them examine the swelling."

"But I have to take care of a patient."

He responded, "Well, take care of him and then go to the emergency room. I think you have an infected lymph node, and we have to check that out right away as we may have to prepare you for surgery."

"What?" I yelled.

"You have to get that taken care of."

"I'm coaching football and teaching," I argued. "I can't take time off that quickly." But after the preliminary examination, they decided that I should come in the next morning to have immediate surgery. My friend, Dr. Leslie Esposito, volunteered to help. Sister Alphonse was there also, as well as the chief of staff.

"I want a local," I had said. "I don't want to be knocked out because I need to get back on that field this afternoon and be in class the next morning."

"You're crazy!"

"No, just shoot me up with Novocain."

They doctored me up so that I was fully awake during the surgery. Suddenly Dr. Esposito pulled out this chunk of meat–a lymph node–and held out the forceps, saying, "Look, here it is."

I looked at it, and as they were sewing me up, I wondered, "Will I be able to go home?"

It turned out I was unable to go home that day. I was too sick! I was on pins and needles because there was a danger that the lymph node was malignant. I remember saying to myself, "My God, if it is malignant, my days are numbered. How do I settle this? To be so young…just about thirty years of age.

I finally decided I wanted to die with my boots on.

The doctor phoned about three days later. "Father, I've got great news for you!" he announced. "It's benign, but you should have a checkup every six months."

To be honest, I've never had a checkup since, but it was a tremendous lesson for me. I began to realize how precious life was and that we could lose our health and planned future at any moment. We should not take these gifts for granted.

I've never known any priest, other than the Cure´ of Ars, more devoted to the confessional than Monsignor Bernard J. Dolan. He practically lived in the confessional. He would be there every afternoon from 3:30 p.m., when St. Anthony's High School let out, until about five p.m. He also heard confessions every Saturday from three to six and from seven to nine p.m. People came from all over to confess to him–high school kids from Maywood, Long Beach, San Pedro, Compton, and South Gate; and college students. He always had a long line of penitents.

When the first Fridays came around, we went to church in the morning, along with two or three visiting priests, to hear confessions from nine to twelve o'clock. Then we would have lunch before returning to hear confessions until about 2:30 p.m., and then back again at 3:30 until about 5:30. In the evening, we were hearing confessions from 7:30 until 9:00 p.m. We really had confessions coming out our eyeballs! In those days, the students came in during both the morning and afternoon hours. We heard confessions almost around the clock. It was a way of giving the students and other penitents a sense of sin, of improving and guiding them. We had to dispatch them quickly because we were busy hearing so many, but we tried to give each one the "gift of the present moment." It was an awesome experience.

I'll never forget my first Christmas at St. Anthony's. It was 1944 and I had just been ordained when the fleet came in from Japan. Did we hear confessions around the clock! I remember on one of these evenings someone came into the confessional. The merchant seaman was invisible behind the confessional screen. As he related his sins and problems, my hair stood on end. He apparently was a rough guy, and he talked that way. He had really been around the block many times. When he finally finished his confession I knew an awful lot more about life. "I want you to make a real sincere Act of Contrition," I said to the man. "Tell God you are sorry for your sins, and I'll give you absolution and your penance."

"I don't know any Act of Contrition," he replied. "I wouldn't know what to say."

"Then tell God in your own words how sorry you are for all your sins and that you will not commit them again. Let Him know how humble you are, how sorry you are. Tell God you want to be a better person."

"Well, OK."

I started out the absolution prayer, and then I heard this guy say, "Oh, God, will you please forgive me because I'm a God damn son-of-a-bitch." I almost burst out laughing, but that turned out to be one of the most sincere Acts of Contrition I have ever heard in my life. Because of this man's tremendous sorrow, I lightened up his penance.

The spirit, the uplifting feeling I experienced just to be able to heal, to help the penitent in those particular crises, can hardly be put into words.

Young people would come in with problems, doubts, and fears. People arrived with low self-esteem, not knowing how much God loved them. To me the confessional is one of the most outstanding ways of manifesting and granting God's mercy. Yes, Jesus healed by performing physical miracles, but the priest through Christ is able to bring about so many wonderful spiritual miracles as the confessional encourages the penitents to confess with a spirit of humility and honesty.

In addition to the confessional, Monsignor Dolan was equally devoted to the Mass. Every morning he would say the 6:30 a.m. Mass. Should he ever happen to miss the Mass because of illness or some inconvenience and one of the other priests didn't cover for him, he would be angry. It was my job to make sure that someone celebrated the 6:30 Mass for him.

He was a tremendous priestly man who loved the Eucharist and the Sacrament of Penance. He taught us by example.

We always ate lunch at twelve noon and dinner at six o'clock. We had to be on time for these meals. Monsignor Dolan would stand at the end of the table, waiting for the priests to assemble. We would arrive in our cassocks, very seldom in our suits. When everyone was present he would bless the food, and then we all sat down.

The conversation at table depended upon his mood. If he didn't feel like talking, there was kind of an awkward silence. At times we would try to break it by bringing up all sorts of things until he made some crisp remark. It was awfully hard to dialogue with the other priests when he was sitting at the head of the table in silence. It caused tension.

Generally I was allowed to come to the table for the six o'clock evening meal sans clerical garb for the simple reason that I was coaching football. By the time I had finished coaching the team, had the players clean up the dressing room, and had driven the bus to return them to school, I would be a little late for dinner.

One evening, a little after six o'clock, I arrived at the rectory still wearing my coaching slacks and jersey. There was an air of tension at the table when I arrived. The other two associates, Father Jerry Cahill and Father Jim Hansen, were very quiet, as was Monsignor Dolan.

Monsignor looked at me. "By the way, Jim…" (Whenever he used the word "Jim" he hoped he would try to soften me up a bit. Otherwise he always called me "Father." It was his way of saying he had possibly made a mistake. However, he was not about to say that he was wrong.) He then stated an incident and related how Father Cahill and Father Hansen had solved it. (Naturally Monsignor Dolan opposed their decision.) "What do you think of these two men's decision?" he asked.

As he was speaking, I remember thinking, "Oh, God, let Monsignor Dolan be right. Let these guys be wrong," because he was really putting me on the spot.

"Jim, don't you think those men are wrong?"

After a moment, I said, "Well, Monsignor, I agree with Jerry and Jim."

"Ye gods!" he exploded. He stood up at the end of the table and shouted, "You guys are one heartbeat, one nervous system, one bloodstream. One of you gets hurt, and you all suffer together. I can't stand it." He walked out without eating the rest of his dinner.

We looked at each other and said, "Oh brother."

I often quote Monsignor's remark whenever I marry a couple. I always say, "Now when you marry you must be one heartbeat, one nervous system, and one bloodstream." He taught us in so many, many ways!

Monsignor had a unique custom of walking for about twenty minutes after lunch and dinner. He wished us to join him as he strolled up and down the sidewalk between the church and the rectory, from the back wall to the front of the church on Olive Street. We would walk two or three abreast, trying to keep a conversation going. This was a challenge as he was a very taciturn man.

Oftentimes we would ask him questions like, "How do you think the boys will do Friday night when they play Mt. Carmel?"

When he didn't answer, we would ask another question. He would walk on for a minute or two and say, "Father, I haven't answered your first question yet."

We kind of got used to that. He had said he was taciturn. That was putting it mildly.

I was inspired by his dedication to the Church–the people of God. The Church was his life. This encompassed its needs, challenges, and vitality. In this manner, he reminded me a great deal of Cardinal McIntyre.

After a period of time I detected one particular idiosyncrasy: he never liked for anyone to say "No" to him. It seemed to embarrass him. He also never liked to say anything was his fault. He could not confess, "I blew it." I learned many positive things from Monsignor Dolan, but I also learned some negative things from him and my father. Both of them were *never wrong*. That's why I would say to myself, "I have a God-given right to be wrong." I always admitted, "It's my fault." To me, refusing to admit one's faults is a sign of lack of self-love.

Monsignor Dolan had one other great passion—football. He did not understand the sport, but he loved to go to the games when either St. Anthony's or one of their future opponents, or "enemies," as he called them, was playing. On a Friday afternoon he would say to me, "By the way, Jim, have you got any appointments tonight, or are you free?"

I would think to myself, *Oh, God.* I knew I had two or three appointments that night, but I also knew that when he asked that question, I had better cancel them without letting him know. Thus, I could be available to drive him to whatever game he wanted to see.

If Anaheim High School was playing Mater Dei High School or Anaheim was playing one of our future opponents at Santa Ana, Monsignor might ask me if I planned to go. I would cancel my appointments for that night, then after dinner I would get behind the wheel. He would leave the rectory, get in the car, and I would start driving. Next he'd take out a cigar, begin to smoke, and not say one cotton picking word. We would drive all the way to the stadium, get our tickets, and then he'd sit next to me in the bleachers, not saying anything, only following the flow of the ball. For example, if the ball was going north, he would be looking north. If it was going south he'd be looking south.

After the game was over, we would get in the car, and I'd start driving home. He'd take out another cigar and smoke. Then he would begin to talk, and he would keep it up all the way home. I felt it was very important for me to be available to him under these circumstances. Basically he was a very lonely man, the kind of person who was always reluctant to ask favors of anyone. He had his idiosyncrasies, but he was a great priest and so good to the fellows.

Monsignor Dolan always preferred the company of men. He really did not seem to enjoy women's company. On one occasion as we were walking near the church and school, some women approached him. One said, "Oh, Monsignor Dolan, we understand you don't like women."

He replied casually, "That's right, Madame! I don't!" and he kept walking.

The rest of us tried to cover up his tracks as best we possibly could because he could be really abrupt.

I recall another occasion of a critically ill man who was a fallen-away Catholic. I had visited him at St. Mary's Hospital in Long Beach to see if I could reconcile him to the church but was unsuccessful. After I told Father Jim Hansen about this, he also visited the sick man, but had no success either. We were telling this to Monsignor Dolan.

Monsignor was very devoted to the sick. He would go to the hospital every day to visit the patients and the handicapped. "You guys are stupid," he said. "I'll go over with you."

So we accompanied him to the man's room. Monsignor looked at the oxygen tent enclosing the patient, who was lying there and breathing heavily. Suddenly Monsignor ripped open the tent's zipper, stuck his head inside, and said, "How about coming back to the practice of your Catholic faith?"

The patient gasped, "I can't breathe! I can't breathe! My oxygen…"

"I'll tell you one thing, young man," Monsignor replied. "If you don't get back to the practice of your faith, you might end up in hell, and you won't be able to breathe anything but smoke and fire. I can help you. How about returning to your faith and receiving the sacraments?"

"Yeah!" he said.

I must say, in this rather bizarre way, Monsignor took care of him. He heard his confession, anointed the man, and brought him back to the practice of the faith. We will leave his disposition to Almighty God.

Yes, Monsignor Dolan was very wonderful in the way that he cared for the sick. By example, he taught us dedication and devotion to them. Among other things, I learned clearly that I was on duty at all times. Whenever necessary I picked up the slack for the other priests and them for me. Monsignor Dolan was kind of a priestly Vince

Lombardi. I understand that when Lombardi was coaching, the players would be so mad at him that they would get together, forming a camaraderie among themselves, to help prevent themselves from being intimidated by Lombardi's anger and strength. I guess we had that same reaction toward Monsignor Dolan. We were determined to meet his expectations or else. He always raised the bar to challenge us to reach our potential.

I recall another night when he came to me as I had just arrived from the school. It was about eight o'clock at night when he said, "Jim."

The moment he said my name I became nervous because I knew it meant he wanted my help.

"There is a couple in the front wanting to see about getting married. I can't stand it," he said. "You go and take care of it."

None of us had our own office. We used any one we could find open. I entered the office to encounter a sailor about twenty-three-years old. Beside him was an elderly woman, perhaps in her sixties.

"We came to see about getting married," the sailor said.

"Are you his grandmother, Madame?" I asked the lady.

"I did not come here to be sneered at," she retorted. "I am the bride to be."

Now I understood why Monsignor Dolan had stormed out of there and told me to take care of it.

Monsignor Dolan had great wisdom and understanding. He also was very decisive. We knew we could go to him with a problem or difficulty and he would listen quietly; asking a question now and then. He always gave a quick, incisive, and clear answer. He was a very prudent, wise and priestly man.

I recall one night when I had received a call from a couple who had marital problems. The difficulty stemmed from drinking. I was still a young priest then.

It was about 10:30 p.m. when I left to go to their home. Once I got there, quite an angry squabble ensued. It was very late by the time

I had finished trying to help the couple. I didn't get home until about 1:00 a.m. I'll never forget coming in and encountering Monsignor Dolan in his bathrobe at the head of the stairs. "Father, where have you been?" he asked.

"I was out trying to counsel a distressed married couple."

"You were totally out of line," he said. "That was a very imprudent thing for you to do. Go to your room."

I did exactly that. I was so mad and upset that I don't think I slept much that night.

The next morning, after I had said Mass and finished teaching my classes, I returned to the rectory. Monsignor came into my room—he very seldom did that—and sat down. "Father, about last night," he began. "I wanted to teach you a lesson. You know you young priests have got to be very careful because your reputation could be compromised in certain areas. That was no hour to go out to counsel a married couple, especially if there was drinking involved. You had no idea whom you would meet when you got there. You should have had some other adult with you, perhaps a police officer, to protect you just in case anything had happened. You are a young and vulnerable priest. I care about you, and I care about the priesthood. That is why I got on your case last night."

"Well, thank you very much, Monsignor."

That was all he said. He abruptly got up and left the room.

He surely did teach me a lesson that night that I will never forget. I have passed on this lesson to other young priests serving with me.


Monsignor Dolan was a magnificent preacher in the old oratorical style. People came from all over to hear him preach.

His material was excellent. His face would get very red and he would almost blow a vein in his forehead as he stood and spoke in the pulpit!

When I gave my first homily at St. Anthony's 6:30 a.m. Sunday Mass, I thought it was pretty good. (We had this custom that the priest who preached at the first Mass did so for the remaining Masses throughout the day.) I came to breakfast right after.

Monsignor Dolan greeted me and asked, "Father, did you prepare that homily?"

"Yes, I did."

"Did you write it out first?"

"I did. As a matter of fact, I even got it typed."

"Well, it was awful," he said. "I'm not prepared, but I'll preach the rest of the Masses. I don't want you preaching that homily again today."

I was furious, just like the time my father told me to grow up and offered no consoling words when the administrators cut football my first year in the seminary.

From then on I was determined to preach well. Monsignor would never say that to me again!

Preaching is like a surgeon preparing for brain surgery, one has to be prepared. I have filed every homily I have ever given. It is beneficial to renew them at times, however. Although much of the material stayed the same, the examples changed. Instead of using "high button shoes" and "gaslights," I would insert "loafers" and "neon lights," but the material was still there!

We didn't get a lot of time off at St. Anthony's. Monsignor Dolan would give us maybe two-and-a-half days off at Christmastime and Easter, otherwise we were on duty. Yes, in those days the associates did not get much time off. In our early years of ordination, Monsignor Emmett McCarthy, my classmate, was stationed at Immaculate Heart Church in Hollywood. Whenever he asked his pastor for some extra time off, the pastor would reply, "Father, check the statutes of the Archdiocese. You have your one day off during the week and x number of days off for your vacation. Those are your only days off." If McCarthy pressed Monsignor O'Donnell again, he would say, "Don't be ridiculous."

That rigidity has changed now, thank God.

We also didn't have our own cars. There would be the pastor's car and one other that the associates shared. We would jockey back and forth about who could use it. This was difficult when there were three associates. Each of us wanted it for our day off and, when it was available, to drive around the parish area. Otherwise, we had to walk. We also had a Brother Philip who would come by once in a while and ask, "Hey Father, anybody have a free car around here that I could borrow?" He was a holy man, one of the most marvelous Holy Cross brothers one could meet, a joy to be with. We would lend him the automobile whenever it was available.

The situation is much different today. Every associate has his own car. He has much more time off. This is good, if it is not abused.

In those days we didn't have a separate bathroom. I had to share one with another priest, and sometimes two. If three of us had the 6:30 a.m. Mass, it could be a little awkward, but that's the way it was. Later on, when I was on the priest council, I recommended that every priest should have his own living room, his own head, and his own bedroom.

"What do you mean by this word 'head'?" Cardinal Manning asked. He was a little upset with me because he thought I was being rather crude. I finally explained to him that in the Navy head meant toilet.

Thank God associates now have their private bedroom and bath. Priests have to have a certain amount of privacy. I think a priest should have a good place to sleep and be allowed to bring adult guests and family members into his quarters. The rectory is his home, not merely the pastor's. Monsignor Dolan always made the rectory a home. We had a great camaraderie. We looked forward to meals. We would kid around, conjuring up pranks and joking about all sorts of things. We had such a great group of priests. It was a very happy household, and it was most enjoyable for us to spend time together. This camaraderie was evident to the people.

One of my nicest possessions is a note from Monsignor Dolan...

I left St. Anthony's in 1957, but Monsignor Dolan once invited me back to give the Good Friday devotion homilies. These were the type of homilies that Bishop Fulton Sheen had once given there. (At times other really fine speakers were also invited.)

I was thrilled to come back. There were student choirs and packed crowds as I preached the three-hour passion devotion homily based on the seven last words of Christ. It was a magnificent event! People were listening to the P.A. system outside because they couldn't get into the church.

I later received this note. "Jim, your strength and your presentation for the three hours was tremendous. You really have grown." It was signed, "Bernie."

I saved that note, and I treasure it because to me it was an enormous compliment, somewhat like Vince Lombardi telling one of the players, "You did a great job!"

One time Monsignor Dolan remarked, "You know, Jim, I've had you with me a long time, and I've never done anything for you."

Although some of his other associates had gone up the ladder of ecclesiastical success, I was still there driving the bus, coaching the football team, teaching, ministering, and doing many other things the best I could. I was kind of a general practitioner.

"Monsignor Dolan, I'll tell you one thing," I said. "You will never know what you have done and are still doing for me. You've taught me two of the greatest things I could possibly learn as a priest: devotion to the confessional and devotion to the Mass and Eucharist.

Now those are tremendous gifts. That's why later I named the hall we built at St. John Vianney Parish "Dolan Hall." I wanted that great priest to always be in my mind and remembered by the people. I remember him every day in my prayers. I respected him; he challenged me, and he challenged all of the priests who were with him at St. Anthony's in Long Beach. He always raised the bar!

During my time at St. Anthony's, there was an incident in my life that greatly enriched my priesthood, making me determined to keep peace in the families to whom I ministered. It was a lesson I learned at home.

My brother and my father were alienated for a number of years. In many ways they were like oil and water, and oftentimes they didn't mix well. They were always knocking heads together. I can recall my dad would at times pound his fist on the kitchen table and say, "Silence is golden!"

"The hell with silence," my brother would say. He might stalk out, or they would get into a verbal tussle. Then my brother often left home, hitting the rails and taking a freight train to Arizona or Nevada. My uncle Mike would go out to look for him, eventually bringing him back. My father wouldn't raise a finger to do it. My mother, of course, suffered during all of this. My sister Mary (who was seven years younger than me) and I would strive to keep peace.

When World War II broke out, I was stationed at St. Anthony's. My father and brother had not spoken to each other for a year or two. My brother was with the railroad police and was deferred from service. I came home one day and found him over at the local pool hall near where he roomed in South Central, Los Angeles, shooting pool with a guy called Shakes. My brother said, "You see that sign where Uncle Sam is pointing a finger at you and says, 'I want you'? Well, I'm choosing Uncle Sam. I've got to help get this war over with. I've enlisted."

"Oh boy, that's fine, John." (This was in 1943 just before I was ordained.)

I celebrated my first Mass while John was away at boot camp in San Diego. Of course, he was unable to attend either my ordination or my first Mass.

The Navy wanted to put John into "special service" as a military policeman because of his background in police work, but he did not want that. "Hell, I didn't join the service to fight my own men," he said. "I joined to fight the enemy." He refused, even though he could have gotten a higher ranking had he joined the military police.

Boot camp prepared him to be a gunman on a Navy ship. He went overseas after finishing his training. I remember one thing he said before shipping out: "They had better not send me to England, because the first Englishman I see, I'll hit."

"Oh come on!" I said. (We had that Irish dislike for the English which my dad and Uncle Mike had instilled in us. We thought the phrase "bloody English" was one word until we were fifteen years of age.)

At that time John was very much in love with a wonderful girl named Betty Bryan. She also was very much in love with him.

Betty was working for Howard Hughes, the producer. I remember visiting her one night when she and John were thinking of getting married. (Soon John would be coming back from overseas on leave.) "Betty, let me tell you about my brother," I said. "You are such a refined, lovely girl, and John is a real tough son-of-a-gun. You know he is rough and very up front; he wants his own way; he is stubborn."

When I finally finished, she said, "Father Jim, those are some of the reasons why I love him."

I learned a lesson about keeping my big mouth shut. I can't tell those in love not to be. When the chemistry is there, love is sometimes stronger than reason. I could only advise.

Soon after, John decided he did not want to get married while still active in the service. He felt he might come back maimed or changed, and he did not want her to be married under those circumstances.

Regarding the relationship of my father and my brother, when John came back from overseas, he'd visit our home only when my father was absent. They avoided each other. We all felt bad about the situation, but my father would not bring up his name, and John would not speak about our father.

One afternoon I happened to come home while my father was out front watering the lawn. The kitchen wall phone rang, and I picked it up. It was my brother John calling from the Port of Embarkation in San Francisco.

We talked. Next he talked with my mother and my sister, Mary. John told us he was going back overseas, that he had drawn the short straw on a very dangerous assignment as an armed guard on an ammunition ship, the LS Dyke [sic]. That was about as perilous a duty as one could have. He drew that assignment because he had turned down a rest and relaxation leave on Treasure Island in San Francisco. He wanted to get the war over.

When I got back on the phone, I said, "The old man is outside watering the lawn. Do you want to talk to him and say good-bye?"

"Put him on."

I went outside. "Pop, John is on the phone. He has a rather dangerous assignment overseas, and he'd like to say good-bye to you. How about it?"

"Yeah, I better go in and say good-bye to the boy." He dropped the hose on the lawn. I watched it snake around before I went over to shut the water off.

When I got back inside the house, my father was still on the phone talking with my brother. I heard him say these words: "Good talking with you, Son, and you take care of yourself. May God bless you and good luck."

There was a tear running down his cheek as he hung up the phone. He went outside, turned the faucet back on, and finished watering the lawn.

I never said anything because I could never speak to my father about personal matters. But they were reconciled. That was the last time my father would ever talk to my brother.

Isn't it marvelous that they were reconciled? How terrible it would have been had they not been reconciled after all that time.

To continue this story, later during my assignment at St. Anthony's, my mother phoned to tell me that she had received a telegram saying John had been killed in action. His ship had been blown up by a kamikaze pilot in the Mindoro Straits in the Philippines.

"I'll be right home," I said.

My mother told me my father was on his way home from the night shift at General Petroleum Corporation and had probably stopped by a marsh in Carson to pick mushrooms. (In those days, the marsh was called "Nigger Slough." Mushrooms grew in its moist soil.)

I drove out there and saw my father off in the distance, holding a hat full of mushrooms. I walked through the muddy grass, its vegetation enhanced by the ever-present cattle droppings. Approaching my father, I said, "Hey Pop, I have some bad news."

"What is it?"

"John was killed in action."

I'll never forget how he dumped the mushrooms on the grass and put his hat on his head. "Well, Son, I better go to your mother."

He walked one way, and I walked the other. I could not console him or he me. I couldn't even talk to him; he was deep into his thoughts, and I was engrossed in mine. He went to his car; I went to mine.

When I arrived home I saw my mother and said, "Gosh, Mom, I'm so sorry."

"God gives; God takes away. Blessed be the holy name of God," she said. "Now can I get you some breakfast?"

\*\*\*

Regarding my attitude toward my father—he told his children that the Fourth Commandment was the most important. If one kept that commandment, all the others would fall into place. It didn't bother me; I just went along with it. To obey him and go along with his ideas made my life simpler. When he said, "No," to something, that was it. One could not fight "city hall." His idea for children was: "They should be seen but not heard."

I respected my father and was proud of him, but I never told him so. He was a hard worker, a good provider, and hospitable to everyone, respected by his peers and friends. I don't remember ever having an intimate father-son conversation or shared pursuits. I was closest to him when training, racing, and conditioning our greyhounds. I never thought anything was unusual with our relationship; I just took it for granted.

I never said "I love you," to him, or remember him saying it to me. The question never came up. It was engraved in my very nature. Certainly he loved me. He was my father. By his example, he taught me compassion for others, pride of heritage, service to God, man, and country. His courage and fidelity to work was obvious. Had he lived beyond his sixty-seven years, I would have liked him to remain about the same. If he had become maudlin or dependent, I would be embarrassed for him and myself. He taught me to be proud that I was an O'Callaghan and that automatically, "I had class."

So many of the qualities he possessed were those of my first pastor, Monsignor Bernard J. Dolan. My father unknowingly prepared me for that assignment. It enabled me to understand and work with Monsignor Dolan for thirteen-and-a-half years. It was a challenging, sometimes even turbulent time and yet very rich in experiences and results.

# THE NEWMAN CLUB

After I had been at St. Anthony's for thirteen-and-a-half years, I said to Monsignor Dolan, "I think it would be good for me to get a new assignment. I'd like to get some experience in a small town, perhaps like Lancaster. I'm tired. I've worked with youth for so long; now I would like to minister to families."

He wasn't keen about the request, but as he was on the archdiocesan board of consultors, he had impact.

"Please put in a request, will you?" I asked.

Well, it turned out differently than I had expected.

I got a phone call from Bishop Bell, who asked me to come down to his office in Los Angeles. "Father O, we have a job we'd like to have you do," he said when we met.

"Bishop Bell, I made a request that I'd like to minister in a small parish. Hopefully there will be a more diversified group of people, young and old. I'm tired of working mostly with youth."

"Well," he said, "we have a difficulty over at Los Angeles City College. The Newman Club has been accused of immorality, gambling, and drinking. Of course, we know it's exaggerated, but we'd like you to go over there and take care of that."

"Wait a minute, Bishop Bell!" I said. "I don't want to go to the Newman Club. I want to go to a small parish."

"No, we'd like you to be Newman Club Director at Los Angeles City College. Think over the request for twenty-four hours."

"I thought I told you how I feel," I protested.

He turned around and looked behind the venetian blinds covering the window for a few moments. When he turned back to me, I said, "Bishop, there is no need to think about it for twenty-four hours because the only reason I have for refusing the assignment is selfish. I'll take it as long as I can handle it my way."

"Well, you have to be prudent," he responded.

"Prudent!" I said. "As Cardinal Bea said, 'We are all trying to be so prudent we are losing our courage, and if we are not careful we will all die of wisdom.'"

He laughed and said, "You can handle it any way you want."

That's how I happened to be assigned not to a small, out-of-town parish, but to Los Angeles City College as the Newman Club Chaplain.

When I arrived at Los Angeles City College to take over my assignment at its Newman Club, I was not too pleased. I entered an old building on the northwest campus corner west of Vermont Boulevard. It was split up into areas for the Jewish, the Protestant, and the Catholic faiths. Our space merely consisted of a semi-hall and an inner office for the priest. It contained a desk, a few book shelves, and chairs. Adjoining the office was a bathroom. The main hall next to our area was not very large, and it was shared by all the faiths.

The place was a rookery. The outside meeting room was battered and when I went into the inner office where I would have my desk, I couldn't believe what I saw. A light was hanging from the ceiling, dangling on a cord, and the desk was scarred and filthy. The chairs were well worn and scattered.

I entered the bathroom and really got angry. The toilet was filthy, the floor scuffed and dirty. It reminded me of an abandoned tenement bathroom. My blood boiled.

I left the quarters and went out into the main hall looking for a janitor's closet. When I found it, I got hold of a broom, a mop, a pail, and an old pair of pants. I took off my clericals and put on the old pants. Luckily I had on a tee shirt. I put some soap and water in the bucket and returned to clean the dirty toilet.

As I was crossing the hall, the rabbi came out. He thought I was the new janitor. At that moment, I did not want to explain. I let him go on thinking what he wanted.

While I was angrily scrubbing and cleaning, there suddenly appeared three young students: one a Costa Rican, one of Irish descent, and the third a sturdy German type. I never said a word, and they never spoke. After looking around for a little bit, they must have realized who I was from the look on my face for they abruptly left. I was really disturbed but slowly went on cleaning up the place.

Within an hour four students arrived, and, without saying a word, they brought out mops, pails, and brooms. They worked alongside me cleaning that pigsty for a couple of hours. When we finished the task, they introduced themselves and I then introduced myself.

This was the beginning of my new assignment.

There were a tremendous amount of students at Los Angeles City College. We had two thousand students to minister unto, but the Newman Club was in total disarray. We tried to put some stability and efficiency into the club. It did not have a good reputation on campus. Most of its students were going to school, working a part-time job, and then returning home. It was called a streetcar campus because they typically didn't have cars. These were kids from the blue collar areas, but they were a marvelous bunch of students.

We tried to put some doctrinal structure into the club by starting and teaching religion classes. The only place I could teach was in the outer hall.

I made a couple of rules for the students. "When you come into this Newman Center, if a girl enters for the first time, you guys stand up. If a girl is carrying books or a package, be sure you help her with her articles." I made up some very definite rules which we enforced—such as no alcohol, narcotics, or smoking on the premises.

The students asked, "Would you wear your cassock when present with us?"

"Sure, I'll do that."

I began to appoint students as temporary secretaries since I had neither a secretary nor a bookkeeper. Then I said, "Here are some census cards; go find out the religion of the students you meet. If he or she is a Catholic, inquire where their parents went to school, and if their parents are going to church and practicing their faith.

They went, checked out many students, and soon brought in quite a number of census cards. I had only been there for a couple of months before students were lined up outside my office, waiting to see me.

I had incredible classes. I initiated many courses at various hours. This was the schedule of classes for the week:

Classes on Apologetics:

| | | |
|---|---|---|
| Monday | 9:15 a.m. and | 1:15 p.m. |
| Wednesday | 11:15 a.m. and | 12:15 p.m. |
| Thursday | 10:15 a.m. and | 1:15 p.m. |

Marriage Course:
M. W. F.          10:15 a.m.

History of Religion:
Thursday night          8:00 p.m.

Confessions:
Mon.through Fri.*     3:00 p.m. and   4:30 p.m.
(*except Tuesday; Also by appointment.)

Rosary Daily:          7:45 a.m. and 2:15 p.m.

Novena:
Thursday          12:15 p.m.

Sociology:
Tuesday          10:15 a.m. and 11:15 a.m.

It was a tough schedule. Whatever free moments I had were spent on student interviews.

I had a lecturer every Monday night. He had been warned that he had only fifteen minutes to speak. If he went over the time limit, I would ring a bell, and he had to sit down. The kids knew the meeting would be over within an hour; we kept it that way.

We held a student meeting every Tuesday night. There were no problems or difficulties even with well over one hundred (and sometimes two hundred) students at each gathering. It was amazing how they policed themselves and kept the security.

We had dances, and students would come from all over the area. We really packed the place. I would pick out ten male students and tell them, "You are pretty 'good looking dudes.' When you come into this hall and see some girls that are not dancing—'wall flowers'—you go and ask them to dance."

In this way we kept all the girls dancing.

The girls had no idea this pressure was on the ten boys. I told them, "We have Blacks, Mexicans, Asians, and other races here. If you don't want to dance with a Mexican or Black or someone of another race that is your business, but don't make an issue out of it."

It worked out well. After establishing ourselves, the group wanted to get more involved with the entire student body.

We worked to get Sheila Conway as editor of the weekly campus newspaper. We also trained students like Joe Bondaman and Russell Lascola to audit classes. They were quite skilled in theology and philosophy, and they would challenge the professor if there was something taught in the classes contrary to our Catholic teachings. Naturally, we kept the teachers on their toes. Dr. Lombardi, the college president, remarked, "How in the name of God can one man do so much? The heads of our departments are not doing as much!" Suddenly the Newman Club became a very prominent and positive influence on campus.

Hank Ennon, who was the football defense coach for the college, asked me if I could help a little, but I said, "I have all I can do."

It was a thrilling experience! I had to go back to the books and study in order to work with these kids. I was with them at every evening meeting except one night. That night when I was not there a small riot occurred. When informed, I was furious. However, I decided that before blowing my top I would listen to what the students had to say.

Apparently some campus member who had a fractured neck had left the hospital. He had been drinking before he arrived at our meeting, and he started disturbing the members. They carefully held him lest his neck be damaged and called the police. They made a great decision and safely subdued him. I was delighted that I had held off my decision to criticize the students without knowing the facts. The students were all very protective.

On one occasion, I was sick for a few days and rested at the Good Shepherd Parish where I was in residence. Those students came in with loads of gifts and flowers. They didn't have much money, but they were the most generous kids one could ever find. The desk I now use has gone with me everywhere. It was given to me by the Newman Club, along with a clock and its marble support. They also gave me the magnificent crucifix that hangs on my wall. Those students who had nothing gave everything. They thought I was the greatest thing since popcorn!

At times the Newman Club members would ask, "Father O, would you walk over to the campus wearing your cassock?" I would walk over there with them looking like Jesus Christ surrounded by his followers!

We trained the young students to go out and speak on street corners where they could challenge Jehovah's Witnesses and other fundamentalist sects. They did magnificent work.

We asked Sheila Conway, the editor of the college paper, not to run for student body president but to stay on as editor for we needed her there. We started electing members to the student council. We began to make a positive Christian impact on the campus.

It was a thrilling, wonderful experience, a means of great joy to me. Also my love of youth and their enthusiasm increased in leaps and bounds.

To tell the truth, the new assignment was one of the most fulfilling experiences of my life. I began to enjoy it as much as I had enjoyed coaching football. On the down side, I had to go back to the books and review my theology, diversified religions, and youth challenges. I worked with these wonderful students with no personnel support and little money. However, the students helped out and really got involved in every way.

They were certainly to be admired. They put a lot of time in the Newman Club and together we enhanced its reputation and built it up to a viable force on campus.

We began to infiltrate our members into the student council and newspaper. Soon we were making some real impact on campus. The faculty and campus knew who we were.

I was there for four really glorious years. I met so many wonderful students. I'm also happy to say that we never had a marriage from a Newman Club student that was not in the church. Further, I think every non-Catholic who took instructions became a Catholic.

I used time well because a number of kids wanted instructions. I would train students to instruct inquirers on a "one-on-one" and "one-on-two basis." When they had progressed through the Baltimore Catechism, they would then bring the catechumens to me, and I would go over the whole catechism with each one. If the catechumens then desired to enter the church, I would see that they were either baptized or made a profession of faith. Thus, they were received into the church. Unknowingly, we anticipated the R.C.I.A program. This whole experience was just outstanding and productive.

At that time challenges were pretty strong on campus from a group named "Fair Play for Cuba." There was also a certain communist influence. We really had to brush up on our faith and the church's stand on communism. I remember one time we had some special reports on communism coming out on the same day we had scheduled a big meeting at one o'clock in the afternoon. Suddenly we noticed we had a lot of strangers there. They were groups from "Fair Play for Cuba" and the American Civil Liberties Union. When we tried to show the film which portrayed the evils of communism, these groups interrupted the talks and film. They took charge and subdued our students. They did it more or less through parliamentary procedure and heckling. We knew nothing about these tactics and our students could not handle them, so in desperation we finally had to call the meeting off. Our kids were really whipped.

At the next meeting, I challenged our Newman Club students and said, "You know we got whipped, defeated, and subdued because of our lack of knowledge. So let's do something about it."

We did not have much money in our treasury; however, we used it to purchase a number of J. Edgar Hoover's *Masters of Deceit: The Story of Communism in America* and distributed them. We also purchased pamphlets, essays, and other material regarding communism and its influence on our American heritage. We learned and understood government and the church's stance on communism and its evil. We had the kids study, read, and become more updated in the knowledge of both their faith and the political situation.

Later on we held another meeting, this time at night. The meeting hall was jammed packed. Once more the same groups came to participate. I was never so proud of our students, because they whipped the tails off of these agitators. The students now were all fired up and knowledgeable about their faith.

Subsequently, Justice William Douglas of the Supreme Court came on campus. He gave a talk regarding the church's stance on birth control, right to life, and other things. We took issue with some of his views, and later our students picketed him outside the school auditorium. When he left the hall, they followed him down to the Hilton Hotel in Beverly Hills where they again picketed him. He tried to avoid them; finally he went back to Washington, D.C.

They wrote him a letter: "Are you really advocating the positions you stated at the meeting in our school, or are you just voicing current opinions?"

He wrote back: "I don't necessarily believe in all the statements I made. I was just voicing current opinions."

It was good these kids challenged him to define his personal stance. They got deeply involved in their faith and in the political situation.

A little later on, Eleanor Roosevelt, for a large fee, was going to speak about communism on the campus. We thought, "My God, if anyone knows how to talk on that topic, it certainly is not Eleanor Roosevelt."

So, we really got our campaign together. We planned how we were going to challenge her views on campus. Unfortunately, right before her scheduled visit I was sent to Berkeley to help to prepare some of the new chaplains for the Newman Clubs all over the U.S. and had to miss her speech.

While I was still in Berkeley, I received a phone call about a new assignment.

My stay at the Newman Club had been a tremendous time. I met the most wonderful young people. I have contact with some of them even now. They were just great young people, always enthusiastic, who loved their faith and went all out to spread it on campus and elsewhere.

Even so, when my new assignment came through I literally kissed the ground saying, "Thank you, Lord!" At last I would have a little plot of land and people to call my own. As pastor; I would be able to work with them to bring Christ to all the area.

I had just become pastor of Our Lady of Malibu.

# THE FIRST SENIOR PASTORATE

Malibu was a small parish of less than five hundred families. The parish consisted of twenty-seven miles of coastline extending inward to the San Fernando Valley. We also had a mission chapel located in Topanga Canyon.

Our Lady of Malibu was nestled in the hills underneath what was known as the "Hughes Think Tank." There wasn't a lot of property (a grammar school, rectory, and a small church), but it was my parish!

The people were rather bohemian and free spirited. In the colony we had the very wealthy that fronted the beach; north of this area was Point Dume, which was rather affluent, also. South of the colony was Big Rock, where many diversified people lived. Then we had the dirt farmers north of Point Dume. Along the Pacific Coast Highway were many merchants and innkeepers. Malibuites were a great mix.

After a few months, I got an Irish terrier. Some of the bohemian people took notice and said that a pastor who had a dog couldn't be "all bad."

Living in Malibu was like living under a microscope. I made a decision never to swim in the ocean; also, I would not go to their homes and socialize because whatever I did people knew about it, and the news spread like wild fire. It was a small community, and the priest was in the public eye. Only after I had been told that I was named the new pastor of St. John Vianney, did I actually swim in Malibu.

It was a prudent decision.

The people were wonderful, but trying to bring them together was difficult. For example, one day I noticed the pews in the church were an ugly black color. I took a pen knife and after scraping through the paint, I could not believe my eyes. "Oh, my God, this is beautiful oak wood," I said. "The pews should be scraped and polished!" I requested that the families in the parish volunteer to do this work on Saturdays.

"We don't do that sort of thing," they said.

"We do now."

It was amazing what they accomplished. They removed the pews, scraped, and then polished them; they became beautiful wooden pews, a delight to the decor of the church.

We had a deck on the side of a naked bare hillside, directly behind the main altar and sanctuary. I spoke to the grammar school children, asking each one to "bring to the church a stone the size of their head. From them we will build a grotto."

We constructed a beautiful grotto behind and over the main altar. (Anyone looking through the church window now can see this natural shrine.) Then we stripped the red velvet drapes covering the interior side walls of the church and confessional entrances. This exposed the natural wood and brick behind the drapes. These few changes added to the warmth and simplicity of the church.

Next we decided we would have coffee klatches after morning Mass. The altar society which we formed was kind of negative when I suggested, "Let's clean the altar and sanctuary every day."

"We don't do this daily."

"Well, you will now."

We united some of the people, led by a wonderful lady, Lillian Holtzman, who was very outgoing and hospitable. Soon a goodly number of other people started participating in our daily coffee, cake, and toast. The ladies and men also prepared and cleaned the church. It was awesome!

The parish itself was quite diversified. There were many writers, some producers, film people (actors and actresses), small parcel landowners, engineers, and merchants. As a whole, they were a mixed bag. I found them to be challenging and interesting.

One of my first great mistakes took place when I initiated a men's club. I gathered all the men I could and announced, "We're going to have our first meeting followed by a dinner."

This group did not socialize well.

There must have been about fifty men who showed up. After the business ended, we held a little reception in the small hall. Later on we went to the Malibu Inn for dinner. My big mistake was having an open bar from six to seven o'clock, with beer, scotch, bourbon, and gin.

Some of the fellows wanted to drink as much as they could during that hour. By seven o'clock, a number of the men had drunk too much. However, they had a marvelous time. After the dinner, they supposedly headed for home.

During the night I kept getting calls from wives asking, "Where is my husband?" When the wife of one man in particular, an engineer, called, I told her to come and get him for he was in the school yard hanging on the basketball standard. He paid a price for that, and so did I. I learned I would have to be more prudent in the future.

I tried to get people from the dirt farms, Malibu Colony, Point Dume, and Big Rock to mesh together and become more of a family. Thank God we were able to do that.

I had a wonderful associate, Father Brendan Nagel, a brilliant young man from Dublin, Ireland. We put on a series of sessions on scripture and theological classes. I told him, "You take the scriptures," because he was brilliant in the Old and New Testaments, "and I'll take the doctrine of the church." The courses were a smashing success. We had one-hundred people weekly for months.

Then we put on another series called, "The Catholic Church and the Protestant religions." We learned more about our faith by studying what the Protestants taught and reflecting on what we believed. We also covered Mormonism, Hinduism, Buddhism, and various other religions and the people ended up very much informed. They enjoyed the classes and the camaraderie.

Unfortunately, in later years Father Nagel left the priesthood. It was a terrible loss for our priesthood, and I am sure a terrible loss for him. It certainly was a blow for me.

As I mentioned before, our parish had a twenty-seven mile coastline. Often I would go out on communion calls and be gone for three hours. I would travel inland, and then along the coast. It was time consuming to reach people who were sick and the shut-ins. I spent much time on the road, where the views were gorgeous.

I was on the Pacific Coast Highway driving north towards Port Dume the day that President John F. Kennedy was assassinated. When the news came over the radio, I was so shocked I pulled off the road. I saw many other cars doing the same.

After four great years in Malibu, Cardinal Francis McIntyre asked me to start a new parish in Hacienda Heights, California. The parish was named St. John Vianney. I was not ordered to take the assignment but did so voluntarily. I told the people of Our Lady of Malibu that I chose to leave them reluctantly but that I believed God wanted me to face a new challenge. They reluctantly but lovingly agreed with my decision.

# BUILDING A NEW CHURCH

There is no book that actually sets out how to start a parish.

On September 1, 1965, I came to Hacienda Heights with some information given to me by my classmate, Father Dick Murray, who had started St. Bernardine Parish in Woodland Hills. He advised me to meet the people, have coffee klatches, and find some other ways to gather them together to seek information.

I visited priests in various parishes in the area. Monsignor John McNamara, pastor at St. Martha's in Valinda, had been a former associate priest with me at St. Anthony's in Long Beach. He felt I was intruding a little upon his parish and was not too welcoming.

The pastor of St. Joseph, Eddie Callahan, was upset because he felt the archdiocese had cut some of the best areas from his parish to form St. John Vianney. Also, he was irritated with Monsignor Jim Mulcahy of St. Louis of France in the Bassett School District, believing Monsignor Mulcahy had been allowed to keep certain portions of his parish while he had not been given the same privilege.

None of the pastors from whom my territory had been carved offered me the census cards of the people from their areas that had been assigned to our parish.

I felt like a chicken running around with its feathers dragging in the rain and no place to go. "For God's sake," I said to Eddie Callahan. "I gave up the parish of Our Lady of Malibu where I had everything organized and paid for. We had great people there. After all, we belong to the same church."

"Well, it's not your fault," he said. "It is more with the way they do things at the Chancery Office."

So I was in a difficult situation.

Fortunately, Monsignor David Coleman at Our Lady of Guadalupe Parish in La Habra was a good friend. He said, "Why don't you come over and stay with me? I'll give you a room and a bath, and you can start working from here."

Fortunately I was able to get quarters in their rectory. He also gave me a thousand dollars to help sweeten the pot for the new parish.

Starting a parish is very difficult because one must have a place to gather the people for Mass.

I met a one-legged man, Bob James, who really helped me get started. (I also had a great friend with one leg in Malibu, Walter Hinkle, a veteran of World War II who had lost his leg in Corregidor. A strange coincidence; they were a great help to me. I was very close to both of these men.) Bob James, a go-getter, understood the challenge and helped get everything under control. He and I went around visiting various factories to see if we could find a place and space suitable for Mass.

Unfortunately, none of the factories were available, or if so, they were inadequate. None of the public schools had a facility open for us either so we were strapped for a gathering place.

Coincidentally, a young man whom I had formerly coached in football, Ted Zimmerman, was head of the adult education program of the Hacienda Heights School District. (He also had been the former football coach at La Puente High School.) When he heard I was in the area, he visited me and said, "Hey, can I help in any way?"

"Man, you sure can...if you can find a place where I can celebrate Mass."

He took me in to see the superintendent of schools, a Mr. Glenn Wilson. When I walked into the office, I'll never forget Ted saying to Mr. Wilson, "We are fortunate in this area to have a man of the caliber of Father O'Callaghan. He's going to be a great resource person here and a great inspiration for the people. We gotta help him."

Mr. Wilson, who was not a Catholic, said, "We'll do what we can."

I really liked Ted's spunk in presenting me.

Unfortunately, without a space to offer Mass, there can be no collection, and without revenue, one cannot get off the ground. I was already borrowing all the money I could get from the archdiocese to help start the new parish.

We heard there might be a gymnasium available up in La Habra Heights, an area situated between Hacienda Heights and La Habra. The situation was not ideal for two reasons: first, this gym was outside of our parish, and, second, there was a serpentine road leading to it. Nevertheless, it was a place in which we could offer Mass.

As luck would have it, we were able to negotiate with the county and finally arranged to rent that facility for Mass.

I would go up to the gym every Sunday morning at about five o'clock. (First I had to put the altar and all the equipment for Mass in the station wagon.) Someone would be there from the county to open the door. Then we set up 750 chairs for the seven o'clock Mass. That took some doing.

In between liturgies, I would celebrate two Masses and hear confessions. I also secured another priest to help me with one or two more Masses. We would clear the parking lot after each Mass and make space for the following ones. It became very difficult in the rain and mud. Thank God it didn't rain too often.

As there was only one highway going south to Whittier, I often had to go out and direct traffic in my cassock to get people's attention. It was a major problem and challenge, especially in the summer months when the surfers were making their way to the beaches, but we did the best we could.

After the Sunday twelve o'clock Mass, we had to take down the 750 chairs and stack them away. I would then get in my car and race to St. Joseph or St. Louis of France Churches to baptize the babies of our parishioners at three o'clock. After the baptism, I would go visit people in their homes.

People were very grateful and helpful.

I remember one Christmas midnight Mass when we decorated the basketball hoop with garlands and brought in small pine trees from the area. It was difficult, but the results were beautiful. The spirit of the people was great!

Mrs. June Schwarz organized coffee klatches throughout the parish boundaries, enabling me to meet parishioners and drink coffee until it came out my ears! We had them every day and possibly twice on Sundays. Ideally, twenty or more people gathered in a home and shared coffee and doughnuts or coffee cake. I would ask the people, "What kind of a church do you want? What is your idea of a parish community? What kind of architect would you like? Would you like to have a parochial school?" I got input from hundreds of people. I wanted to get to know them by name. It was a back breaking job, but worthwhile.

I learned that the people desired a big, beautiful church of modern Spanish design built on the property facing Turnbull Canyon Road. The archdiocese gave us almost fourteen acres of land for our parish site. The minimum sum was around $160,000. Cardinal McIntyre, a very wise man, had purchased it way ahead of time. The parish now had to buy that acreage back from him at low interest, but at least we had it!

We started to get the parish together. The people desired a permanent church. I did also, but Cardinal McIntyre said that he wanted us to build a temporary one. I knew once we got saddled with `a temporary church, we could have it for thirty, forty, fifty, or sixty years. It might remain a temporary church forever. So I had to really fight for our permanent church.

I went out and took a survey of the City of Industry and all the diversified factories situated there. Then I told the cardinal, "This place is going to grow, and it won't depend on aircraft or war. It has many diversified industries. The parish will grow and we need to build a church for at least 1400." That became another big battle. Eventually he changed his mind.

Next it was hard to get him to agree with the roofing material. We wanted to put on tile; he was against it. We wanted a portico in front of the church; he was also against that.

He had lots of definite ideas. Although Cardinal McIntyre

w a s  a  g r e a t  businessman, I don't think he had a great artistic sense. He had his own ideas of beauty. He certainly was a firm, determined man.

Finally, we were able to settle on building a permanent church. It was a tremendous blessing. I couldn't wait. Celebrating Masses every Sunday in La Habra Heights had been extremely difficult, time consuming, and back breaking. I think for one entire year of Sundays, I never had one off.

Tired of commuting from La Habra Heights, I asked Monsignor Ben Hawkes, the chancellor, if I could purchase a home in Hacienda Heights. Despite the generosity of Monsignor Coleman, it was very difficult to live out of our area. I wanted to get into Hacienda Heights and live among the parish people. Finally, Monsignor Hawkes said, "You can buy the home, and we'll loan you the money for it."

Of course, we eventually had to pay it back.

I purchased a home for $32,500, at 1515 Janlu Street. At the time, it was the real estate office for homes being sold in the area.

I remember asking for air conditioning for both the house and the church. It gets very hot in Hacienda Heights during the summer; air conditioning is a blessing.

"My God, what are you talking about?" Monsignor Hawkes said. "Do all the people out in that area have air conditioning?"

"Look at the homes around you here, Monsignor! Do they all have air conditioning?" I asked. "Even if all the houses around the chancery office don't have it yet, you do. What's the problem with me having it, also?"

He let that remark go by. We installed air conditioning in my home.

I kept meeting with the people during coffee klatches, gradually finding out what they wanted. They were very definite. They wanted a modern Spanish church, and they wanted the grounds to be beautiful. They desired a vibrant Catholic parish.

The area was mostly Anglo at that time. There was also a good sprinkling of Mexicans. There were no Asians and only a few Blacks.

As a whole the parish was quite well educated. I would say half of the adults were college graduates. I liked this educational level because I had been ministering to college people in the Newman Clubs. However, I just liked people in general. I met a very dynamic group of people at the coffee klatches. We started to work on getting our plans organized for the church and parish plant. Everyone was motivated, but we had one real challenge: raising the money!

I wanted a census taken to determine how many Catholic families were within our parish boundaries. I appointed Jack Nelson as the commander-in-chief of the census committee. Bob James and a number of other members were assigned along military terms. The men were appointed colonels, captains, majors, and lieutenants. We decided to carry out a survey of the entire area assigned to us by the archdiocese. The men went from door to door–God love them–and worked hard, accomplishing this task within two weeks. We finally came up with over 1500 families. This was a great start.

Some families had been going to St. Martha's, others to St. Joseph's, yet others to St. Louis of France. Now that their new parish was St. John Vianney, they were instructed to go to the gymnasium (our temporary parish church). This was very difficult for many. Some decided to remain in their own parishes until we could provide them with a feasible place for Mass in Hacienda Heights.

A conflict started among the parishioners. Many wanted a parochial school as well as a church; therefore, we decided to ask the archdiocese for permission to build both. It was granted.

Soon I was called in by the Hacienda Heights Improvement Association for a discussion regarding any proposed parish building and site. "We are very proud of our area here," they said. "If you are going to build a new church in our area, we want you to keep up with our standards of local beauty and environment."

We had a banquet with them one night. "Ladies and gentlemen," I began. "I just left Our Lady of Malibu where I was pastor, and we won a national prize for the most outstanding small landscaped church in America. You are going to have to strive to keep up with us when we put our parish together. It will be beautiful!"

Jack Neiland, a landscape architect, was a parishioner. He was very helpful. We started landscaping the whole area, cooperating with

Mr. John Bartlett, who was our architect for the project. Formerly, the thirteen-and-a-half acres had been an orchard, but it had been stripped of the orange and avocado trees and left absolutely barren. We planted over 120 pine trees, along with many other types, around the perimeter of most of our boundary area.

Unfortunately, vandals would sometimes come in at night and pull out the newly planted trees. Martin Giordano, our maintenance man, Cristobal Arellano, our gardener, and I would go out there the next morning to replant the trees before they died. It was a back breaking and challenging task.

When I see those beautiful trees now, it is inspiring. They are about one hundred feet high or more, and it looks like they have been there forever, but actually they were planted about thirty-five years ago. They are absolutely beautiful.

Next we put in the grass separating the parking areas. Finally, the construction of the church began. The architect did a tremendous job on the church and school. We gave the people the modern Spanish architecture they requested.

I had asked the cardinal for a church that would seat 1400; he finally agreed on 1200 after we presented him with the projected future of Hacienda Heights. I then asked if we could have stained glass windows.

"Are you out of your mind?" he replied.

Joe Moss, an accomplished artist from Laguna Beach, and I persuaded the cardinal that the price was right and the faceted glass would be most beautiful. Finally he agreed as the price was reasonable. Moss designed our magnificent windows. I think they are as beautiful as any I have ever seen. They tell the story of St. John Vianney's life at Ars, France.

The finished church turned out to be really warm and devotional. The people loved it and love it still. It was all brick, wood, and faceted glass. The rear of the church from the altar was less than 80 feet; its width was 118 feet. Everyone felt close to the altar.

Some people had asked why we weren't going to build a cruciform church. But I told them, "No, I want people in front of us and close to us so that when we offer Mass and preach we can see each person and each one can see us. I want a sanctuary close to the worshippers."

The people put together one tremendous church. We were very, very proud of it.

One of the biggest difficulties at the beginning of the parish was the absence of the Blessed Sacrament. We were able to purchase a residence for myself, but I was not allowed to reserve the Blessed Sacrament there. In case of a sick call, at any hour of the day or night I had to drive out to St. Joseph's in La Puente to get the Eucharist from their tabernacle, and then return to Hacienda Heights to administer the Eucharist to the sick person. I was always hoping to finish before the sick person died. I felt the tremendous need and hardship of living in an area where the Blessed Sacrament was not permanently housed.

We finally got the tabernacle installed and reserved the Eucharist there; Christ was living among us. Without it, I felt the "presence of the real absence!" But once the Blessed Sacrament was with us, oh, how I rejoiced! I can't adequately express how it felt knowing the Lord was always there dwelling among us. The Lord had come to dwell in Hacienda Heights in the midst of His people and was there upon our altar.

Next we had to discuss whether or not we'd have a grammar school. I took a survey of applicants for the second grade, asking how many would apply. We had two hundred children eligible for it; however, I could only seat forty or fifty at the most. Somehow I would have to choose fifty out of the two hundred. I wondered what should I do—put markers in a bowl and allow the first fifty pulled at random to attend? Everyone wanted his or her own child enrolled. *Maybe*, I thought, *we had better not have a Catholic school.*

That's when the cabbage hit the fan. I spoke to Cardinal McIntyre about it. He said, "You have to have a parochial school."

Actually, I think our people as a whole would rather have had a good CCD program because we couldn't possibly get hundreds of kids into our school. I thought it was too great an obstacle. I believed it was better to concentrate on the families rather than on the school. He said he would take that under advisement, and that I should gather information and report to the board of consultors.

I will never forget the day I was in Palm Springs on a golfing vacation with Emmett McCarthy, Dick Murray, Frank Roughan, Davie Coleman, and Jim Pierce. I got a phone call saying that the cardinal wanted to see me immediately. I was to address his board regarding the school at one o'clock in the afternoon on Thursday.

I was in the midst of my vacation, a vacation which I really needed. I said, "Oh Lord!" but I drove home, got my materials together, and presented myself at the chancery before the board of consultors.

When I faced Cardinal McIntyre, he was adamant. "Father O'Callaghan, I understand you don't want to build a parochial school."

"Well, it's not that I don't want to build a parochial school." I responded. "It's just that we have too many grammar school students and there won't be enough space for them. We'd have to choose and reject. This would irritate and disturb many of the people whose children would be rejected. I think we should concentrate on educating the families and the children as a whole in a CCD program."

Nevertheless, Cardinal McIntyre wanted the grammar school. He began by asking the council about it, and then I presented my case. Finally, the council members presented their input, also.

The first one to dare to dissent against the cardinal was Monsignor Bernard J. Dolan, my former pastor. The cardinal really turned on him and lashed out. The next man to come to my proposal's defense was Monsignor William North. The cardinal jumped all over him, too. Then another priest, Monsignor John Clarke, spoke up for me. I think there were four out of the twelve for my proposal, but the cardinal ripped into each one of them. Then he told me that his mind was made up. "I want you to have that parochial school."

"Well," I said, "Cardinal, I'll accept the fact that you want a parochial school. I'll obey you, but I have a God-given right not to agree with you."

"What do you mean you don't agree with me?"

"As pastor of the parish I have better judgment regarding our peoples' needs than you do."

Then he really blew up. "How dare you insult this august body of men here—these experienced consultors—and me! How can you say that? I'm so angry that I'll let the board take over this meeting."

But he never did. The doors were open, and the chancery personnel in other offices could hear the ruckus from the council meeting.

"I know where my people are coming from," I continued, "and I am not in favor of a parochial school under our conditions and circumstances."

"You are intractable."

"No. I shall obey you, but I have to state my opinion."

Monsignor Paul Stroup was seated next to me. "For God's, sake, Jim, knock it off," he said.

"Paul, keep your own peace. I am fighting for what the people want, and by God I have the right to say what I'm going to say."

I had begun to pack up my gear, when the cardinal asked, "Where are you going?"

"Well, it's over."

"Stay where you are," he ordered. He looked really angry. Finally he said, "You do as I say."

"Archbishop, I will do as you say," I repeated. "I just want to state that I don't agree with you, but I will obey you." I felt really ticked off as I was exiting.

Just as I was going out the door he said softly, "By the way, Father O'Callaghan, we have been very hard on you."

"Don't worry about it. I shall take my hostility out on a golf ball." I went back to Palm Springs to lick my wounds. I may have been beaten down but I had not been totally vanquished yet. When I got back from vacation, I thought it through and told myself, "I'm not buying into this without a challenge."

I told the people about the cardinal's decision even though I had been warned by one of the consultors, "Don't do that, Jim, because if you do you are going to cause more problems with the cardinal. He's adamant on the school business."

"I want to let him know what the people really think," I replied. "I asked the people to vote whether they wanted a parochial school or a CCD program. The result was that about 85 percent said they were in favor of our CCD plan, mostly because they couldn't get all their kids in the school."

So, I gathered my materials together again, and I called for an appointment with Cardinal McIntyre.

As I entered his office he looked at me and said, "You again?"

"Yes," I replied. "I want to give you some information I have regarding the parochial school question."

"What do you mean?"

"Here it is." I laid my findings on the desk: "86 percent of our people are in favor of not having a parochial school because many would be unable to enroll their children in the school."

He looked at me and said, "I'm amazed."

"I tried to tell you this, but you were so angry I couldn't get it across."

"We'll take this on a trial basis, and you need not begin a parochial school."

"Thank you, Your Eminence," I said, and then I walked out. I respected Cardinal McIntyre even more after that because I could confront him and give him opposing ideas. He would challenge a priest and cut him down if he was wrong, but he also could use objectivity. In my case he finally said, "You have my blessing."

Subsequently, I had phone calls from everywhere. "Jim, that's great!"

So we did not have to start a parochial school. That saved us a lot of money which could be put into other areas. Otherwise, many future plans could not have been developed as the money for them would have been absorbed by the funding of a school, its staff and maintenance.

By this time the church design was completed. Mr. John Bartlett, the architect, and I went to present the plans and a model of our future church to the cardinal and the building commission.

Cardinal McIntyre again disagreed with us—this time about the portico in front of the church. We wanted a porch to shield against the sun and the heat, but he didn't like it. He got so angry that he broke a small portion of the model. He said, "I do not like the structure and facade at the front of the church. It is ugly."

"It's all a question of beauty, Your Eminence. I like it, and beauty is in the eye of the beholder."

"You do as I say," he replied.

"I will," I said. But it wasn't over!

Later, I went to his office and brought him a sketch of the future church, including the front portico he had disliked. "Didn't I condemn this before?" he asked.

"Yes, you did."

"I like it now."

At least I could work with him and get him to change his mind if the ideas and plans were valid and properly presented.

Until space for religion classes was built, we had to catechize many hundreds of parish children in various areas. We taught some of them in garages throughout the dispersed parts of our parish.

I went to the public school system and asked if I could rent a few of their rooms for catechism, but I ran into a stone wall because our area was predominantly populated by fundamentalists. "It's not our policy," they said. "You can't do that."

I told the people, "Let's go to a school board meeting; we'll get our proposal on the agenda. I want all of you to dress to the teeth, and we'll go down there, using the steel fist in the velvet glove approach."

We stacked the school board meeting with our people, presented our request, and got on their future agenda. Amazingly, they later changed their policy. For $5,000 yearly, we were able to rent or lease rooms in different schools where we could meet and start teaching our kids CCD classes. This enabled us to eliminate instructing them in garages.

Then the next question came up: "Can we have some of our guilds meet in the schools?"

"No," they replied. "You will either have to rent the rooms or find activity locations elsewhere because, after all, yours is a church activity."

"What are you talking about?" I responded. "You have Boy Scouts and various other organizations meeting in your schools for free. The mothers' guild is not totally religious. It is a gathering of a group to help our church."

They still said no.

I selected another place in a public school and planned to have our women's guilds meet there. I had asked local School Superintendent Russell Ribb if we could have it for free.

"You will have to pay a fee," he replied.

"You allow Boy Scouts and other groups to meet in public school rooms without a fee, so why not us?"

He still said we should pay a moderate fee so I told Jack Nelson, "Take this check to Russell Ribb and tell him I am going to take this matter to the pulpit and print it in the bulletin, asking why they allow the Boy Scouts and other groups to meet in the public school rooms and not us."

Russ Ribb said he would take up the matter with the county counsel.

"The county counsel has one opinion," I told him. "But I'm not going to depend on it. We also have archdiocesan lawyers, and we shall get an opinion from them."

Russ sent the check back via Jack Nelson, my representative, and said, "You can have it for nothing."

We were able to use the school facilities through that approach. The public schools seemed to cooperate more and more with us, especially once the members of the school board told them: "We are here to build up the educational moral atmosphere of the entire area of Hacienda Heights. Hopefully, what the church teaches will result in better students, who will be more conscious of their obligations to be c a r i n g, r e s p o n s i b l e, a n d honest young men and women who are respectful of their teachers."

From that time on the school board changed its attitude toward us, and we all got along well. We began to visit the public schools, and a good mutual spirit has prevailed in Hacienda Heights during all of the last twenty-seven years. We have a wonderful public school system here, and the Church has been very much a part of it. Our priests have been welcomed on campus, and we have worked hand in hand with all the school personnel.

Later on I asked Cardinal McIntyre if we could build a rectory once the church and school were built. I wanted to live next to the church. That, of course, was another challenge.

He gave us permission but put us on a limited budget, so we had to bootleg a few things, such as a wall around the rectory and plans to make it look bigger, more hospitable, and decorative. We hoped for the best. The main thing was to keep the cardinal away from the parish site. He had been in New York where lack of space made every inch functional. He also was very definite about his convictions. As I mentioned before, he wanted the foundation of the church close to Turnbull Canyon Road. He also wanted the school built quite close to the church. There would be very little space separating the two buildings.

"For the love of God, I want a big space with trees and grass between the church and the school," I said. It was essential to keep Cardinal McIntyre away from the site until the foundations were laid.

When we had that done, he came out to check the property. As he was driving through the site, he remarked, "I thought I wanted the school built in this area, and now you have this big space separating it from the church."

"Oh is that what you wanted?" I replied, "I'm sorry. The foundations are in now."

He let that remark pass by, thanks be to God.

We also recessed the church back about thirty feet to provide for funerals and wedding processions in front of the church. Like St. Patrick's Cathedral in New York, the cardinal wanted our church front practically on the street and sidewalk. I must say, Cardinal McIntyre never forgot what he had previously decided upon or stated should be done.

Unfortunately, our property had no access to the west. There was an Assembly of God Church located on an acre and a half fronting the west side of the parish. I talked to the minister and learned that he was dissatisfied with how the Assembly of God board was hindering his plans for building a library complex. He made it clear that this property could be open for purchase.

"I'd like to purchase that property as it would give us western access," I told Cardinal McIntyre. "Their minister told me it would have to go through the Assembly of God's board of deacons. I have spoken to Mr. Purcell, the chancery official, about our need for it but have made no progress."

Once I got so exasperated when I received no answers from the chancery office that I slammed the phone down on Mr. Purcell and said, "I've had it!"

Immediately, there was a return phone call. "This is Cardinal McIntyre. Have you got a problem?"

"Yes, we have a problem! You people downtown make judgments and don't know what's going on out here."

"I'll be out there tomorrow morning at ten o'clock."

He did indeed arrive with Mr. Dick Purcell, the head of escrow. When they pulled up in front of my temporary rectory, the cardinal said, "Now, Father O'Callaghan, you get in my car, and we'll drive around and analyze the situation. I don't want you to say anything to me, and I won't say anything to you until we size it up. After we size it up I want you to reason a little, compromise a little, and so will I. We will see if we can come up with a solution."

So, we drove around and looked at the property and also the area on the west side where many of our people lived. We then discussed it with Mr. Purcell. Cardinal was cordial; he could see the need to obtain the Assembly of God's property and open up access to the parishioners living on the west side. He said, "All right, you can purchase that Assembly of God property. However, they are asking $117,000. You will not give them one penny more than $70,000."

At least we now had a goal.

It took a lot of negotiation to deal with the minister who favored us, as did some of his deacons. We made one compromise after another. Astoundingly we purchased that most-needed property. It now has a building named "Dolan Hall," in memory of my mentor, Monsignor Bernard J. Dolan. The purchase price was $70,100.

Amazingly, we accomplished the entire project for the low sum of $800,000. Such buildings today would cost almost four or five million dollars. We were very fortunate.

# PRIESTLY FELLOWSHIP

The heart of the St. John Vianney Rectory was actually our dining room table. It is where we discussed our homilies, promoted fraternity, and shared our ideas and convictions. The conversation was never dull. It is quite important for every priest's home to have a good cook. Tasty and well-prepared meals inspire camaraderie and good fun. It is the one time the average parish priest is able to get together to communicate and socialize with his fellow priests. Other times priests are each busy with their own ministry and obligations. Our parish of over five thousand families made many demands upon the ministering priests.

We never had a head of the table chair throughout our years at St. John Vianney. I always felt that everyone seated at the table was on an equal basis and had a right to his opinion. Therefore, it was open season for anyone who sat there.

Over the years I was blessed with the most wonderful young priests who made enormous contributions to our parish. Many of these young men went on to higher studies after being honed and prepared by our people. In some ways this was unfortunate because their studies in theology, philosophy, spirituality, and dogma took them away from parish ministry and placed them in the academic and spirituality formation, far from the parish level. I always felt this was kind of a disservice to God's people because these priests were so great at ministering to them. However, our cardinal knew what he was about. He needed these men to help train others for parish ministries.

Even though I was not able to go on a real sabbatical for fifty-two years, these bright young men taught me where the church was going, the current development in theology, scripture, liturgy, etc. They were well versed about Vatican II and the following developments in the church. My expertise was experience, and I could challenge them from that perspective. I had practical knowledge of what would wash and what would not wash, what would happen or what might not happen. Experience does teach much! We had great, great times.

Normally many of the things that happened in our parish were due to the wisdom, vision, challenges, and understanding of these young priests. They made a definite impact upon our parish pastoral life. When I looked at the mosaic of our parish life, I saw it had been put together from their contributions and ideas; just as different colorful bits of colored marble constitute a total picture. This model identified our parish life and sought to meet its goals and challenges. What these young men had done was incredible. They had given St. John Vianney Parish its character, tone, love, and depth. My role was to permit, challenge, and correct them, and, if they erred, to encourage them to bury their failures, learn from them, and move on.

This was also true of our sisters, deacons, lay ministers, and parish organizations. They initiated many ideas: everything from the Basic Family Program to the Martin De Porres Center, from spiritual organizations to cultural groups. If the parishioners wanted to initiate a new group, I would say, "You may have any organization you wish in the parish, provided it is permitted by our Holy Father the Pope and our Cardinal. You may start them and do the work and ministry that follows. However, I need not be a member of any one of these organizations. If I choose not to join the charismatic group, or St. Vincent de Paul, or the Filipino Catholic Association, that's my right! Please don't attempt to lay any guilt on me. You have the right to those organizations. I am in favor of them! But count me out if I choose not to be a member." The associate priests also had this choice. The decision worked out well.


It was quite incredible to witness the zeal and enthusiasm of our associates and to share their difficulties. At times they would tend to get frustrated or discouraged. After all, most of what priests meet during the course of their daily activities is negative: a marriage problem, a kid in trouble from a narcotic addiction, an alcoholic husband, a psychological illness with a wife, a rebellious kid, a disturbance in school, someone in jail for a crime. Much of what comes to our office is a challenge and can drain one.

There also were a lot of wonderful things going on in our ministry: preparing people for marriage, hearing confessions, baptisms, first communions, counseling, and instruction of potential converts. Oftentimes we discussed these challenges at meals or at sessions in the rectory home. I could reassure them things were going to be all right despite opposition or lack of enthusiasm from some of the parishioners.

I remember one particular night when Father Jack Stoeger came in with Sister Joann. They had been having coffee in the dining room and both were at the point of tears. Each of them separately had taken a lot of flak that particular day. I could see they were discouraged, so I said, "Let's have a little wine and cheese and talk about this." I got a bottle of wine and three glasses, and we had an hour's discussion. After that we were all laughing because we knew we were in this together and that we couldn't take all of life's challenges too seriously. After all, God is still in charge.


How well I remember another occasion when I came into the rectory after finishing evening confessions in the church. It was about ten o'clock at night. Father Jack Stoeger was sitting on the kitchen counter, eating a piece of cake and drinking a glass of milk. Father Douglas Ferraro was sitting at the kitchen table having a Diet Pepsi.

"My God, what a day I had!" Father Stoeger said to me. "Listen to this." He spelled out all the problems he had had to confront and try to solve that day.

Father Ferraro then remarked, "You ain't heard nothing yet." He listed the challenges of his day.

"Let me tell you what I encountered," I said. "I'll top you both!"

That's how we talked through many of these things, sharing each other's challenges with a great spirit of sympathy, camaraderie, and understanding.

We also had the privilege of having a retired priest named Monsignor Denis O'Duignan live with us for seven years. We called him "The Monsignor." He had been a pastor in Kansas City, where he had built a parish from scratch, been an official in the marriage tribunal, and worked with Catholic Charities. He was a charming man of all seasons. We met him through Father Ferraro, who had invited The Monsignor to spend his retirement with us.

"You earned your monsignorship as a young priest," I told him. "I had been appointed monsignor through osmosis. After all, every other member of my class was designated one. How could they turn me down since I wasn't that bad?!"

He was our monsignor! He brought so much wisdom and understanding to the table. He also liked the ladies. "My God, Monsignor, this priest has a father besides a mother," I would tell him. "Why don't you ask about him?" It was always the ladies and the mothers.

Monsignor O'Duignan would sit at the table discussing history and the classics with Father Joe Shea, who was a bright young man. They regaled us with their knowledge of history. They might start with Sparta in Greece and then go through all the battles of our Civil War, describing the campaigns and war strategies of Generals Sherman, Robert E. Lee, and Ulysses S. Grant. Both priests also loved Aristotle and Caesar. At times all of us would join in, questioning and challenging them.

Any subject was allowed at our table: politics, religion, sports, sexuality, narcotics, ecumenism, etc. One time a visiting priest came to our table. Someone brought up the area of sexuality and we got into a heated discussion. "I don't think that topic should be discussed at this table," he said.

"Father, no one controls or monitors discussions at this table," I told him. "If this bothers you, you can leave and have your meal either up in your room or in the kitchen. However, you will not regulate what is discussed here."

He chose to remain, and later on he got involved in the discussion himself. It was always open season. Priests must be able to express themselves. Young priests had to realize the temptations and struggles of the older priests. Older priests had to realize what challenges young priests were facing. In this way we were able to better understand each other.

We really enjoyed each other's company and it showed in the parish. Sometimes one of the younger priests or I might drop by for a glass of wine at dinnertime on our day off so we would not miss that evening's discussion.

One of the greatest tributes that I ever got as pastor of our parish was when Father Lawrence Baird came home one night and said, "You know, Father O, come nighttime, when I turn into the parish driveway to put my car in the garage, I say, 'Oh my God, I have come home.'"

Our table was sometimes blessed by the presence of our wonderful parish nuns: Sisters Rose Ann, Joann, Theresa, Lydia, Mary Ann, and many others. They brought so much, both intellectually and spiritually, when they came for meals. We shared and shared alike.

Other times we had lay people at our table. It was a tremendous privilege to have lay persons who both informed and challenged us with their questions. Medical doctors Louis Marchioli and Carlos Espinosa often added their expertise.

A wonderful spirit of happiness prevailed around our table; the camaraderie was outstanding. This spirit of hospitality is so necessary today for priests. Monsignor Dolan had taught me this a long time ago when he said, "Father, as an associate I want you to be at our dinner each evening except on your day off." At times Monsignor Dolan could be very taciturn, but he was right on target in other ways!

My rule for the priests was: Be on time for meals. This is our private time together. Give each other forty-five minutes to an hour to communicate and socialize. If a person comes in and wants to see you at twelve or six o'clock, let them wait until after lunch or dinner because it is imperative that we be together.

Naturally, a sick call would preempt everything. It is incredible how people hate to wait for priests for even a half hour, but they will wait three or four hours to see their doctor. The sad part is since there is no charge they sometimes think they are doing us a favor by coming to us. People have to learn and respect that priests need each other's company.

When a new pastor was assigned to St. John Vianney upon my retirement, he had his own table so he gave the old one to me. I placed the table and chairs in my brother-in-law and sister's dining room at their home in San Clemente. About two months ago, several former associates—Father Lawrence Baird, Father Fred Gaglia, Father Joe Shea, and Father John Montejano, a newly ordained priest from our parish—gathered around that table. We were having a great discussion when someone exclaimed, "My God, this is the old table from the rectory! Things are the same! We need each other, we enjoy each other, and God loves this table."

All in all, I think priests in every rectory should work very hard to make sure that the priests are present at meals, have a good cook, and share each other's joys, disappointments, and anxieties. Yes, the table means so much to a priest's life and ministry.

Hermes Pan, Fr. O, Mrs. O'Callaghan
Mike and Mary Kevany, 1950

Fr. O

The temporary church
La Habra Heights
Gymnasium, 1966

St. John Vianney Church
Hacienda Heights, CA
Ground breaking, 1967

Construction picture
St. John Vianney Church

Rory and Parnell

Blessing of the animals
St. John Vianney, 1980

June and Egon Schwarz with Fr. O, 1972

The Rectory Table

Fr. O and friends

No sport too challenging, 1979

Father Jim Hansen at podium
One of Fr. O's many Roasts, 1974

Variety show, 1975

The ordination of Fr. Cahill, M.J., 1986    Fr. Tom Cahill, 2011

Fr. O presenting St. John Vianney Parish    Fr. O making a point
Book to Pope John Paul II, 1986

Priestly friends (l to r), Frs. Albert Bahouth, Lawrence Baird, John Montehano, Fr. O, JackStoeger, Joe Shea, Kevin Kostelnik, 2001

Deacon Jesse Martinez, Msgr. Timothy Nichols, Fr. Christopher Terry O.P., Msgr. O, 2001

Fr. Joseph Shea, Sr. Joann Heinritz,
Fr. O, Fr. Jack Stoeger

Sr. Mary Ann Scanlon,
G.S.J., (above)

Sr. Theresa Harpin,
C.S.J. (below)

Jean Bernhardt, Fr. O,
Cindi Bernhardt, Fr. Shea, 1997

Sister Leonella, 1997

Hermitage Big Sur, 2000

Valerie Sinkus, Irma Martz,
Fr. O, Sister Joann at the Hermitage

Monsignor James O'Callaghan, 1995

# PART THREE:
# EVERYDAY SAINTS AND SINNERS

# THE WOUNDED HEALER

Years ago, at the persuasion of Father Jack Stoeger, Sister Joann Heinritz, and Father Joe Shea, I left St. John Vianney parish for seven weeks to study at the Jesuit Theology Center in Berkeley, California. I lived at the Chardin House, which was the resident home for both the Jesuits who were on sabbatical studies and current Jesuit theological students, plus other guests. As a diocesan priest, I was allowed to be a guest.

One day, I remember discussing "woundedness" with Father Michael Buckley, a Jesuit theologian, and Father Jack Stoeger, my former associate. Father Buckley, S.J., had given a talk titled "Am I Weak Enough to be a Priest?" to the young Jesuits preparing for the deaconate. That title really turned me off. "I can't buy into that," I said. "Because my ideal is: 'Don't show weakness if you wish to make things happen. Be in charge.'"

I was not convinced by their arguments. Later I came home to continue my ministry. As always there were challenges to be met, solutions to be found, obstacles to be overcome. If I failed, I buried it, tried not to make the same mistake twice, and went on, not letting it affect me too much.

What little did I really know!

The Lord has very wise ways of dealing with us. Some years later I was on the sixth hole of the El Monte Golf Course. I had borrowed a graphite shaft driver to obtain more distance in my old age. I still remember hitting the ball right down the middle of the fairway when all hell broke loose. It seemed as if my back fell apart, and my legs were in terrible pain. It was all I could do to stagger off the course, get into my car, and drive home. That was the beginning of the end as far as my athletic activities were concerned.

I consulted the doctors, especially my orthopedic surgeon, Dr. Michael Esposito, and his father, Dr. Leslie Esposito. They ordered some X-rays taken, and both physicians recommended back surgery. They brought in a neurosurgeon who worked along with Dr. Esposito. I was operated on for six or seven hours at St. Mary's Hospital in Long Beach. They took bones from my hip and put them in my spine, hoping that all would work out. This was actually the second surgery I had had on my back over a period of ten years, both the result of imperfect golf swings. When I came out of the surgery, my recovery didn't go too well. I had to be in a cast for months; the pain was constant. I was out of control. Previously I had pictured myself confined to my bed, telling myself, "Because of my pride, someday the Lord is going to put me down in a bed, totally helpless, under the influence of narcotics with a catheter up my penis and nowhere to go." And that's exactly what happened.

I remember one day in the hospital when an old Italian friend of mine, who had never been sick a day in his life, came to visit. "You know, Father O, you ought to be grateful you are not blind," he said.

I could have nailed him to the wall. Not knowing how I felt and never having experienced a debilitating injury, his remarks seemed so insensitive. I learned from that remark never to tell a suffering person, "I know how you feel," because no one but the sufferer does. It is better to be quiet than make inane remarks.

I spent many days in the hospital and finally went home to the rectory where the other priests looked after me. Since I had my back casted, I was more or less helpless. The priests would remove the cast, take me to the shower, and wash and bathe me. They would have to replace my cast as I lay on the bed. I was totally dependent on others, and it was hard being so out of control. I was fighting it all along, especially because I was in pain.

I couldn't sleep; I was taking Halcyon and other narcotics. It was challenging to only lie in bed or stand. I could not sit up or ride in a car for almost nine months. I forgot what it was like to be outside at night in the dark. After a while, I began to get very depressed.

People would come to visit me, but I wasn't anxious to see anyone, including my family members and special friends. No matter what I did or to whom I was talking, it seemed that the pain and discomfort was like a silk stocking over my eyes. No matter what I said or what I looked at, I was conscious of that silk stocking.

As time dragged on I became more and more addicted to Halcyon. I could not sleep at night at all. I envied the priests who could go to bed and sleep while there I was confined to my cast, lying sleepless in bed. I could not get out of bed unless someone supported me, and then I would walk with the cast on my back.

The only consolation I had, if any, was to offer Mass every day flat on my back in the bed. I would invite people from the Corpus Christi Center (the business and social center of our parish), and three or four would assist. That helped. I said my Divine Office, prayers, and rosary every day, but it was an effort. When I finished, I was glad it was over.

I couldn't read or watch television. Uninterested in anything except reflecting upon my own woundedness, I felt totally helpless. Sister Alphonse from St. Mary's Hospital in Long Beach, and my doctor, Mike Esposito, decided that perhaps I should go to the pain center at Long Beach Memorial Hospital. Hopefully this would help me cope with my pain.

The center's staff united each patient with others suffering from excruciating pain. One man I was assigned to was a garbage collector from Las Vegas, the father of ten, about fifty years of age, who had been in charge of dumpsters. Somebody had put a lot of bricks into a dumpster, which was against the law, and then put brush on top. Not knowing it was filled with bricks, he elevated it over his head. It broke and crushed him. This man was in excruciating pain. What a noble man he was! A real Christian, he loved Christ, and he frequently quoted the Bible and received strength from it.

The second man I was assigned was an electrician from Downey. He had a lot of pain throughout his arm and shoulder. We all tried to help him, but he broke down mentally and had to go to the psychiatric ward.

The third man was a Muslim from Kuwait. He, too, had great

stress and pain. He was a tremendous man. He prayed hard and accepted God's will.

The fourth person I had was a young Mexican mother of two, and she was also in excruciating pain. We five banded together, relating to each other's needs. We tried to console and help each other. I would go talk to them at bedtime, trying to encourage them. They in turn helped me. One thing we had in common was pain!

We tried biofeedback. We participated in discussions, listened to music and sounds of water. We had counseling to relax us. They gave us narcotics.

I stayed away from narcotics, even the sedating drinks, and life went on very slowly, monotonously, and painfully. We heard various lectures on pain control. One day a professor gave us a lecture on pain, and when he had finished I said to him, "You know, professor, you telling me how pain is, is like me telling a woman how it feels to be pregnant. You are not with it at all."

"You are right, Father. I'm not in the pain that you're in," he replied.

This regimen went on for quite some time. The challenge to face reality came one midnight. I will never forget it.

I had been really depressed. During my illness I could not look at a crucifix and say the words, "Lord, I accept whatever it is that is happening to me." I could not accept it. I didn't want to be wounded.

That particular night I had been unable to sleep. I started walking down the hall in the hospital until I passed the area where the cancer patients, the paraplegics, and the emergency cases were housed. I asked myself, *What am I doing here? I don't belong here. I take care of these people.* Then it occurred to me: *You are here because you are one of them!* That's when the cabbage hit the fan. I believe that was the lowest emotional, psychological, and perhaps spiritual point in my entire life.

I went back to my room and sat down on the bed. Still unable to look at the crucifix, I began to reflect on a favorite prayer of mine that I had come across in *Thomas Merton's Palace to the Path of Nowhere*, written by James Finley, a Trappist brother. I frequently recited it: "Prayer is the distilled awareness of the presence of the Father who tells me, imitate my Son and the Holy Spirit will enable you to make it happen [sic]." I reflected on this prayer over and over again, but I kept questioning, *Oh, God, what kind of a father are You? I have given my life as a priest; I try to do the best I can in my priestly life.* I was feeling very sorry for myself!

Then I reflected on the fathers of infants. I have had the privilege of baptizing babies and watching them in their father's and mother's arms, totally dependent. I knew that God had said He loved us even more than a mother or a father loved his child, and I knew those children were totally dependent upon their fathers, loving them unconditionally. If their fathers and mothers did not take care of them, they would die. I thought, *If God loves me even more than these parents love their children, then I should love and be as dependent upon God as these children are upon their parents,* but I still could not bring myself to that acceptance.

Then I reflected, *God, I realize now You do love me because You created me, You sustain me, and You have given me Christ to show Your love for me.* I thought in terms of prayers offered in awareness of the Father's presence and said, "OK, I am present to You, Father, You who say, 'Imitate my Son.'" As I reflected on that, I remembered God ordering Abraham to sacrifice his son Isaac.

It really tore that old man apart as he walked up the sacrificial hill, Isaac by his side. Abraham agonized over this, but he was a man of faith. He was going to do what the Father ordered. When Isaac wondered where was the ram they were going to sacrifice, Abraham said nothing. When they got to the top of the hill, Abraham drew out his sword to kill his son in a tremendous act of faith. But then the Lord spared them both. They spotted a ram caught in the bushes. Abraham told his son, "Get the ram, and we'll build a fire." They killed it, and that was the sacrifice. Abraham's faith was certainly tested, but God spared the man's son.

Then I reflected upon Jesus in the Garden of Gethsemane. If anyone loved the Son, it was the Father. He truly loved his Son with an unimaginable love, and yet we find Christ in the Garden undergoing tremendous torture, the apostles falling asleep, and everyone deserting Him. Abandoned, almost at the point of despair, He breaks out in a bloody sweat; crying, "Father, if possible let this chalice pass from me. Don't have me go through this." The Father said, "Do it [sic]." Christ submitted and went to His passion and death for us. So, I thought, *My God, if You can demand that of Your Son, whom You love beyond any other individual or person in the whole world as part of the Trinity, then certainly You can demand this of me.*

I said, "Lord, I do believe You love me, that You ask me to imitate Your Son, and that the Holy Spirit will sustain me. Help me to somehow get through this. I am aware of Your presence. I'm trying to imitate Your Son, but when is the Holy Spirit coming?"

Gradually, over a period of days, it occurred to me to go and visit and dialogue with the patients, nurses, helpers, staff, and visitors. Everybody we meet in the hospital—whether it is a nurse, doctor, or staff member—has a story. I decided to go out and minister to them. Gradually some of the pain left as well as some of the depression. Finally, I was allowed to go home.

When I got home, I began to hear people's stories there, too. A prayer group came to me and said, "Can we pray over you?" I was never much for this charismatic prayer business, but I said, "All right."

About forty-five people came into the room, and they placed their hands upon me, praying that I might be healed. I didn't exactly have faith that it would happen. However, shortly after that I began to feel a little better. I could stand a little longer on my feet; it was less painful than before. Then Cristobal Arellano came in with a group of his Mexican men and said that they would like to pray over me. I respected him as he is a very spiritual and wise man. As they prayed over me, I asked God to help me.

Whenever I went to see Dr. Michael Esposito for follow-up care, I had to lie across the car seat, and then stand in a corner of his waiting room until he could see me. I still could not watch television and was uninterested in the newspapers or magazines. I was committed to nothing except getting through my Mass and prayers. All this was very difficult. I kept asking God, "When is relief coming?" I started a novena to our Blessed Mother, asking Mary to intercede so that somehow I would be able to sit and drive a car and not have to be always lying down and having people looking after me.

Slowly but surely the pain began to subside, and now, through God's grace, I can drive without pain and work in my office. I'm unable to do any kind of active sports such as swinging a golf club, but I'm able to minister, say Mass, get along by myself at home, and walk. I'm so grateful to God, our Blessed Mother, and all the people who prayed for me. I now say a novena in thanksgiving every day of my life. I can't explain this healing to scientifically-oriented people, but God definitely stepped into my life. Did He teach me a lesson? Oh, He did. The positive results of all of this are the following.

Formerly I took care of people who were ill or sick, but it was with the attitude of a disciplined soldier. If I got a sick call at three o'clock in the morning, I didn't want to leave my warm bed. I didn't say, "Isn't it beautiful? I'm going to take care of the sick." Heck no! This was three a.m. But I went out to minister to the person, and when I came back after having helped the sick person and having administered the sacraments, I was always grateful for having been able to do so. But back then I didn't have a real understanding of compassion.

Now, being a wounded person, it's a little different. I see people hurting, and I have an idea of what they are experiencing. I will never in my life tell a sick person, "I know how you feel," because I do not know how he or she feels. Only God know how they feel.

I was celebrating a Sunday Mass at St. Dorothy Church in Glendora some years ago when my attention was drawn to a young woman brought to church by her family. She was both mentally and physically handicapped. Her features were contorted and in constant motion. Perhaps thirty years of age, she was physically and mentally incompetent. When I first noticed her, after my wakeup call, I approached her parents and said, "God love you all! It's so marvelous to be in the presence of such beauty, such loveliness, and such innocence." Then I embraced the little girl and kissed her. The parents began crying. I said, "What a grace she is!" Neither I nor my ministry was the same anymore.

Now when I minister to the sick and the dying I never ask, "How do you feel?" I am a handicapped person, and the Lord in His wisdom had to bring me to my knees to learn compassion. Yes, I can't play golf, surf, hunt, and fish anymore. I have been stripped of these pleasures. However, I am able to swim. The YMCA knows me well. That keeps me in shape. I am in the water for one hour five times a week. If I can, I tread water and swim with the aid of an aqua jogger, not touching my feet on the bottom. This strengthens my legs and puts no pressure on my spine. How grateful I am to God for bringing me to my senses. I believe I am a more grateful and compassionate person now. I can truly say that God gifted me via this back injury by bringing me to my senses. I think I'm a better priest and a more candid person. I know I'm a more compassionate one. Now I truly see the beauty of being wounded. Christ was wounded; He is there with me. I am wounded, and I am united with Christ's woundedness. I hope and pray to get better as the years go on. It certainly has been an experience for me to learn to be a wounded healer.

## CINDI BERNHARDT

In the course of a priest's pastoral ministry, we meet some remarkable people. One of the most amazing, courageous persons I have ever met was Cindi Bernhardt, a girl from our parish. This dynamic girl had just graduated from Nogales High School and had been accepted to attend a college in Colorado. She was a fine student, gymnast, and cheerleader, an extremely beautiful girl. Her flaming red hair and personality made her very visible.

In 1981, she was so happy to attend school that in the spirit of fun she did a back flip for her girlfriends. Unfortunately, she somehow fell through an open window and landed at the base of the building. The fall broke her neck, making her a quadriplegic, unable to walk or use her hands.

While in physical therapy, she learned how to draw and later paint with a brush in her mouth. She perfected her skills over the course of several years, and her work was exhibited in public and private collections. Cindi also became a member of the Association of Mouth and Foot Painting Artists.

I could not believe the courage, faith, and humor of this magnificent young woman during her therapy. Fortunately, she had a mother, Jean, whose love and support greatly assisted and sustained Cindi. She also had two lovely sisters. Her father had died in the interim, yet throughout all her trials Cindi had taken a position of absolute courage. She attended college and worked with handicapped children. She also established a handicapped society. Her courageous and faith-filled attitude influenced numerous people. She spoke at church services and seminars, giving inspirational talks, and in so doing traveled all over the United States. She positively impacted many individuals and groups. The incredible thing about Cindi was that whenever one met her, she had a smile and a good word. She was always positive, cheerful, and ready to interact.

Her paralysis was obviously difficult to bear, but her attitude encouraged us to look at our own lives and ask, "Where does she get this strength?" Cindi certainly got the strength through her faith, from her indomitable will, and from the support of her family, particularly her mother Jean and friends. Instead of being a millstone around her neck, this tremendous handicap had been turned into something very positive. I often thought if Cindi had gone through college and become a teacher or social worker, or perhaps a wife and mother, she would have been the best! But in God's plan, she has reached thousands of people; as a quadriplegic she has been a source of inspiration to countless families, men, and women, indeed to everyone whom she meets. At a time when people strive to lower the bar of challenge, she has raised the bar and gone beyond it. One could not meet that magnificent young woman and not be inspired to go out and be a better person. Her faith was deeply rooted.

Some years ago, when I had that very difficult surgery on my back and was left pretty much immobilized, I remember her mother bringing Cindi for a visit. Smiling, she said, "Father, you came so close to being paralyzed. Be very grateful to Almighty God for the condition you are in." All I could think was, *Thank you, God, and especially for the inspiration of this wonderful girl.*

It was inspirational to see her out on the lawn in front of our school, teaching from her wheelchair. What a gift she was to the people while counseling the elderly and the sick, or to those witnessing her in front of a large audience, asking them to accept God's will in their lives. This came from a source that was absolutely magnificent. Cindi was every inch a lovely, feminine woman. She was every inch a holy little person with the courage of a lion. Knowing Cindi and her mother impacted my life in a positive way. It made my challenges seem small.

When people complained they found it difficult to get to Mass on Sunday, I oftentimes remarked how ashamed they should feel in the presence of Cindi. She came to Mass every Sunday in her electric wheelchair and upon receiving Holy Communion made me think, *Oh, God, she is a sign for all of us to reflect upon.*

Today what I'd like to say to her is this: "Cindi, I am so proud of the picture Father Joe Shea and I had taken with you at a party we attended at Dom and Sandy Niccoli's home–your radiant smile prevails. You are a blessing to our parish; you are a blessing to me as a priest, and you haven't begun to touch the thousands yet. God bless you."

## MACHO MAN

Being a parish priest is an exciting, challenging, and stimulating role. In our age of technology, from computers to Internet, the American church seems to reflect a business image. Personally meeting with a priest is akin to waiting for your number to be called in an ice-cream parlor, or maneuvering through receptionists who hopefully have pulled your census card—if one exists.

As priests become an endangered species, the prospect of eyeballing one of us or having a personal conversation becomes even more remote. There is no time or opportunity for storytelling. The tragedy is that the lack of priests and the impersonal attitude of so many people add to the dilemma. A breach is developing between the clergy and the people of God.

One wonders how Christ ever accomplished His mission sans phones, computers, files, and discs. Someone said, "The life of a parish priest is a series of interruptions"—how true! Such was Jesus' life. The Master possessed compassionate people skills, and so must parish priests.

Acquiring this gift greatly depends upon one's zeal for hearing people's stories. We must see people as individuals, not numbers or problems to be solved. To know the faithful is to share in their joys, sorrows, expectations, and disappointments. The key is to love them and see in them a part of oneself. As John McDonald, a boyhood friend, said, "A piece of us is in every person we will ever meet."

I have compassion for the priests who must minister in an administrative capacity. For many it is a real burden and sacrifice, but it must be done. They are deprived of much of the love a grateful people lavish upon caring priests. They do not hear the stories and share the broken hearts as well as the celebrations and joys of their people, much like what Christ experienced in His daily encounters with the people, so well described and expressed in the Gospels. How often people's lives challenge, enrich, and inspire our homilies, giving dimension to our priesthood. We bring Christ to them, and they certainly bring Christ to us.

In the fabric of my fifty-seven years of priestly ministry, let me share one simple story.

"Macho Man" was a big guy, a truck driver by trade, with a body tailor-made for a big rig. He lived in the *barrio* with his wife and children, surrounded by numerous relatives and friends. The parish basic family program reached out to the "unchurched"—fallen-away Catholics and those who had slipped through the cracks. Macho was caught in this network.

On a typical census call, the family was encouraged to participate in the church of their origin. Macho's family was a mixed bag. All had been baptized, but few had received their First Communion or Confirmation. We also learned that Macho and his wife had not been married in the Catholic Church. However, the family was receptive and, whenever possible, Macho participated with his family's weekly home visitation instruction. After some time he expressed interest in making his First Communion with his children. This request was presented to me. Our meeting was the beginning of a mutually rich experience.

Not only was Macho big, but he was also sincere, humble, generous, and loving, an in-your-face honest guy. His wife understood and loved him dearly. Once the necessary papers had been procured for their marriage in the church, things fell into place. We set a date for their confession, Macho's First Communion, and their subsequent marriage validation.

Macho and his wife lived as brother and sister for a short time in preparation for the reception of these sacraments. They humbly went to confession, and then they received the Eucharist the next day. The date for their marriage validation had been set, the preparation and paper work completed. They were ready to receive the sacrament of matrimony.

Macho was dressed in a tux on the evening of the marriage ceremony. It fit him like he was blown into it. He was proud, anxious, and excited! The bride, in her fifties like Macho, was dressed in white and blushing with joy. They were surrounded by their children, grandchildren, and friends. The wedding was a joyous occasion, and the church was electric with the excitement of the event.

The mutual trust, love, and devotion as they pronounced their vows inspired me and impacted the family and guests.

As Macho and his wife marched down the aisle after the marriage, the rafters resounded with the cheers, good wishes, and *vivas* of their friends. Never did I witness a happier couple! Afterwards we all returned to their home to celebrate. Cerveza, margaritas, enchiladas, tortillas, and *musica* were enjoyed.

At next morning's 9:30 Mass, Macho, followed by his wife, came forward to receive Holy Communion. With a big grin, he said, "*Mi padrecito*," as I gave him the Eucharist.

"*Cuerpo de Cristo*, Macho Man." I said as he beamed with happiness.

The following Tuesday, I was awakened by a 4:30 a.m. phone call. Macho Man had had a severe heart attack and was unconscious. I quickly dressed, grabbed my oil of the sick, and drove to his house. But I was too late! I could hear the distant ambulance screaming its way to Queen of the Valley Hospital. I started chasing it, but it seemed that every stop light was against me. When I arrived at the emergency room door, I was directed to the trauma center, and there, lying on a gurney—strapped, stripped, huge, unconscious but alive— was Macho. The trauma team—nurses, attendants, and all—were desperately trying to save his life.

As I moved among them, preparing to anoint him with the oil of the sick, I thought, "How privileged am I!" The trauma team was zealously striving to save his physical life and doing all they could, but as a priest I was prepared to ready Macho for his entrance into eternal life. His body, like all bodies, would die, but his soul would live forever. What a privilege to prepare him for his passing!

I moved in among the medical team, conditionally absolving and anointing him, and then gave him the Apostolic Blessing. He died shortly afterward.

As I drove home, I reflected on the events and God's divine providence. I realized that to deal with a person like Macho Man, we must understand his background, his feelings, and his weaknesses, and we must share our own vulnerabilities and failings. This enables the other person to understand that we share some of his emotions and difficulties.

Later that morning, I visited his home—it was wall to wall carpeted with his family and friends, all there to comfort and care for the wife and family. When I entered their crowded, simple home, their eyes sparkled with gratitude. I was their priest, whether they were gang bangers, the unchurched, or devoted faithful. I thought, "This is where I belong." I felt like Christ in the midst of His followers.

The wife asked everyone else to leave the bedroom as she wished to speak to me privately. Our conversation was a great, faith-filled dialogue. She was resigned, ready to face the future, and so grateful for their recent conversion.

At times like this people need not a doctor, lawyer, social worker, or psychologist but a caring priest.

I buried Macho, as I have buried many others, but he will always be a part of my life. The joy of this little incident is one of the many stories that make up the mosaic of a parish priest's life. O God, what a calling is ours—and not only for now, but for all eternity!

## ELVA FREEMAN

This is really a faith enigma story. During the 1940's, St. Anthony's High School held a great basketball tournament for high school girls. They came from all over the archdioceses of Los Angeles and Orange to participate in this tournament. There might have been about twenty to twenty-five teams.

Two weeks before the tournament, I was asked to teach the girls at St. Anthony's to double post. In those days the basketball games were only on half court. Girls could play one half of the court on offense and the other side of the court on defense.

I met Elva Freeman while getting acquainted with the players. She stood out from the others as a superb athlete—very sure of herself—a natural-born leader and an outstanding student. I explained some things that could be done with the team regarding the double post and set plays, but she rebelled. She was used to running the team her own way and did not accept direction. I told her, "You do it my way, or you don't play on this basketball team." So she quit. She had some idea that I would go chasing after her and bring her back, which I did not.

Some days later she contacted me and said, "All right, I'll do it your way, and we'll see what will happen." She returned and worked out with the other girls, and she was outstanding.

Elva and I still had a lot of conflicts after that, but basically she followed my direction. She lived alone with her mother, whom she apparently dominated. It was a single-parent home, and she was its queen.

During the course of the tournament, we gradually became friends. It turned out later on that the only one she would actually listen to or obey was me.

Her I.Q. was tremendous so she had many opportunities for her college placement. When she told me that she thought she would like to become a Maryknoll nun after graduation, I responded that I didn't buy that at all. "You have such a strong will," I said. "You are the type of person who will only obey people whom you respect. In a religious community or in the work area you will oftentimes run into people who are bosses that you can buy or sell. However, you just can't cause conflict because you feel that you are superior to them in intelligence, or ability, or whatever it may be. I can't recommend you to the Maryknoll convent."

The specific convent Elva desired to enter was on the Hudson River in New York. She kept after me, and finally I told her I would write a letter on the condition that I would inform her counselor that I could not recommend her fully, so it was up to them to make the decision. Elva got all her papers together, applied, and was accepted into Maryknoll; however, she was only there three months when they asked her to leave because of insubordination and difficulties with obedience. So she returned to me, saying "I want to sue the Maryknoll nuns for putting me out."

"Come on, get on with your life and forget it," I said.

Somehow or other she put aside her anger and pride and went on to university to study. She was a brilliant college student, and after she had graduated she would occasionally call me. "I'd like to meet you at the airport," she would say. "Can you pick me up?"

"I don't pick up any young female alone." (In those days a priest didn't ride alone with a woman.)

She would be furious when I sent someone to pick her up at the airport. Afterwards we might go down to the beach to throw a football around and just have fun. Also, we would talk about her future plans.

Elva went up the ladder of financial management rapidly. One day she called to inform me that she was going to work in Japan.

When I next heard from her again, she wrote, "I'm going to get married." (She was going to marry a military captain she had met over in Japan.)

"Tell me about it," I said.

After she gave me more details about their relationship, I said, "For the love of God, don't get married. You are not going to make it because with your will, it's going to have to be all your way. Marriage is a two-way street. So I'm against this marriage."

However, she did get married.

As I had anticipated, it didn't last long. They divorced and she came back to the United States. She brought with her a couple of beautiful teakwood Buddhas, saying, "These are yours."

"I'll take them on lend-lease only." I replied. (I still have them.)

Elva went back to New York and began to rise in the business world. We lost contact until she was in her forties. Unexpectedly she phoned me one day and said, "I'm building a house on the Hudson, a beautiful home. I make a six-figure salary, and I'm alone. I want you to know, too, that I no longer believe in the Catholic Church, and I am an atheist."

That really surprised me.

I wrote her and then contacted her on the phone.

"I get as much joy and kick out of sitting in front of my fireplace and gazing at my navel as you do when you sit before the Blessed Sacrament," she said.

Well, what could I say? Her mind and will were set in concrete. "I'll keep praying for you," I reassured her.

Some months later I heard from her again. She had been diagnosed with cancer and was in New York's Roosevelt Hospital.

My first concern was her spiritual wellbeing. "Will you see a priest?" I asked.

"I don't want to see any priest."

I had a good friend, Father Frank McKay, a Maryknoller, living in New York. I contacted him. "Will you go and visit Elva Freeman?"

He made a point of visiting her. As soon as he walked into the room, she said, "I know who sent you. It was Father O'Callaghan. No way! I am not coming back to the church, and that's it. I'm happy in my atheism. I am OK."

Of course he contacted me after this rebuff. "It's no dice with her."

I kept phoning her, but got absolutely nowhere.

Late one evening I got a call around midnight, and she said to me, "Father O, I am dying. I want you to know that you will receive a telegram from my doctor saying that I have died, am being cremated, and then buried in some cemetery in New York. That is it, but I want you to know about it."

"For the love of God, Elva, say, 'God please forgive any sins I may be guilty of. I do love You. Help me to reach my eternal salvation.' Will you please say this prayer?"

As I recall she was quite adamant, and I could not move her. I again encouraged her to make an Act of Contrition, but she said, "I don't believe." So she was coolly, bravely going to her death.

A few days later I got a call from her at midnight. "Father O, I think this is it. I want you to know because you are my friend; you have always been my friend."

I think I was the only one that ever fully opposed her and made some impact, hopefully for the right reasons. I loved that young lady. Shortly afterwards, I received a telegram from her lawyer in New York. "Elva Freeman is dead, cremated, and buried."

I felt terrible because there was nothing I could do. In every Mass I have offered up since that time, I remember Elva Freeman specifically for the repose of her noble soul, and I hope that Almighty God is merciful to her. He alone could understand her. The question comes up: Can one who does not believe in God go to heaven? I have a real struggle with that and hope that somehow in God's divine mercy He will save her. Only He knows her love and motivation.

It is amazing what a precious gift faith is. It's astonishing what decisions people make, the paths they walk, and in thinking of Elva I can never forget the impact she made on my life. Also, because of her denial of the faith, she has given me an even greater urgency to protect and preserve the faith for others and hopefully for my own sake, too. I commend her in my prayers and hope that someday I shall meet her in the Kingdom of Heaven.

## Gary Cooper

"My name is Rocky Cooper, and I would like you to meet my husband next Sunday. He is a shy man but would like to get acquainted with you."

The woman introduced herself to me after the 10:30 Mass at Good Shepherd Church in Beverly Hills, California. I already knew who she was, but I was surprised by the request. I told Rocky I would be happy to meet her husband.

Although I had seen Gary Cooper on the RKO lot, I had never had the pleasure of personally meeting him. Apparently, that was going to change.

I knew that the movie star no longer was a candidate for conversion since he had been received into the Church some years previously by Father Harry Ford, a former associate priest at Good Shepherd. Nevertheless, after celebrating Mass the following Sunday, I walked out to the patio behind the sacristy. There, standing larger than life was Gary Cooper, along with Rocky and their beautiful daughter. As I approached, Rocky said, "Father," I would like you to meet my husband, Gary, and our daughter, Maria."

With a crinkly grin, Gary Cooper stuck out his big hand and

shook my hand warmly. He was tall, tan, friendly, and cordial. However, Rocky was right, he did seem shy. We talked briefly, and then I moved around greeting other parishioners. Later that afternoon, I received a phone call from Rocky. "Would you like to golf with Gary? Do you have the time?"

I told her I'd be free later in the week, and a tee time was set at Bel Air Golf Course for the coming Friday.

In the meantime, I started wondering if Rocky was pushing me on Gary. I already knew that he was stricken with some form of cancer. (The news had been in the paper.) However, I did not know the seriousness of his condition.

I phoned Rocky on Friday morning. "Please forgive me if I am wrong," I said. "But it occurred to me that perhaps you might be imposing me on Gary, and this I would not like to do. If so, I would like to cancel the golf game."

"Oh, don't do that," she said. "He is already gassing up the car. He really is looking forward to playing with you."

Gary picked me up shortly afterward, and we drove the few miles to Bel Air. He was pleasant, warm, and a good conversationalist.

As we teed off, it was obvious that Gary was weak. Despite his determination, I could see he wasn't up to playing eighteen holes. Instead we crisscrossed the course, seeking out open holes to eliminate distance and avoid a wait. We had a great time joshing and kidding each other—neither of us challenged the pros.

After the game, he drove me to the rectory. "Let's do it again!" he said in parting.

Soon afterward, Gary Cooper checked into Mt. Sinai Hospital for exploratory surgery. He asked me to come by and visit.

The night before the surgery I stopped by the hospital at about ten o'clock. I will never forget entering his private room. He was alone; family and friends had left. *What an enigma!* I thought. The great actor and celebrity was lying on his bed, deep in thought, with his hands under his head. He had on a red bathrobe.

"Hi, Gary," I said softly. He opened his eyes, delighted to see me. We talked for quite a while. He was calm, resigned, and ready for the upcoming surgery.

"Tomorrow is the big day, Father," he said. "They are going to open me up. I certainly hope all goes well."

I reassured him that he was in my prayers and in God's hands. We shook hands and I blessed him before I left.

The next morning they operated, viewed the extent of the cancer, and closed him up. It was inoperable. Gary returned home shortly afterward. Later, he phoned and asked me to drop by

I drove to the Cooper home, a beautiful Holmby Hills one-story house on three hillside acres. Rocky greeted me at the door and brought me to the living room, where Gary was standing with Maria. "Gary," I told him, "I am so sorry." I will never forget his response.

He smiled, put his arms around Rocky and Maria, squeezed them, and said, "You know, Father, God has really blessed me in this life. He has given me so many wonderful gifts. I have a loving wife and daughter, and God has surrounded me with many sincere friends. I have no complaints. If God wants to take me now, it's OK, because God certainly has not shortchanged me."

*This is a man of faith!* I thought. We talked for a while, and then Gary said, "Could you drop by to see me again?"

"I will be seeing you," I reassured him.

During the weeks that followed, I visited several times. Then one day, I received a rather urgent call from him. "Father, could you come by and see me because something really bothers me, and I need an answer."

"Sure, Gary," I replied. "I will come by this evening."

I went to his home very late that night. He was dressed in a pair of loafers, dungarees, a white T-shirt, and a dark blue pullover sweater.

"I am so glad you came because this is what concerns me: You know I only became a Catholic a few years ago. Why is it that ever since I've become a Catholic, I feel so much more sinful than before? Why am I much more conscious of it now?"

At the time I didn't know where I got inspiration (now I know it was the Holy Spirit), but I asked, "Gary, do you have a flashlight?"

"I do."

"Will you get it for me?"

He quickly brought me a flashlight, and I asked him to sit on a chair at the perimeter of the room, away from the main lamps, where it was quite dark. I looked down at him. "Gary, that sweater you are wearing is a beautiful sweater. It has no imperfections."

"What do you mean?" he asked. "I am sure you will find some specks and lint on it."

"I cannot see them, but now I'll beam the flashlight on your sweater."

I shined the light on the sweater and there were, indeed, some hairs, lint, and a small stain. They stood out against the background of the dark sweater. "You know, before your conversion, you were somewhat in darkness," I said. "You were not reflecting too much on your own personal life and on your relationship with God. Now, since you are filled with the love of God, the slightest fault becomes much more apparent. And, in the light of that love, you are more aware of God's love for you. That is why you *think* you are a much greater sinner than you were in the old days."

"Oh, thank God," he said. "That makes sense, that really makes sense."

The answer left him at peace. We talked a while longer before I went home feeling grateful that, in a small way, I had been of help to him.

Gradually, his body deteriorated from the cancer. I remember visiting on another day when Gary said he'd just had a talk with Ernest Hemingway. Ernest, then bedridden in a hospital, had called Gary and said he was going through some hard times. "I'll bet I make it to the barn before you do."

"Aren't you a Catholic?" Gary asked.

"Well, yes, I am, I guess," Hemingway replied. "But I am certainly not practicing."

Gary then spoke to Ernest about returning to the Church and the faith.

"You know, Gary," Hemingway said, "I could always make an

Act of Contrition. I learned that from my catechism training as a kid."

To Gary, it was an indication that Hemingway's faith had never completely left him.

While visiting Gary on another occasion, I could see he was in enormous pain. I'd brought a small steel crucifix about three inches high and two inches wide, and I gave it to him. "I want you to hold this," I said. "And when the suffering gets intense, squeeze that crucifix until it hurts and then unite your sufferings with the sufferings of Christ for the good of souls. This will make your suffering more meaningful." He took the crucifix and held on to it tightly…and he began to understand.

Slowly Gary got weaker. Since I was scheduled to give a retreat at a girls' high school in San Diego, I had to briefly leave town. It was a three-day retreat, and I was committed to it. Shortly before it began, however, he died. It was May 13, 1961, just six days after his sixtieth birthday. Although I had to miss being present at his funeral at Good Shepherd Church in Beverly Hills and his internment at Holy Cross Cemetery, I certainly knew in my heart that a good man had gone to God.

As a priest, I have prepared many people for death. But I have never met a person more resigned and better disposed for death. Not because he was Gary Cooper, but because, in his own humble way, he loved God. No wonder the Swedish newspaper, *Svenska Dagbladet*, reported, "He had the soul of a boy: pure, simple, nice, warm…he was the incarnation of the honorable American."

Sometime after his death, Rocky said, "We want to give you something of Gary's in remembrance of him." She gave me his golf clubs. They were long-shafted clubs, custom-built for a lean, tall man.

Later on, I recall reading an article in one of the popular magazines. The well-known author had written that when he had visited Gary in the actor's late illness, he noticed that Gary was lying in pain, gripping a small steel crucifix. The writer knew nothing of the significance of the crucifix, but Gary did, and so did I.

I am sure that when Gary met Christ, he was greeted as a friend—

someone who had grown to know and love Jesus. Following Christ can be a tall order for a superstar, but Gary Cooper seemed tailor-made by God for the task. Like Christ, he remained meek and humble of heart to the end.

## HERMES PAN AND THE CIGAR BAND

Sister Leonella was one of twenty-seven sisters in the convent attached to the parish and she was quite influential. Since Sister Leonella had never met Hermes Pan, some of us decided it would be fun to play a trick on the sisters.

When Hermes came for a visit, he was told: "We will introduce you as a bishop from Nigeria."

"What?"

"You can pull this off," I assured him.

So we dressed him as a bishop. We had the correct garb, except for one thing: He didn't have a ring. So we got a cigar band and glued it on his finger.

Fathers Jim Hansen, Jerry Cahill, and I took him over to introduce him as the new bishop from Nigeria. The sisters were thrilled to death to meet him. Sister Leonella, who was always so perceptive, asked, "Well, Bishop, where is your diocese?"

"It's in Nigeria," he replied. "I have been sent there from Rome. I'm working among the people in this little village and instructing the priests regarding Roman affairs. Oh, by the way, I'll let you kiss my ring."

She knelt down and kissed his cigar band; the other sisters also kissed his pseudo ring. Then they began to question: "How many priests do you have in Nigeria, and how are vocations coming?"

Hermes was answering the best he could. Suddenly it dawned on them that they were being taken. They never forgot Hermes and the cigar band they all had kissed with sincerity!

## RICARDO MONTALBAN

Ricardo Montalban has made many charitable appearances for worthy causes. When I started St. John Vianney Parish in Hacienda Heights, we put on our first big dinner, hoping to raise some funds to really get the parish off the ground. I asked if he'd come out, make an appearance, and give a talk to the people. He graciously agreed and won them over with his charm, his love of the faith, and, of course, his beautiful wife. If ever a man has been faithful to his wife, his religion, his family, and the industry, it was Ricardo Montalban.

If someone would say to me, "Who from the film industry would you recommend to talk as a strong, fine Catholic and a good example?" I would always reply, "Ricardo Montalban for he is the best—'*un buen hombre*.'"

## FATHER THOMAS CAHILL

One of the finest priests I know is Father Thomas Cahill, a member of the Miles Jesu community. At this time he is pastor of Santa Maria Reina Parish located in Ponce, Puerto Rico. His journey has been a long and eventful one.

He graduated from high school as the president of his class; Father Joe Shea, a classmate, was vice president. Tom opted to go to the college seminary for philosophy. After two years Tom dropped out of philosophy, left the seminary, and became rather disillusioned for many reasons. He was uncertain about his future. His parents were successful and would aid him in any pursuit he chose; however, he wanted none of this. He had a problem with material things and had a great attachment to the virtue of poverty. He felt that poverty was the answer to a lot of life's questions and that one had to relate to the poor.

So he left his family in search of his own identity and destiny. He traveled to South America, India, Europe, Israel (working in a kibbutz), and Mexico, trying to find his life's purpose. His father and mother were supportive of their only son among five sisters. Although his father had a wonderful business that Tom could have easily fit into, they really wanted him to become a priest if it was God's will. They prayed and went to daily Mass, hoping that their young son would find his goal. He would come home occasionally from his wanderings and visit the family.

On one occasion, he dropped in to see me on his way to Corona. He came in bearded, dressed in a sweat shirt, dungarees, and sandals. He carried a copper pot and had a knapsack on his back.

"Where are you going?" I asked him.

"I'm going to join my friend, Joe Fedora," Tom replied.

"I can take you. I would like to meet him."

The priests at the St. John Vianney rectory were impressed, amazed by Tom's passion for poverty, his clothing, his backpack, and the copper pot. He was most amiable and lovable when they engaged him in conversation,

After driving him to Fedora's home, I met and immediately liked the man. He was a fine young Catholic. The two of them had planned to bum their way down to Mexico City to work in an orphanage. Although their transportation to and housing there would be up for grabs, that's the way they operated.

(Later on Joe Fedora would become a Maryknoll priest. He has done marvelous work in South America and also at the Maryknoll office in the United States.)

After they parted, Tom continued his wandering. During his travels his mother and father celebrated their twenty-fifth wedding anniversary. They were in London at the time, staying in one of the chicest hotels. They hoped that by sending out letters Tom might possibly pick one up and discover where they were staying. When the couple arrived at the hotel, they sat in the lobby for a few moments, waiting for tea and sweet cakes while their baggage was being delivered and their room prepared. A moment later what appeared to be a bum with a long black beard came through the hotel's entrance.

He held a copper pot to his chest, carried a knapsack on his back, and his feet were sandal clad. Of course, the concierge at the desk said, "Get him out of here."

Jack Cahill rushed to the desk. "That's my son."

"He cannot come in through the front door," the concierge responded.

Instead he let Tom in through a back door.

Tom and his father climbed the back stairs to his parents' room, where he showered and dressed in Jack's clothes. He later accompanied his parents to dinner. After a short stay, Tom left and began to travel through France, working in the vineyards and enjoying the countryside.

On one of his rare homecomings I visited him and merely mentioned, "It is very important, Tom, that you receive a spiritual direction. Find out God's plan for you." But he was not in favor of doing this. He was on his own and avoided direction, totally caught up in his poverty kick. I reminded him that doing much for the poor and being compassionate is good, then added: "You know, Tom, there are other kinds of poverty. My priestly poverty is that I'm so busy with people in the ministry I have no time to spend my salary. My money is piling up. It is my lack of time that is my poverty. You have nothing but time, and I think in some ways you are squandering it by not having a more proper spiritual guidance in your life. Get a spiritual director."

But he did not.

Later on, when the parents of one of Tom's good buddies, Mike Krulak, died, Tom went back to New York to visit and console him. He also met up with Joe Fedora. Both Mike and Joe had become priests. They were a tremendous influence on Tom and greatly aided him regarding his faith and vocational difficulties. At a later date Tom went to India where he worked in Mother Teresa's Home for the Dying for about three months. That made an enormous impact on him.

In his wanderings Tom came across a Father Alphonso Duran, the head of the Miles Jesu organization. It is a very militant group of young men and women which includes both single men and women, and married couples.

He became interested in joining the Miles Jesu and was put on a really tough schedule by Father Duran. Tom had to do hard menial labor in a shoe factory and received no formal academics. During this time he lived under the strict rule of the Miles Jesu. After a year or so he was allowed to study philosophy and theology and did very well.

He spoke a smattering of French, and, of course, he was fairly adept in Latin and English. After some time he joined the community of Miles Jesu, and they sent him to Rome to study. He entered the Angelica where he studied theology. He was a wonderful student and learned to speak fluent Italian. I often remarked, "When the time comes for ordination, Tom, I'll be there.

It seemed an incredible voyage to where he was finally called to priesthood. Father Joe Shea and I went to Rome as guests of Jack and Theresa Cahill and attended Tom's magnificent ordination by Pope John Paul II. In all there were seventy-six priests ordained.

Afterwards Jack threw a big breakfast party for Tom where I was first introduced to Father Duran. Jack had said to me, "I'm not too keen about that director of his. Would you check him out?"

Jack and I both understood Tom needed a firm and solid superior. "I'll be glad to sound him out," I replied.

When I met Tom's spiritual director, although younger than I, he seemed a real tough hombre. During the course of the breakfast, Father Duran privately asked, "Father O'Callaghan, are you checking me out?"

"You got that right," I replied.

"Did Jack Cahill ask you to observe me?"

"He sure did."

"Well, what do you think?"

"I think you are a son of a bitch."

"Well, you are a son of a bitch, too."

It was true: we read each other well. I liked him immediately. He was just the superior that Tom needed. A no-nonsense man who would encourage Tom to fly right, challenge him, and give him

163

proper direction. Father Duran was a committed man who practiced chastity, poverty, and obedience. He was a great priest.

While we were in Rome, Joe, Tom, and I were permitted to concelebrate Mass at St. Peter's tomb. It was an enormous thrill to be with Tom Cahill, celebrant, and with Joe as concelebrant. Later on we went to St. Paul's outside the walls, and the three of us offered Mass on the tomb of St. Paul. Thus we honored two of the greatest figures in the Catholic Church.

At first Tom did a stretch in India. He was able to get a passport under the guise of being a student at the university (which he was); it enabled him to work with the youth groups in his area. He lived in a mud hut teaching catechism to the impoverished youth. Later he returned to the Miles Jesu to serve in various capacities.

At the present time he is a pastor based in Puerto Rico, at a beautiful parish with three other Miles Jesu members, doing remarkable work among the Puerto Ricans. Tom is so full of zeal. Every time I see him and look into his faith-filled, compassionate blue eyes; he makes me feel bad because he is so good.

One time Father Joe Shea and I went to visit Tom in Puerto Rico. We surfed, laughed, and had a lot of fun. Tom had always been a superb athlete. Father Joe and Tom played one-on-one in basketball, and I saw that the old drive and competition were still there. We wanted to make sure Tom was getting some proper exercise and was in good shape. He was! He ministered in an area which was low-income and challenging. I particularly noticed the enormous influence he had among the men; many of them participated in the liturgy. He had an enormous church with thousands of people attending Mass.

I remember years ago when we were starting St. John Vianney Church and having a hard time getting money. Tom and his father happened to be at Santa Monica beach when they saw a man drowning in the surf. Tom went out after him and helped to bring him to the beach where he was given mouth to mouth resuscitation. The man turned out to be a millionaire belonging to the same country club that Jack Cahill did, the Los Angeles Country Club. Of course, the man was thrilled to be alive and very grateful. He asked Tom, "What can I do for you, son? Can I help you with college?"

He replied, "No."

"Can I give you a set of golf clubs?"

Tom said, "No, but if you really want to do something, you can send a little money to my friend Father O'Callaghan who is starting a parish in Hacienda Heights."

This man then sent a check for five thousand dollars to our building project to install a stained glass window in St. John Vianney Church.

With more priests like Tom, the church's future will be secure. It is my deepest joy to have fanned just a bit the glowing coals of his priestly heart. The Cahill family is proud of their son, brother, and uncle, and so am I!

# FATHER JIM HANSEN

When a friend such as Father Hansen dies, I wonder, "Where and how will this man be replaced?" I loved having him around because he would always be upbeat and charm any group. With his dynamic personality, one could fade into the background and just enjoy his presence and humor. His great heart would dispel any possibility of envy.

As pastor at St. Anthony of Padua Church in Gardena, he was loved by the entire city. While on his way home from a Confirmation ceremony at a nearby church, he fell asleep at the wheel for a few seconds and drove right into a large eucalyptus tree. It was a horrible smashup. The paramedics brought the Jaws of Life to get him out as he was trapped. Freeing his hands he gave them his personal card on which he had scribbled, "Take me to the Little Sisters of the Poor Hospital. I am a Catholic priest; get me a priest."

When I saw him in intensive care the next day his body was totally crushed. But not his spirit! I said to him, "I hope you are not going to die, but you may. Let's you and I say the prayers of the dying."

"I don't want to die," he said.

"Come on, Jim; let's say the prayers of the dying."

He was kind of reluctant, but finally he said, "OK. I'll do it. I'll accept God's will."

So we recited the prayers.

Then he said again, "Really, Jim, I don't want to die."

To distract him and change the thought flow, I said, "By the way, we are putting on a musical comedy[2] at St. Vianney Church, and we'd like you to participate."

"Yeah, I'd love to do that."

"Could you do a quick stand-up comic and dance routine?" I asked.

"What is the date?"

I gave him the date and my blessing.

Shortly after that he suffered an embolism and died.

Before his burial took place, priests, firefighters, law enforcement officers, and the sheriff formed an honor guard around his casket. The city of Gardena had printed up a huge billboard saying, "Father Hansen, we miss you, we love you, and we are so sorry." The influence that man had in the entire area was unbelievable.

I gave the homily at the funeral Mass, expressing how often men of his stature, intelligence, dynamism, and talent can intimidate others in authority or those of little stature who dislike being in the shadows. "It is sad that a man of this caliber could not have been utilized better by the church." I made that statement to the bishops in the presence of the archdiocesan officials and Cardinal Manning. It caused quite a

---

[2] We named the musical comedy "*Hansen's Follies*." It was put on by Sandy Niccoli, Wilma Dela Cruz, Jo Papara, and some other parish members; it was a great success.

stir, but this great priest deserved it all.

I remember Father Jim Hansen every day of my life. (His mother's maiden name was O'Callaghan. She was from Green Lake, Wisconsin.)

He had been torn by having to choose between the theater arts, medicine, or the priesthood. He opted for the priesthood. What a blessing for us all! This was the death of a truly great priest. I offer my Divine Office every morning for the souls of two of my dearest friends: Father Jim Hansen and Father Jerry Cahill. They will always be remembered among the truly great priests of our archdiocese.

## ARCHBISHOPS AND CARDINALS

During my many years as a priest I've had the privilege of serving under four ordinaries: Archbishop John J. Cantwell, my ordaining bishop, and three Cardinals—Francis McIntyre, Timothy Manning and Roger Mahony.

I was ordained by Archbishop Cantwell, a bishop who was considered very conservative and autocratic. The local pastor was in charge of the parish, but we all worked under the archbishop. He had the final word.

In those days parish associates were called "assistants." They were assigned to assist the pastor in the parish, who would then determine their tasks: mostly confessions, census taking, and teaching duties. The pastor enumerated our schedules, duties, and privileges.

One had certain rights as an assistant but not many. I remember Monsignor Dolan once telling us at dinner that the "only right an assistant has is the right to a Christian burial, and sometimes I doubt that." Of course, he was kidding, but there was a lot of truth in it also.

There was very little room for discussion because the pastor was the lord and master of the parish. It was his responsibility, and he was very much aware of his authority, dignity, and role.

The chancery office, or "downtown," as it was referred to, was the powerhouse. It was presided over by the archbishop, his board of consultors, and other chancery office officials.

My first meeting with Archbishop Cantwell was when I was serving Mass in the cathedral with a fellow seminarian, Pat Burke. I wasn't much of a server and neither was he, but we were assigned to serve a High Mass that Archbishop Cantwell was celebrating. During the introductory part of the Mass he was reading from the heavy missal book that was placed on a steel book holder which Pat was holding for him. It wasn't exactly in the proper position so the archbishop pushed it—almost autocratically—in Burke's face. This made me angry.

A little later we accidentally spilled the coarsely ground incense on the marble floor surrounding the altar. We heard it crunching under the feet of the archbishop and his assistant priests. The archbishop seemed really bothered. When Mass was over, the master of ceremonies sought out Pat Burke and me. "Where are your coats?"

"They are in the sacristy in the servers' closet," I replied.

"I'll get your coats, and then you two get out of here. The archbishop was very upset with you two clumsy servers."

We really made an impact!

The next time I had an encounter with the cardinal was on a very rainy day at the seminary. As there was nothing else to do for exercise, I was jogging on the long incline in front of the main building when suddenly a limousine driven by a Filipino chauffeur appeared. Archbishop Cantwell was in the back seat with his sister, Nellie, and an Irish terrier. The limo stopped next to me, the rear window rolled down, and his lordship's face appeared. "What are you doing?

"I'm running...getting some exercise."

"You are a stupid man," he said. "Get out of the rain, and go back to your room."

I had no alternative. I peeled off, jogged to my room, and took a shower. I was a little upset, but in those days there was no such thing as a democracy.


Archbishop Cantwell had a great vision of the church. A prelate of his times, he was in power. The pastors were in charge of the parish but subject to the archbishop and to the chancery office and its officials. There were few lay people working in the chancery and things went along very smoothly.

Cantwell was a man of great knowledge—a little on the pompous side—but his position led to his having supreme authority over the archdiocese. He was in charge, and we knew it!

The archbishop governed a smoothly operating church with plenty of priests, sisters, and brothers. Almost every parish was staffed by an Irish pastor. Sometimes people would ask, "Do you have to be Irish to become a priest?" How greatly that has changed!

The people were subservient to the church and very loyal. This was Pre-Vatican II. I found him a devout, intelligent, but aloof prelate, a product of what was, at that time, an authoritative church. He left a challenging and growing archdiocese to his successor Cardinal McIntyre.


That was my first introduction to the hierarchy. Those were the days when people would say, "There are three infallible statements: (1) The pope says it, (2) The priest says it, (3) The sister says, it, and that is it."


The second cardinal under whom I had the privilege of serving was Cardinal McIntyre, who succeeded Archbishop Cantwell. (He was elevated to cardinal shortly after he arrived in Los Angeles.) He was the first cardinal from the western states named by Pope Pius XII.

Before entering the seminary, he had a career in finance in New York. This very astute man was ordained in his thirties.

In his early priesthood, he trained under Cardinal Spellman in New York, working in the chancery office until he was sent to take over the church in Los Angeles. The assignment certainly was a tremendously important challenge for him. He became the ordinary and was now on his own, no longer subject to Cardinal Spellman.

The beliefs and views he had of the church were conservative and deeply felt. He was ever loyal to our Holy Father, the magisterium, the Eucharist, and Mary. By nature he was a confrontationist, and we knew it! He was a no-nonsense person who desired facts and results. As a speaker he was dry with no great sense of humor as far as I could see. His life was the church. He loved all it stood for. He was indeed a churchman.

I encountered his decisiveness in our first Diocesan Synod. Father Tom Kiefer, Father "Doc" Sammon, and I represented the young priests of the archdiocese. As a Newman Club chaplain I was trying to present the need for the church to sponsor, promote, and aid the growing Newman movement in our secular colleges. Cardinal McIntyre disagreed with my proposals; Monsignor Edward Wade, formerly Archbishop Cantwell's secretary, tried to defend my position. He was asked to sit down by Cardinal McIntyre and told to let Father O'Callaghan speak for himself. I spoke, but I made little or no impact.

As pastor of Our Lady of Malibu I was involved in a possible land trade with the county. A few experienced real estate men, a lawyer, and a few others were assisting me. I trusted them but did not know all the details. I had phoned Monsignor Ben Hawkes concerning an escrow, but the cardinal picked up instead. He asked me pertinent questions about the escrow which I could not answer. I told him I trusted my experts.

"I will not OK a deal based on your 'trust' of others," he told me. "I want facts. Because of your lack of facts, Father, the deal is off."

At first I was angry, but later I wrote him a letter and said it was the best whipping I had received since my father strapped me at fourteen years of age. "Now I know why you are Cardinal Archbishop of Los Angeles and I am pastor of Our Lady of Malibu Parish." I determined from that day forward to always have facts for Cardinal McIntyre.

Since my parish was about to construct a convent, the architect and I met with the cardinal in the chancery office. After a discussion he asked the architect for the grading plans and said, "Please excuse me for a few moments." The cardinal got out a pad of paper and a slide rule from inside his desk. After some calculations he looked up and asked the architect, "Since when does water run uphill?" The embarrassed architect left to revise the figures, and the cardinal then said to me, "Father, when you ask an architect a 'foolish' question sometimes you get a foolish answer."

For my last project in Malibu I researched everything (the future population, plans for improvement, sewage, proposed emergency projects, transportation, etc.) After answering his questions, the cardinal said, "You have done your homework, Father. Go ahead with the project." I was proud of his affirmation.


I first met Cardinal Timothy Manning when I was a second year philosophy seminarian at St. Patrick's Seminary, Menlo Park, California. The cardinal had often vacationed in England while he was studying in Rome. At times he was a guest of my cousins Sean O'Callaghan and his sister, Noreen. Sean was stationed in Harrow, outside of London. (He was later canon of a beautiful church there. He had also been a teacher at St. Edmund's Ware.)

Sean was a graduate of London University. Noreen graduated from Oxford University and was teaching in Brighton at an exclusive school for girls of upper-class English families. They were two very bright, wonderful, and hospitable people.

When Cardinal Manning came back to the United States from Rome, he dropped by St. Patrick's Seminary for a visit. Apparently my cousins had spoken to him about me. I will never forget him coming up to my second floor corner room. I think he experienced a cultural shock as he entered my threshold. Unfortunately, at the time I was breaking the seminary rules in two ways: I had washed my jock strap and it was hanging in the window drying out. I also had the sports sheets spread out on my desk. Both offenses were against the rules. When he came in he must have realized I was totally different from my gentle, cultured, brilliant cousins. I did not make much of an impact. After that I didn't see much of him until he became cardinal archbishop.

When he was in charge of me as a pastor, I found him to be a very sensitive, highly intellectual, poetical, and gentle man with a great affinity for the Irish. His homilies were all based on the Scriptures and just beautiful. He had a brilliant mind, was a lover of the classics, and was as sensitive as a violin. He was more at ease with the Irish priests than he was with the Americans. This deeply spiritual man was thin and aesthetical. Although very conscious of the fact that he was the cardinal archbishop, he was humble in his own way.

My difficulty with him was that I am very confrontational, and he did not like confrontation. Unfortunately, sometimes he took the confrontation personally. For me an opinion is an objective fact, either right or wrong. It has nothing to do with loyalty. He seemed to have a sense that opposition indicated a lack of loyalty.

I recall very well that I was to be present when we were having the first Confirmation in our parish. Unfortunately, the cardinal wanted to change the date, postponing it for three weeks. This would interfere with my scheduled fishing trip in Panama with Fathers Murray, McCarthy and DeJonghe. When I found out (through his secretary, Monsignor Clement Connolly) that the cardinal wanted me to change my vacation plans to accommodate his schedule, I called up Monsignor Connolly and said, "That's fine if you want to switch the Confirmation date, but I want you to know I will not be there."

"Now wait a minute!" he replied. "You have to be there when the cardinal comes to the parish for the first time."

"I've got an obligation to my buddies. We have planned a trip to Panama, and I'm going fishing. The only way I will stay is if the cardinal orders me to stay."

Well, he did not order me to stay so I went on the trip. He was really upset with that and took it personally.

I remember coming back from fishing and being told that the cardinal's Rome trip had been canceled. He had had the free time after all.

A short time later, I went to the Confirmation at the church of my classmate Father Walsh, and the cardinal was there. I walked up to him. "Your Eminence, how are you?"

Rather coldly, he said, "Hello, Jim," and then he left the room. I could see he was upset.

Bishop Johnson was also there with him and actually was doing the Confirmation. "Hey, Jim, the cardinal is upset with you. You better go in and make some kind of peace," he remarked.

"OK."

I went into the room and spoke to the cardinal: "I understand the Confirmation at St. John Vianney in my absence was beautiful."

"It was great!"

"It goes to show you, Cardinal, you didn't need me there. I have qualified young priests who can take care of everything. I was not needed."

"They did extremely well."

"I want you to know that at the very exact time that you were celebrating the three o'clock Confirmation, I was in Panama with a hook up on a marlin. To be honest with you, I would have much rather had a hook up on a marlin than to have been there at the Confirmation."

He just didn't know what to say.

Six months after that we had a dedication in our parish. Again the date was set for a time I couldn't be there. I called up Monsignor Connolly and said, "Can you rearrange this?"

"You've gotta be there. The cardinal is coming."

"I'm not going to be there because I have a prior commitment." It was the same old story. "Unless the cardinal orders me, I'm not going to be there."

When he came for the second time and I was not present, he was really upset! But I believed I was merely fulfilling my rights. The next time I saw Monsignor Connolly in his office, he said, "You have really hurt him."

"What do you mean?"

"He's upset because of the way you treated him."

"Wait a minute! Why didn't you protect me? You know me."

"I am just a conduit."

"You are more than that," I replied. "You should have explained the situation."

"The cardinal wants to see you. You had better go in and apologize."

I went into the cardinal's office and said, "Your Eminence, if I have hurt you, I am very sorry. There was no mean intent."

"You have really hurt me."

"Forgive me! Whatever I did was because I felt justified in what I chose to do."

That settled the matter, but he was never quite comfortable with me.

Another time he came out for a Confirmation and was much more amenable.

Later we were having some very special people being confirmed, and we asked permission to have it done by Father Joe Shea, at Father Shea's request. Unfortunately, Cardinal Manning understood it as if I were taking over. Father Joe, God love him, went to the cardinal and said, "Father O'Callaghan had nothing to do with this small Confirmation; I am in charge of this. If there is any fault it is mine."

That seemed to calm things down a little bit. Later the cardinal came out and confirmed those twenty people for Father Joe because the cardinal wished to be there.

After that it became more peaceful, and we got along a little better. That is, until Father Ferraro wanted a Toyota car. He said, "I'll call Monsignor Hawkes to ask for permission to purchase the Toyota."

"I wouldn't do that if I were you because he won't deal with an associate," I said.

He went ahead anyway and called Monsignor Hawkes, who said, "No way! Don't talk to me! Your pastor should be talking to me about this."

So I called up Monsignor Hawkes. "Father Ferraro wants to buy a Toyota."

"Why does he want a Toyota? Why don't you go to the Kaiser Brothers Dodge dealer? We have a fleet of Dodges."

"Well, we have a businessman in the parish who is an executive with Toyota, and he can get us a deal as good as anything that you can get from Kaiser Brothers. Are you saying we can't buy anything but American cars?"

"You will have to go to the cardinal on that," Monsignor Hawkes said.

"What! I need to see Cardinal Manning?"

"Yes."

So I called up Monsignor Connolly, got an appointment with the cardinal, and went in to see him.

The cardinal met me in his little office parlor. "Jim, it is so good to see you! How are you?"

"I'm fine. I am here on a very foolish request. You know, here you are cardinal archbishop of all of Los Angeles, and I am a pastor of a large parish, and I have to take your very valuable time to ask you whether or not my associate can get a Toyota. It's like someone going to the head of IBM and saying to this C.E.O., 'May I have your permission to raise the urinal in the men's room six inches?'"

He didn't like the vulgarity. But he said, "If I say you can have it, then Monsignor Hawkes will be upset. If I tell you that you can't have it, you will be upset."

"I won't be upset! You tell me one way or the other, and I will accept it. That doesn't bother me."

"Well, let's pray and think about it," he said.

"I want to get it now, before the prices on insurance go up."

"I'll tell you what you do. Pray on it, and I will pray on it, and I will let you know."

I couldn't believe it.

I went home, and he ultimately said, "You make your own decision."

So I had Doug go out and buy a Toyota. Then I wrote a letter to the cardinal, saying, "Your Eminence, I listened to you, took your advice and guidance." On the bottom line I wrote: "P.S. Father Ferraro really loves his new Toyota."

All these little things understandably upset him. He was sensitive and took things personally. But he was also a brilliant man, very compassionate to the priests, especially the sick clergy. He had great gifts which I certainly do not possess. Later his greatness really came out when he developed cancer of the spine. This man suffered tremendously, yet bore it with patience and courage while at Norris Center, U.S.C. He died magnificently and humbly, setting a terrific example for all of us. He showed us how to handle suffering.


I had mentioned in the past that Cardinal Manning was a suffering bishop and I would remark at times, "For God's sake, get off the cross and lead us into battle." That was my perception of the cardinal at that time, but it was a prejudiced point of view. He was truly a wonderful priest, a man of God. He was certainly a product of Archbishop Cantwell, who was very proud of him. Archbishop Cantwell and his sister, Nellie, loved Cardinal Manning like a son. They prepared him to become a bishop. Later on he was elevated to archbishop and finally the cardinal of Los Angeles.

Cardinal Manning left an indelible mark on our presbyterate and Catholic population. Humble in life and courageous in death, he will not be forgotten.

*** 

In 1985, Cardinal Roger Mahony, the Bishop of Stockton, California, replaced Cardinal Timothy Manning, becoming the third cardinal in the archdiocese of Los Angeles, a territory extending from Santa Maria to Orange County.

As a young seminarian Mahony had worked for his father's family poultry farm in North Hollywood. He cared for the chickens and also sold them to markets throughout the area, delivering them to the buyers in a small truck.

Cardinal Mahony was a man of tremendous gifts, with a bright and retentive memory. He was skilled in theology, scripture, and the world of computers, Internet, and ham radios. His mind and imagination were highly active. He was open to new ideas and challenges. He also spoke fluent Spanish. He was comfortable with the wealthy and powerful yet at home with the needy, minorities, and underprivileged.

He was not an athlete, but had he taken up golf, he would have matched Tiger Woods. He would have made his golf game happen!

He knew the stress and challenges of the workplace. As a gadget and fix-it man, he could do everything from electrical wiring and plumbing to general maintenance. He was also a skilled helicopter pilot.

Like Cardinal McIntyre, he was confrontational by nature. One must have done his homework in order to challenge Cardinal Mahony on any issue from migration to the quality of Notre Dame football. By nature he was also a reserved, compassionate person. In private company he was unobtrusive, a good listener, and aware of the other's needs.

Although he accepted opposition well, he had his own mindset. He might ask one's opinion, but frequently his decision was already made. He was a churchman; the Catholic Church was his life. He had the courage to make a decision regardless of opposition. But like all of us, he was not always right.

The Cathedral of Our Lady of the Angels was the result of his vision, courage, and determination. Like all great leaders he could pull the trigger, putting his neck on the block regardless of the opposition.

He had a temper, and when he was irritated it showed. Before he cooled down, he would send out his midnight missals (i.e., letters). Many of us had been the recipients. However, when confronted with the facts he was quick to admit when he or something was wrong.

He had a great love and concern for the Catholic Church. This meant both the people and the institution. His prayer life, devotion to the Eucharist, love of our Blessed Mother, plus his loyalty to our Holy Father were part and parcel of his nature.

Cats were a great part of his recreation. He had a quiet but subtle sense of humor. One of the irritating facts in his life was the length of Shane O'Neil's (my fox terrier) nose. At Chancellor Terrance Fleming's fiftieth birthday party, the cardinal left the head table and walked to the table where I was seated among nine others. He bent over my shoulder and whispered in my ear, "Cut two inches off of Shane's nose," and walked away. The people at my table were wondering what important message he had given me.

Once I received numerous brochures from plastic surgeons located on the west side of Los Angeles, encouraging cosmetic surgery for Shane's nose. It took some time on my part to realize that our cardinal was responsible for sending these brochures. How I retaliated is between the cardinal and me!

## MYLES CONNOLLY

In the early 1960s, when I was pastor in Malibu, California, the Malibu Colony area was part of our parish. As I said before, many film writers, directors, and actors lived in the Colony. Their homes overlooked a very exclusive area of the beach. Among them was Myles Connolly. His residence was located right on the oceanfront. He was a very distinguished looking man, a film writer and author by profession, and the father of a lovely family. He and his family were exemplary practicing Catholics. At some point in our friendship, Myles developed a heart condition that required hospitalization and surgery. When he returned from his operation he was not responding well to the procedure. It was my pleasure to visit him, bring him the Eucharist, and minister to him as a sick parishioner.

I shall never forget that whenever I went to Myles' home to bring him the Eucharist, although he was very weak and should have been in bed, he really edified me. When I arrived at the door I would find him kneeling on the threshold, clad in a very beautiful dressing gown, cravat around his neck, freshly shaven, and his gray hair perfectly groomed. His head would be lowered in adoration. I would say, "Myles, you are a sick man! Please don't leave your bed. Let me bring you the Eucharist. You are endangering your life. Please don't do it." His wife would be in the background, but she did not interfere.

He would respond with words of profound faith: "Father O'Callaghan, when my God comes to Myles Connolly's home I want to be on my knees in adoration of Him as He enters my threshold. Please allow me to receive my God in this way."

That tremendous act of faith really impressed me.

Later Myles went back to the hospital for further surgery. I visited him the night before he underwent exploratory and, if needed, corrective surgery. While I was alone in the room with him we talked about a lot of things. At one point, he mentioned, "You might know, Father, I have written this small book, *Mr. Blue,* which has been well received by many readers. It is a tremendous application of our Catholic faith." (Incidentally, *Mr. Blue* is still in circulation and many thousands have read this magnificent book.)

He added, "If God spares me, this is what I would like to do: The crisis that I see for our church now (in the mid-1960s) is one of faith. Health permitting and God willing, I want to write a book presenting the challenges to our faith and perhaps suggesting some solutions. However, I must go into surgery in the morning, and may God's will be done."

I stayed with him for some time that night. He was well prepared with the last rites of the church and the Eucharist. Finally I departed.

As I left the room I said to myself, "My God, what a man of such great faith."

He underwent the surgery the next day, but unfortunately he did not survive.

His lovely wife came to prepare for the funeral. She had a faith equal to Myles's. "We want to bury my Myles in Our Lady of Malibu Church," she said. "There will be many film people coming—producers, writers, actors, and directors; also, many Jewish friends and other non-Catholics. Myles would want me to make a statement on the resurrection."

We had a very simple funeral. The little church was packed with all of his friends and admirers. He was buried in a wooden casket, in the brown robes of the Franciscan Order. (He was a member as a lay person.)

His wife came beautifully dressed in white with an orchid pinned on her lapel. She wore a lovely spring hat. One would have thought it was Easter Sunday morning when she and her family walked down that aisle to take their place in the pews. That funeral made a tremendous impact on his many Jewish, secular, and Protestant friends from Hollywood. His family's belief in the immortality of the soul was self-evident. It brought out so beautifully the reality of their faith which helped them accept Myles's passion, death, and future resurrection. His death was a beautiful and courageous one. They knew for certain Myles went to his glory.


Myles was one of the most magnificent men I have ever known. What an impact he made on the film industry, on our parish, on me, and on all those who knew him! His lovely wife and family reiterated his beliefs. They were a family of faith, a faith that is so desperately needed in our world today!

# THERESA NEUMANN

When Hermes and I were traveling in Europe in the late 1950s, we were interested in seeing Theresa Neumann, a well-known stigmatic who lived in Konnersreuth, Bavaria, from 1898 until 1962. We had been told she ate no food, drank no water, and received the Eucharist every day of her life. On the Fridays of Lent and Advent she underwent the passion of Jesus Christ, bleeding profusely. The main thing about her bleeding was that the blood ran on the hand, arm, and leg, like when Christ was on the cross. She had a wound on her side, as well as wounds on her head. She spoke various languages when she went through these terrible experiences. At the same time she was able to give prophetic statements about people's lives.

Hermes and I ventured into Germany and up to Bavaria. As we drove about looking for her home town we saw some American G.I.s in a truck and asked them, "Do you know how to get to Konnersreuth?"

They told us they were from Texas, and then asked, "Are you looking for that gal that bleeds and who eats nothing?"

"Yeah, that's the one we're looking for," I said.

"You keep going up this road, and you will find her."

So Hermes and I drove our little Citroen up into the town and found the parish rectory where the pastor, Father Naber, lived. He was a splendid man with a reputation for tremendous holiness. As we were talking to him, lo and behold, who walked into the rectory but Theresa Neumann herself! She was a short stocky woman, about five feet four or five inches tall, wearing a large bandana that framed her face. What struck me most was looking into her eyes; they were most luminous ones I have ever seen. They seemed to look right through me. They reminded me of Pope Pius XII—both had the same penetrating focus.

As the pastor was introducing us, I reached out my hand to take hers and she very gingerly put out her hand. Then I was kind of shocked. I saw open wounds covered by a thin membrane, as if a scab had just been removed from them. On the palm of both hands there was a strip of tape, no doubt a protective measure to cover the wounds.

We talked with her for a little while and asked if we could meet with her again. "Well, I have work to do in my garden," she said, and then she left and went outside.

We spoke some more with Father Naber. "This is a very holy woman," he told us. "She is a remarkable person. She lives with her father and takes care of him."

But the most amazing thing about Theresa Neumann was she was reputed to not eat or drink anything; all she ever consumed was the consecrated daily host. Although she would lose considerable blood during her ecstasies, she looked stocky and well fed. This caused great speculation among the clergy and people. When the German troops entered Konnersreuth, Hitler put her under surveillance for a while. Later he told the intelligence people to clear out of there. He couldn't understand what was going on.

The Catholic Church also put her under surveillance by nuns. Since the cause of the woman's beatification was being considered, the Church was concerned about the type of surveillance that had been done. They also decided Hitler had not conducted a complete investigation.

I recall a Jesuit friend of mine, an army chaplain in Germany, who was a realist. He doubted her authenticity. One day some soldiers prevailed on him, "Why don't you go check her out? At least go and see her."

When he got there, he found a bunch of G.I.s gathered around the bed where she lay bleeding from her wounds in one of her ecstasies. One reached out his hand. She held it and said, "Young man, you are in the state of mortal sin. Your salvation is in danger. Go to confession, and please get your act together."

The chaplain overheard. "My God, it startled me, so I went out and reviewed my conscience to see where I was. Soon I decided, 'I think I am in God's grace and I can go in and see her.'"

At that time, German snipers were everywhere in the area. Since all the officers that wore insignia seemed to be picked off he wore no insignia whatsoever on his G.I. uniform. Remarkably, when she took his hand, she said, "The hand I touch now is the hand of a priest." She added, "Father, take care of your people, be good, and bring Christ to them."

He told me it left him in shock.

In the late afternoon Hermes and I tracked her down and found her doing some gardening work at her father's home. There was a little girl with her. Theresa spoke about our Blessed Mother and we discussed what she was doing. Finally, she said, "I must be about my work. You realize that God demands an accounting of every fifteen minutes that we spend."

"My God," I said. It shook me up. Hermes and I looked at each other—we had better get to work, too! We left her then and went about the town viewing her church and neighborhood. It was a typical country village.

Hermes had his camera with him and had been filming most of our trip through Europe. He decided to photograph her even though she had said she did not wish to be photographed.

"Don't do it, Hermes," I said. But he did it anyway, filming her as she was walking around and speaking to people. However, when he had all the film developed, everything about the whole trip came out magnificently except for Theresa. Anything with her was one huge blur. In reading about her life I have found that others who have tried to photograph her have stated that they had gotten nothing but a blurred picture, except for those photos taken with her permission.

I attended one Mass at which she was present. She had a special place in a little alcove back behind the altar where the congregation couldn't see her. Because there were so many curious people around, she wanted to have peace and quiet. I had my eyes on her when she emerged and knelt for Communion, but when the moment came, I could not look at her. Sometimes, it was said, the host would leave the priest's hand and rest on her tongue. On another occasion, there was a case of where there were three hosts in the tabernacle and she wanted to receive the Eucharist but she was not able to at that particular time because there was no priest available. When the priest finally went to give her the Eucharist, he found there were only two hosts in the tabernacle. She had already received the host in her own home. Apparently, it had come to her. These were a few of the incredible things said about her.

Once two priests, both monsignors from Iowa, came to see her, Hermes and I met with them and we all went together to talk with Theresa. Later on she said one of these three priests had two guardian angels, but I didn't think too much of it until I came home and mentioned it to Cardinal Timothy Manning. "There is a tradition about that," he said. "Any priest with two guardian angels will become a bishop."

"I never heard that before," I said. "I'm going to keep in contact with these two monsignors."

So I did. Lo and behold, one of them was made a bishop.

Theresa had some difficulty with the neighboring bishops. They were not too much in her favor because they wanted her to be more affable to the people and convivial with the pilgrims. She said firmly, "No, I do not wish to do those things. I am not a religious, and you cannot order me to do it. I am acting as I see fit."

Some of the bishops were a little bit resentful because she wouldn't follow their wishes; however, she was an amazing woman, and Hermes and I were deeply impressed with her. I have never forgotten her as well as the G.I.s who encountered her. She made a tremendous impact on them, also.


As far as stigmatism is concerned, she reminds me of Padre Pio a great deal. The church today is considering what an individual's stigmatism really means. Does it confirm she is holy or perhaps a living saint? Although she remains a very controversial figure, I was delighted to have had the opportunity of actually meeting her and to be able to pass her story on to others. Most important of all is that she was deeply involved in the Eucharist. It was the source of her spiritual life and hopefully ours.

## FATHER JOHN MCNAMARA

Priests are human, too. We had a very serious-minded associate at St. Anthony's named Father John McNamara, a graduate of Holy Cross College. He was especially engrossed in theology and philosophy. He loved to read theology, scripture, and the classics in Latin.

He occasionally smiled, but other than that showed little emotion. At times he brought out the worst in me. I wanted to disturb him. Because he was always so conscientious, serious, and mild, I wanted to shake him up. He brought out the needle in me.

Father McNamara usually retired at about ten o'clock at night, wearing an old-fashioned nightgown. Before he got into his bed I occasionally would precede him fully clothed and lie on it, pretending to be asleep. When he came in he would say, "Jim, that's my bed. You are sleeping on my bed! Will you please get off?"

"Zzz!"

"Now I know you are kidding me. You are not asleep. Please get off my bed!"

Of course, I would not. The next thing I knew he would pull on the covers and try to sneak his little body into the bed while I would continue to snore. "Now, Jim, you gotta stop doing this!" He was always very embarrassed and much too kind to say, "Get out of here!"

I used to go on with the charade and later quietly leave.

One night Father Hansen and I hid a vacuum cleaner under his bed. About ten minutes after Father McNamara got into bed, we turned it on from outside of the room. The motor roared and its light flashed. What a reaction! Terrified, he came running out.

Father McNamara was a delightful man. One night I was inside church when a drunken sailor came in. It was during Lent, and the sailor was making the Stations of the Cross. As he walked along the aisles of the almost empty church, he was saying, "You goddam Jews, you crucified my savior." He kept blasting the Roman soldiers. His outbursts went on and on as I watched and listened.

Suddenly, Father McNamara came into the church wearing his winter overcoat. By this time the sailor had gotten to the twelfth Station of the Cross and was trying to pull it off the wall. I grabbed him, took him to Father McNamara and said, "This little priest just loves you." Crying his eyes out, the big guy grabbed Father McNamara in a bear-like hug. As always, Father McNamara's demeanor, kindness, and lack of humor really highlighted the scene.

He was a great little priest. Later on he founded St. Martha's parish in Valinda, which is adjacent to Hacienda Heights.

The priesthood, like every other walk of life, has rich and unique characters.

# True Confessions

In our lives as a priest we encounter many things that really touch our sense of humor. The Confessional is a great source. Here are a few anecdotes that in no way break the seal of confession…

I remember hearing the confession of a little girl who was preparing for her First Communion. As she sat in the chair opposite me, wearing a beautiful dress, her feet barely touched the floor. A tag on her dress stated, "My name is Sandra. This is my first confession."

"Well, now, Sandra," I said. "Tell me your sins.

"I called my good friend Susie a bitch."

She nearly blew me out of the chair when she uttered the swear word. I tried to control my laughter. "You wouldn't call her a bitch again, would you?" I asked.

"No…but she is a bitch."

I told her never to call her or anyone else that name. She was so wise, yet also polite and innocent.

I recall another incident hearing the confession of eight-year-old child. Concealed behind the confessional screen the little voice admitted to telling lies, hitting her baby sister, and disobeying her mother. When the confession ended, I asked the little penitent to be obedient, to be nice to the little sister, and to tell the truth. I then asked, "Are you sorry for all those sins?"

"Yes, Father, I am very sorry for all those sins."

"Now when you go home will you be a good little boy?"

"No," I heard the child say.

"You must not commit those sins again, and you should be sorry for your sins, or I cannot forgive you. Will you ask forgiveness and go home and be a good little boy?"

"No," the child again said.

*What's going on?* I wondered. So, I asked, "Will you please tell me why you will not go home and be a good little boy?"

"Because I am a little girl."

We can make some great mistakes in the confessional!

I was hearing confessions one very busy afternoon when a penitent came in and confessed marital conflicts. This monologue went on and on behind the confessional screen. Finally I started giving advice, hopefully in a spirit of charity and kindness. "Now when you go home, please, for the love of God, be good to your wife. After all, you love her and must respect her."

"I *am* the wife," the person responded.

That was more embarrassing than the little girl incident! I wanted to sink into the floor. I began to understand why this person was having so many problems with her spouse!

\*\*\*

One day I was standing in our church aisle making the Stations of the Cross when a man came in with two women. One appeared to be his wife and the other was a younger woman. When he saw me, he approached. "My gosh, I haven't been here for fifteen years," he remarked. "This parish has really come a long way—the new buildings and the landscaping, etc." He then asked, "What ever happened to that angry old Irish pastor who used to be in charge?"

"You are talking to him, man."

He tried to cover up that remark, but how does one counteract the truth?

Sometimes nothing more can be said!

\*\*\*

One year while setting up a fishing trip at La Paz, the boat broker offered us a proposition. After arranging the boat and crew he looked over the four of us: Fathers DeJonghe, Murray, McCarthy, and me. "By the way, gentlemen, I have four really luscious young girls, only sixteen or seventeen years of age," he stated. "They are really fresh. How about it? Would you like to have them for the night?"

"You son of a bitch, you're a pimp," McCarthy said. "We are four Catholic priests!"

The broker crossed himself, saying, "Oh, I'm a good Catholic! I'm a good Catholic!"

"You are nothing but a pimp," we replied.

We did get the boat but tried to straighten him out so that he might fly right.

I recall another time when I was with fellow priests—McCarthy, Murray, and Bishop Johnson—scouting for a fishing spot in Baja, California. Since there weren't any roads, we were driving on riverbeds when we discovered a little place called Buena Vista, which is now a well-known fishing resort.

As it was lunchtime we went inside a local primitive diner. There were about twenty men, mostly fishermen from Newport and Balboa, California, seated at a table. They invited us to join them. After we sat down the talk started getting pretty raunchy. Then it really got out of line! So McCarthy said, "Gentlemen, you could not possibly embarrass the four of us, but we can embarrass the hell out of you. We are four Catholic priests."

They were absolutely shocked.

I want to add this: We spent four days with those fishermen, raising the bar for them. They became good firm friends who later wanted to have an annual dinner at Newport to renew our friendship. They were a great bunch of guys.

The characters at Pinas Bay were a colorful assortment, but they all had one thing in common: a love of marlin fishing—the hunt, the hook up, and the catch. It was amazing.

There was one guy at the resort, the supervisor, who was a Catholic of sorts. His reputation was rather sordid. He said he had fallen away from his practice of the faith.

He once told us about an incident that had occurred during the off season.

A hurricane arose and huge waves were coming in from the sea while simultaneously an earthquake was shaking the jungle behind the resort. There was rain, lightning, and a great upheaval of trees. Trapped by the sea in front and the jungle behind, this guy was so scared that he cried out to God to save him.

"I found myself running down on the shoreline stark naked, with a gun in my hand, not knowing what in the name of God I was doing! I just wanted to save my life. I was begging God to forgive me and save me. Gradually the waves receded, and the earthquake quieted down. It seemed like a miracle."

He may have had a conversion for a while, but soon he was back to his old self. Perhaps another catastrophe might bring him to permanent repentance.

## HOUSEKEEPERS: CANDIDATES FOR SAINTHOOD!

One of the most important persons in a parish rectory is the housekeeper. A good housekeeper who is warm and friendly creates a warm and friendly atmosphere in the rectory. These qualities help make a home for the priest's staff.

When a housekeeper is interviewed for the position it is helpful if she is in good health and a widow whose children are grown. It is important that she be at peace with herself and enjoy hobbies such as knitting, or reading, or watching television, is interested in sports, or whatever so she will not be bored with leisure time and content where she is. Naturally, her time off and vacation days are important. It is also helpful if the housekeeper is a motherly type because she can certainly relate to the needs of the younger priests and also understand the idiosyncrasies and interests of the pastor. Good housekeepers certainly make rectory living much more palatable and much more delightful than it would be without them.

*** 

Monsignor Bernard J. Dolan had a sister, Margaret, who was the housekeeper at St. Anthony's rectory in Long Beach. Our staff had five priests. Margaret really shielded us from the monsignor. She knew how tough her brother was. However, she made sure that the cook served us good food, our laundry was done, and our rooms were well cleaned. She spread an air of hospitality, making the rectory a home. We priests loved and respected her. She lived and cared for her brother and the priests for many years.

In my early years as pastor, a German woman named Frieda Kalschmidt was my housekeeper. I met her son, Helmut Gaylord, while he was a student at Los Angeles City College and a member of the Newman Club. He was in love with a fine girl named Helmi Schelken.

I met Frieda while I was preparing the couple for marriage. She informed me she would like to be a housekeeper as she was a widow and was free. What a delight! As soon as I was named pastor at Malibu I asked if she would come. She was the most magnificent housekeeper one could have. She wanted to do all the cooking and housekeeping. My associates and I were delighted. She took care of the house, the garden, and the cooking. Oh, the delicacies that she could bake, especially her apple strudel! How hospitable she was! Frieda was such an industrious worker that we would hardly get a handkerchief away from our noses before she would snatch it and have it in the laundry. Like her son Gaylord said, "Boy, she is one hardworking woman."

I also had a dog while living in Malibu. She really cared for Finn McCool. The two made the house extremely warm and comfortable.

She loved to cook and feed people, from Fred Astaire to Judge John Merrick. She never worried about how many were going to be for dinner. Later on, when I left Malibu and came out to St. John Vianney as its founding pastor, I was able to bring her with me. Here again she made a tremendous impact upon our parish, rectory, and our priests. Her prudence, cleanliness, love of the priests, love of cooking, and caring manner certainly helped us all! She was just one magnificent woman. When she left to open up a delicatessen in the San Fernando Valley it was a sad day, a real loss for us because she was the ideal cook and person!

We were then blessed with a new cook. Clarisse was a non-Catholic lady in her sixties whose husband had just died. She was a superb cook and a wonderful housekeeper. (We also had an upstairs maid who did all of the laundry and cleaning.) Clarisse took care of the needs of the priests and provided a good diet for them, and she made everyone feel at home.

She liked to watch films and loved sports, particularly baseball and football. Dinner was at six o'clock, but oftentimes the priests would come in early and drop by her room, which was adjacent to the kitchen, and talk baseball. We had many wonderful times stopping by in the afternoon for a cup of tea and to talk. She would be very pleased as she enjoyed company, and it showed. Clarisse was the ideal housekeeper.

Then there was the other side of the coin.

After my sick leave, I was assigned to the Holy Name parish in Los Angeles. Its pastor had a cook who was a real tragedy. In the first place, she was an inadequate cook. Second, she was quite slovenly. Since she had a husband living at her home, the other associate and I couldn't figure why she preferred living in the rectory.

She had great influence over the pastor. He was a brilliant but simple man. She was very good to him, but we didn't exist as far as she was concerned. I remember the food was not very delectable; however, the pastor was economical and liked to keep the grocery expense down. She did this for him.

One night, I approached the pastor and said, "You know, Monsignor, you are a wonderful holy priest, but you don't understand your priests' needs as far as food is concerned. If I fed you straw and rabbit pellets you probably would think it was shredded wheat and caviar."

"I think you are out of line," he replied.

One time I asked, "Could we possibly have strawberry shortcake with whipped cream on it?"

"No! You can't have shortcake; it's out of season," the cook said.

I knew the berries were in season so I made an arrangement with the nuns who lived next door. I asked them to prepare me a strawberry shortcake with whipped cream and to deliver it at exactly 12:25 p.m. the next day.

As anticipated, the following day monsignor came back from the chancery office in time for lunch with us. At 12:25 p.m., just after we finished our main course, there was a knock on the side door and a

MONSIGNOR JAMES A. O'CALLAGHAN, P.A.

hand reached in holding out a beautiful strawberry shortcake.

"Thank you!" I said, and placed it on the table. Then I looked at the pastor. "There, Monsignor, is your strawberry shortcake."

"Where did you get that?" the cook asked. "Those are out of season."

"Madame, this was created today, and it's a lovely shortcake." I turned to the monsignor, "Would you like a piece?"

"Oh, yes."

I gave him a nice slice. The monsignor really enjoyed it, but the cook was steamed.


I had worked with the monsignor for quite a few months, when one day he said to me, "I think you are a great associate, but I have one complaint. Why do you leave about three nights a week around ten o'clock and don't come back until twelve? I don't suspect you of anything, but what's happening?"

I replied, "To be honest with you, my father and mother live on Sixty-third and Main Street. I go home so I can eat some good food which I'm not getting here."

He didn't know what to say.

As I said, the cook was sloppy. I came in one day and said, "Monsignor, I want you to see the kitchen. Look at the dirt here. Look at her room. It's filthy, too. Also, she should be living at home with her husband rather than caring for us."

But he wasn't convinced. He really trusted her and liked what she was doing.

When the monsignor made a trip to Ireland, he left Father Michael Condor, who was first associate, in charge. I said, "Mike, I can't take this lady anymore."

I went and told her, "You are fired! You're out of here!"

She left rather indignantly. However, we hired a very lovely cook to replace her. When monsignor came back from Ireland, he adjusted to the new cook, the better food, and the overall cleanliness. Sometimes one has to step in and make a change. She was not the cook for our rectory.

After that we had a few others. I remember one who was a very good cook but a heavy smoker. Bonnie didn't like me at all—which is understandable!

We paid her well. She had her hobbies: knitting and painting. Although she was very content to be in the rectory, her smoking habit was a bit difficult. Then she began to get rather bossy. When another priest was assigned to the rectory, she didn't like him either, which took the pressure off me because she turned her ire towards him. Of course, I loved that.

Something really funny happened one night.

"Could I have some brown sugar for my tea?" he asked her.

"Why do you want brown sugar?"

"I want some; will you get me some?"

She went into the kitchen, came back, and dropped a small bag of brown sugar on the table in front of him. He was ticked off. I was amused, but she was out of line. *How can I ask her to leave in a good way?* I wondered.

I went to her one day. "You know, Bonnie, you are a wonderful woman; you have great taste and talent, and you are very good at knitting and painting. However, I don't think we priests are fulfilling your needs. You deserve a better atmosphere and priests who understand your pursuits and talents. We think it would be better for your own happiness if you would find other employment."

"You know that is awfully nice of you to say, Father. I shall."

And she did. That way we were able to end the relationship easily and happily. She got another job, and we had a more peaceful atmosphere in the rectory.


Another time we needed a cook, I contacted a Beverly Hills agency, and they sent out an applicant for a trial. She came with the highest credentials.

I was living in my own home on Janlu Avenue since the rectory had not yet been built. She had quarters adjacent to the kitchen: her own room, bathroom, and sitting room. One night, at about nine o'clock, she began screaming loudly. Hearing the cries one might

194

have thought that I was abusing or attacking her. I ran out of the house and contacted two members of the Knights of Columbus. "Would you come here and escort this woman out—baggage and all?"

We took her back to the agency. Sometimes we have no idea whom we are hiring and must be very careful. She was not a winner! She was not fit at all.

Once I tried out a cook from El Monte who had said, "I just love working for priests." She didn't have any general references but we had very busy priests to feed. Our schedules were such that we came in at six o'clock at night just in time for dinner. Before that, we had said Mass, given instructions, and planned projects, all of which kept us very busy. The three of us generally ate from six to seven; immediately after we had office appointments. We also had other things to prepare for, people to be instructed, and cases to be resolved. There was no spare time to prepare meals or do housework.

"I am a good cook," she had told me. "To show you how much I appreciate working for you, I shall create for you my specialty—a blueberry pie."

"Tremendous!" I responded.

What happened was unbelievable. She spent four hours preparing the pie. There were blueberries squashed on the floor, in the sink, in the oven, and all over the stove. What a disaster! The blueberry pie was never baked!

I called in a couple of fellows to escort her back to her home. We now laugh over the incident. Good cooks are hard to come by yet they are so essential in the rectory.

The rectory should be a home for the priests, giving them an opportunity for camaraderie, dialogue, and joy. It is imperative to have good meals and to be hospitable. I learned this truth from Monsignor Dolan, who had said, "When on duty, strive to make it a home. If you need anything special, have the cook order it. I don't want you eating your meals, other than on your day off, outside of this rectory. I want us to eat together because we are family."

We always dined together. Meals were prepared for breakfast, lunch, and dinner.

Normally we ate breakfast early because of the Mass schedule. That was a quiet time for reading the paper, checking the sports page, reviewing the things that would keep us busy that day. At other times, the priests would come in to have a cup of coffee, kick things around, and josh.

However, sometimes one has to draw the line.


I had another excellent cook. Oh, was she a gourmet cook. But after about three or four months, she began to act as though she owned the rectory. She became a mother superior encroaching upon the lives of the priests. It became her rectory. I told the priests, "Be awfully good to her; treat the cook as you would your own mother. Don't be hard or antagonistic. Be kind and gentle, but she is not in charge of you." Beyond the gourmet cuisine she was getting too bossy and demanding.

I remember one noon I came home, and the secretary said, "There is a Maryknoll priest in the office waiting for you."

The missionary priest was there to see about making an appeal for money from our parish. "Welcome, Father," I said. "It's twelve o'clock. Let's have some lunch."

I brought him into the kitchen and said to the cook, "This priest is a visiting missionary, and he will have lunch with us."

She turned to me. "Why wasn't I informed? No one told me this. Why do you surprise me with something like this?"

"Just put a little water in the soup," I said, trying to be a little humorous.

"You should have told me."

Of course, it was insulting to this priest. "Well, if you don't mind, Helene, I'm taking Father out to lunch so you won't have to water down the soup," I said.

I took him out to lunch and we discussed his appeal request. Afterward, I went back to the kitchen and said, "You just insulted a missionary priest. It was embarrassing for him and me. Now I'm giving you a two-weeks' notice so *sayonara*. And be a little more considerate the next time."

One can't allow the cooks to set the tone for the household or control the priests. That time we discharged a very good cook. But hopefully she learned a lesson, and she would be more amenable to helping priests in the years ahead.

Monsignor Dolan gave me really good advice about dealing with household personnel. "When you are dealing with priests, if direction has to be given to them, don't use a secretary, don't use a cook, don't use a lay person, but give them the order directly, eyeball to eyeball. If you can't do it in person then use the phone. If you can't use the phone, only as the last resort leave a note." I have done this all of my life. Monsignor Dolan was so very honest and direct. He knew what priests needed, and he wanted their respect.

We treated the cooks very, very well. When the priests or anyone else in the household had a birthday, we celebrated with a cake. This helped to promote a home atmosphere which the priests and lay personnel enjoyed. Our priests could invite their friends for dinner anytime; we just asked that they give the cook adequate notice.

When we would go on vacation or be off for a few days, oftentimes I would suggest to the priests that it was important to bring home some little gift for the cook and the upstairs maid. These presents made them aware that father had been thinking of them when he was gone.

When a priest comes back from vacation he should also look for something that has been done. For example, I would tell the upstairs maid, "My, you cleaned my rug so beautifully! You straightened out my desk...or this or that." Compliments go a long way with all personnel, making them feel part of the household. All of this is so important since we are dealing with human beings. Also, the rectory needs the feminine touch and good solid housekeepers to provide it.

One time I got a male cook who came highly recommended. For a while, I didn't see inside of his room. He was a very busy person and not a bad cook, but he was odd. One time I took a look inside his room and saw it was littered with junk. No wonder he had never let me come into his room! That was not the kind of a person to have around because he just didn't fit in. We have had good male cooks, but normally women provide a better home atmosphere.

Today the task of priestly hospitality is more difficult. We have so few priests, and oftentimes the rectory is limited to one or two at most. I think it is vitally important for them to have good meals, three times a day: breakfast, lunch and dinner. If there is more than one priest in the household, they should eat together. This promotes hospitality and communication.

Great housekeepers are a true blessing and hard to come by. I remember dining one time with Monsignor Cawley, who was rector of the Cathedral, and about eight or nine assistant priests. We had been talking about priests when Monsignor Cawley stated, "You know, good cooks are hard to come by. You can always get rid of an assistant, but not a cook, for they are really difficult to find!"

I want to express my appreciation for our cooks and the part they played in the lives of our priests. They kept the house warm, hospitable, and orderly. They helped create a home! Many should be canonized saints! God bless the good cooks and upstairs maids.

## QUEST FOR A CHIHUAHUA

This is a story of a nun in her late seventies and a Chihuahua. Sister Leonella had a little Chihuahua pup named Seamus. She was truly attached to the little dog, as were all the other sisters. Recently, she phoned me from Ojai, very distraught because he had died.

I felt compassion for her and remarked, "Well, Sister, I'll see what I can do."

I didn't tell them what I was going to do but started my search for Chihuahuas. How difficult they are to find! Ever since the *Taco Bell* ad with the little talking Chihuahua came out, everybody wanted one. I searched in vain. Then I finally made a contact in an area above Santa Clarita where a lady had a number of puppies available. They were expensive, but I decided I would go out there and check it out.

In the meantime, God works in strange ways. A friend, Susana Espinosa, came to my home, and I informed her of my search for a Chihuahua. She told me that she thought a mutual friend of ours, Rose Lee, might know someone who had some. I thought this was absurd because I couldn't imagine that Rose Lee, a very delicate lovely Korean lady, would have any connection to Chihuahuas. But as I was arranging to drive to Santa Clarita, I received a call from Susana who said, "Rose Lee tells me that her housekeeper breeds them and has a number of them available."

I was having a difficult time believing this so I said to her, "I'll tell you what we will do. Get the address, and when this lady returns home from work, we'll go see her."

At 8:00 p.m. Susana came by, and we drove to the lady's home.

Thank God t h a t Rose Lee had mentioned, "You'll know it's the right house when you see a lot of cut branches out front," because it was on a very dark street in Rowland Heights. We rang the doorbell, and there appeared Rose Lee's cleaning lady. I couldn't believe my eyes when we stepped into the room. The walls were covered with mounted heads of animals—everything from deer, elk, moose, and even a large stuffed black bear, standing erect and baring its teeth. This room was a taxidermist's dream! I said, "Lady, are you sure you have Chihuahuas?"

"You come with me now, and I will show you," she said.

Yes, indeed, this was Rose Lee's cleaning lady. When I went into another room, I noticed the house was extremely clean regardless of all the animals, stuffed and living.

She showed us two little six-month-old puppies in the bathroom. I picked up one of them because it had a straighter nose and more definite Chihuahua features. "I'll take this little one." It was black, white, and chocolate.

"It's a great little dog," she said.

"Does it have papers?"

"Yes, but to get them you'll have to meet the man I am living with and he doesn't feel comfortable with priests." (The couple was living together but had no civil or religious marriage.)

"Well, I want to meet him."

We went back into the room with all the stuffed animals. When he came in, he seemed very uneasy, until I said, "I admire all your stuffed animals."

"You like them?" he asked. "You appreciate them?"

"Yes. I'm a bit of a hunter. I've been to *Chihuahua, Gomas Farias, Delicias*, etc."

All of a sudden his reserve vanished. "You hunt? You…a priest? You fish, too?"

"I fished many times for the big marlin in Baja, California, and in Panama."

"*Grande marlin*? How long was the biggest fish you ever caught?"

I told him.

"How much did it weigh?" he asked.

I told him it was a three-hundred-pound black marlin. All of a sudden everything changed. The next thing I knew he was very warm and outgoing, and he turned to the lady, saying, "This is a priest! He hunts, he fishes! A priest likes our house. He is *hombre*."

The next thing I knew, another man came into the room with his wife and three children. They produced a number of rosaries and religious articles, asking if I would bless them, which I did.

Word must have gotten out that there was a priest here because suddenly more people appeared with religious objects.

Again there was a knock on the front door. Apparently, the head of the house, Uriel, had called a friend who drove a tow truck geared for freeway accidents. The driver appeared, saying, "Father, please excuse me for my dirty clothes. I just came off work. I have my big tow truck out in front; would you do me the favor of blessing me and my truck?"

"Sure, come on in." I blessed him, and with holy water I blessed his truck and asked God to preserve and take care of this good man.

We then went back inside the house. All of a sudden it was like everyone was happy and warm, and we were enjoying each other immensely. What struck me was that all these lovely Mexican people no longer were ill at ease because the priest was there. They were happy because they had found a priest who was a human being who cared for them and was interested in the things they were involved in.

"I understand, Rosa, that you are not married in the church." I said.

"No, we are not married."

"I'm going to approach your husband."

"No, he will be very upset," she exclaimed.

"Let me handle this. This is my turf. You come with me."

I then said, "Hey, I want to talk with you, Uriel. You were not married in the church."

"I know. I had a previous marriage in Mexico."

"We can get that clarified. Are you willing to marry Rosa in the Catholic Church and do this right?"

"Yes, I'll be very happy. Will you help us?"

"I will do what I can."

By this time they had filled out all the papers for the pup: its breeding, medical report, etc. We signed them and then I asked Uriel, "How much do I owe for the dog?"

"Nothing!"

"Wait a minute! No, no, I want to pay for this dog. I didn't come for that reason. I can well afford to pay for this dog."

"Oh no, Father, this is for you, for the good sisters!" he said. "We want the sisters to have it. Let me show you the other dogs, too."

We went out in the back yard, and there must have been fifteen Chihuahuas, from six months to three or four years old, inside a big kennel. They were yipping and yapping, but the pen was clean, neat, and secure. When we finished admiring them, I picked up the Chihuahua pup. "I'll bring this to the sisters, and they will be very, very happy." I blessed them and bade goodnight to everyone.

On the way home I thought, *Isn't it amazing how God works? The nuns' search for a Chihuahua brought me to this couple's home, where they had an opportunity to meet a priest, help the nuns find a dog, and now they are willing to have their marriage taken care of in the Catholic Church. I had also met new friends, blessing them as well as their rosaries and holy pictures.*

Upon returning home, I called the sisters and announced, "We got the Chihuahua."

They came down the next day to get him. Of course, I had named him Finian, but these stubborn sisters insisted on calling him Jamie. We'll see how things end up.

Anyway, the sisters were delighted. "They gave us this!" They could not believe the family's generosity. The sisters have sent them a painting which Rosa and Uriel now have in their home. Hopefully, with the aid of Susana Espinosa, who speaks beautiful Spanish, I can help the little group.

It was amazing how a Chihuahua helped bring a family to God and also happiness to the sisters!


## CHALLENGES OF THE NEW MILLENNIUM

After fifty-nine years in the priesthood, I regret that I don't have twenty-five more years of ministry. I find the world in which we live to be very secular. If ever priests were necessary, now is the time for apostolic and zealous priests.

Vatican II began the tremendous change that is taking place in the Catholic Church today. There is now a great involvement of the laity ministering in the church and doing it well. We also have many deacons administering some of the sacraments. Then there is enormous participation of our laity in Catholic grammar schools, high schools, colleges, social services, and administrative positions, even trickling down to the kindergartens. However, in the midst of all of the tremendous lay involvement it is the unfortunate fact that vocations to the religious life have greatly declined.

As I look at the young people today, I realize we are living in an extremely selfish age. In the old days we often asked ourselves, *Lord, what do you want me to do with my life?* Instead, today the young people at college and high school levels are asking themselves, *What do I want to do?* Very often vocations are jettisoned or set aside because of one's own selfish or personal needs.

I find that the vocations generally come from families that have had hard times. This is especially true in large families where individuals have had to make do for younger brothers and sisters and sacrificed many things for the good of the whole family. In our nuclear families, there now seems to be much more selfishness, less discipline, and infrequent self-sacrifice.

As I reflect upon our present parishes, I see a tremendous influx of people from other countries. When we started St. John Vianney Parish back in 1965 the vast majority were Anglos. Although there were some Mexicans, Asians were hardly seen. Unfortunately, we did not have many Blacks, either.

But how things have changed in the last thirty years!

Although we still have a great number of Anglos in our parish, there has been an increase of Hispanics. They are the prevailing majority and a marvelous influence. Asians also have entered. (The largest Buddhist Temple in the United States is located within our parish boundaries.) In addition to Filipinos, other cultures, such as Vietnamese and Samoan, are entering into today's local parishes.

This presents a tremendous challenge for the priests. It is very important to be bilingual. Speaking Spanish and English, especially in California, is essential. Many liturgies are now in Spanish, English, or a combination of both.

We have a great need of seminarians. Over the last year I've had the privilege of giving retreats to seminarians at all levels. It is amazing to visit our major college and theology seminary, St. John's, in Camarillo. One would think he was entering the third world because most of the seminarians are non-Anglos.

When dealing with non-Anglos—whether Chinese, Filipinos, Blacks from Nigeria or other parts of Africa, and especially the Koreans—I encounter young men who do not have our mindset. They reason differently and are unfamiliar with the various cultures. It takes them quite a while to understand our thinking and how we approach things. It is difficult for people of different cultures and nationalities to come to understand each other, which is especially challenging if they are living within the same rectory or school. This takes time and presents a hardship. Yet I must say they do well and develop into marvelous priests.

In the 1930s and '40s, our missionaries went to bring the faith to the Blacks in Nigeria and other parts of Kenya. Now the products of those missionaries are bringing the faith to us in America and Ireland (Ireland is also running dry as far as vocations are concerned.) They are sending missionaries out throughout the world.

Recently I gave a retreat to twenty-seven first-year theologians. Among them were five Anglos, the other students were from Africa, the Philippines, Vietnam, and Mexico. Hopefully some from that group will be ordained.


There are tremendous challenges for our seminaries and the church today. I think it is very important for new priests to return to the sacramental life of the church. When we look at the beautiful life of

Christ we find He was always out among the people, ministering to them.

We are now living in an age of computers, Internets, voice mail, etc. Oftentimes when we contact a rectory it is very difficult to reach a live human voice. Instead we usually hear something that is on a tape or see some computer website. It is very difficult to directly contact a human person. In the old days people just came in, and they saw the priest. It's not that way anymore because of the lack of priests, the use of our modern technologies, and our huge parishes.

It is also important for our priests not to be involved in affairs of the parish that can be taken care of by lay men and women, i.e., parish finances and business management; and handling all of the other things that must be done around the church, such as the building management and caring for the grounds. This would leave the clergy free to minister to the people. This is what Jesus did. The beautiful thing about Christ was that He went around healing the sick, raising the dead to life, forgiving people their sins, and distributing the Eucharist.

Three of the most tremendous gifts we priests possess by right of our ordination are absolving the sinner, anointing the sick, and con-secrating the Eucharist. In hearing confessions we sometimes bring the dead to life; in anointing the sick we prepare them to meet their God if He calls them in death; and above all we bring the Eucharist, the body and blood of Jesus Christ, down upon our altar. What a tremendous privilege we priests have! That is what we do! All the other things are incidental in the light of these great sacraments.

The greatest responsibility of a parish priest is to be a holy priest. Perhaps there never has been a holier parish priest than St. John Vianney, who was not a brilliantly educated man, but he certainly was a holy one. As I contemplate the archdiocese and reflect on the past years of my priesthood, I am impressed and moved by the holy priests. What a positive influence they made upon their parishioners! The humble priests were the holy priests that really affected the people. They didn't have to be tremendous organizers; instead they led with sincerity, humility, and love. They were there for the people, and I think that we priests have to be concerned with this truth: We must hear people's stories.

I have often thought that some of our seminarians would do well to forego the constant studies and spend some time meeting the public—for example, working in a department store or perhaps pumping gas. In that way they would develop human relations skills. I find that so many of our priests now are not especially concerned about hearing the stories of the people, yet everybody out there has one. All we need do is to read the Scriptures and follow the life of Christ, especially as portrayed in St. Luke. How it challenges us! Jesus walked and talked among the people, and He was a tremendous inspiration. We, too, must be people priests.

Also, in going about our administrative and sacramental life, we must teach the importance of the sacraments.

Our greatest privilege is offering up the holy sacrifice of the Mass. I think that it is important for us to prepare homilies that relate to the people. We should be informed about the latest films, be aware of sports, politics, business, the conditions of the poor, racism, whatever, so that we can bring these topics into our homilies. Then the people in the church will say, "By God, Father knows where we are and what's going on in our lives!" A good one doesn't have to be brilliant; all we have to do is read some of St. John Vianney's homilies to see how he touched the people because of his sincerity, his love, and his understanding of people. I think that is vitally important for us today.

We have to make penance and the confessional available. I notice that people are sinning as much as they ever sinned, perhaps even more. Many churches have cut down on the hours we give to the sacrament of penance.

We hear confessions every day at St. John Vianney. People come from all over on weekdays to go to confession, sometimes even from fifteen or twenty miles away. This is because we are available. I think the greatest thing for me since Vatican II has been face-to-face confessions because there I am meeting the sinner eyeball-to-eyeball. I would say ninety-five percent of our confessions are face-to-face. When we talk to someone, normally we don't put the lights out in the room. We want to see the person's facial expressions, body posture, and gestures, as well as hear his or her ideas and feelings.

It is amazing how many people come to confession, young and old. I am so delighted they come. They have a sense of sin and a love of God, and oh how we can build up their egos by saying, "My God, you are here! The Lord loves you." I encourage them. I often teach young people how to shake hands. I make eye contact and say, "You're here, and God loves you so don't feel that you are this or that because, after all, when you come to me for confession, it is merely one sinner talking to another. I go to confession just as you do."

I am delighted with this tremendous sacrament of penance. I think we have to make the confessional much more available at hours that are more convenient for the people. Of course, again this takes priests. If they could be relieved of other responsibilities, then priests could have more time for confessions.

Where the church is heading today, I don't know! Is the future of the church going to involve married men, or is it going to include women priests? I don't get involved in all those issues. My firm belief is this: It is up to the Holy Father. It's up to the Church to decide, and whatever decision the Church makes, I will follow.

As far as celibacy is concerned, it has always been difficult for me. But I truly understand its efficacy and power. Maybe someday the Church will permit it to be optional so one can choose to be celibate or to reject it. For me it is a positive force; one sacrifice I can give to the Lord and say, "Lord, this is a sacrifice. I give it to you not as martyrdom but as something that is very meaningful to me." I know it may sound selfish, but in doing this I also realize that no one owns me as a priest except God. Therefore, I am available to Him as He chooses. I follow the guidance of my lawful superiors. This gives one a tremendous sense of freedom. Is it difficult to remain celibate all of one's life? Oh, yes, it is! I thought after twenty, thirty or forty years it would be easy. Well, I'm going on eighty-five now, and it is just as tough now as it was when I was twenty, thirty, forty, and fifty. But I can say, "Lord, with Your help, Your strength, and Your grace, I can give this gift to You and be available to the people and hopefully make an impact in their lives – as well as sanctify my own."

As I reflect on the church and the priests of today, I see the priesthood as a tremendous vocation. We say, "God will provide priests," and this is true, but I think we have to invite more young men to come to the priesthood. The greatest sales pitch for priests is to see that we are happy together and in love with our vocation. If we revel in our priesthood and have a great happy life, that joy will show in the parish, and the young men will be edified and challenged by it.

We priests must spend more time with our youth, encouraging them and showing the joyfulness of our challenging lives. This will certainly influence them to consider seriously the priesthood and the religious life. I also tell the people, "You worry about wanting grandchildren and want your sons and your daughters to marry, but there is nothing as beautiful as a priest or a nun in the family."

Father Joe Shea, who was my associate and a very close friend, had twelve brothers and sisters—all together, there were seven boys and six girls. When his father, a wonderful man, died, Father Shea's six sisters walked down the aisle with their spouses at their father's funeral, the six sons carried the casket, and the mother was behind the whole group, smiling beautifully. And there in the sanctuary was her priest son, greeting the family and giving his father to God in the holy sacrifice of the Mass. My God, what a tremendous scene that was!

I know for a fact that I myself am not the most loved member of my family, for I am an austere kind of person. But I celebrate the marriage of my nieces and nephews, take care of crises in the family, etc. They come to me; I am there for them. It is amazing what a priest means in a family, and any father or mother should be grateful to have a son or a daughter in the religious life. I have never known a father or a mother who regretted giving a son or daughter to God as a religious pursuing a sacred vocation.

Having been ordained in 1943, I have had the privilege of going through Vatican II and all its subsequent changes. It has not been difficult. I have been in Black parishes. I have been in Hispanic parishes. I have been in mixed parishes. I have been a Newman Club chaplain at the college level and taught ethics at St. Vincent's College of Nursing. I have done every type of work the church has asked me to do.

I coached football and basketball. I have hit the streets taking census, given retreats at every level, done everything and enjoyed every bit of it because I did it for the love of Christ. I am not working for our archbishop or the pope. I am working for God under their jurisdiction and authority. It has been a tremendously happy and fulfilled life.

My simple trust in the Church has enabled me to lead and instruct the people through all its changes. My guides and inspiration come from the Holy Father the Pope, the Magisterium, the Eucharist, and Mary. Any priest who obeys them will be tremendously effective. All the priests I have known who were really successful adhered to those particular lines. I can say this for myself as it has been my life all the way. Devotion to Mary is tremendous for the priest, but now I seldom see religious saying the rosary.

I think it is essential for people to see us at prayer. In the church, in the rectory, in the chapel—let priests be men of prayer who lead the people in prayer. When I see a lawyer studying his briefs and working hard I am delighted that the lawyer is taking care of his clients. When people see a priest at prayer–a devout and holy priest– they know this man is certainly bringing their welfare to Almighty God.

I have learned a lot over the years. If people ask me to bless a rosary or bless their car, I take it very seriously, and I ask them to pray for me as I bless the religious object.

The priesthood is a tremendous life, and I thank God that He has called me to it. I know that God loves us and that the Church will prevail. God will provide for all the needs of the Church in the future. My only regret is that I don't have thirty or forty more years to give to Christ. He has certainly blessed my life and made me both very happy and, hopefully, an effective priest.

# PART FOUR:
# TRAVELS

# GOING FISHING

It's very important for a priest to have a regular day off. It's also extremely vital that each priest have priest friends who enjoy the same exercises, pursuits, and interests. I have been blessed with good friends before and since my seminary days. Years ago an associate priest only got one day off a week. My priest friends and I tried to arrange to have our free time on the same day so that we could recreate together.

We decided to take Mondays off in our respective parishes. For example, we would tell a parishioner, "If you want one of us to conduct a funeral, our services will not be available on Monday; however, one of the other priests can do it. In this way we were able to get together to play golf on this "our" day.

Sometimes golf is jokingly referred to as the "eighth sacrament." The priests who golf together stay together and enjoy their mutual ribbings, challenges, and discussions.

Enjoying other recreational activities together is another means of bonding. The priests that I associated with also enjoyed hunting, fishing, and surfing. We spent many of our early priesthood summers in Baja California, going south to La Paz to fish for striped marlin and dorado. Later on we traveled even farther south to Rancho Buena Vista. Ultimately, we arrived at Punta Colorado and the tip of Baja California, San Jose del Cabo. We experienced some truly great fishing expeditions during that time, catching countless marlins, dolphins, rooster fish, etc. I wasn't the greatest fisherman in the world–the other priests were better than I–but sometimes luck was on my side.

During the course of our fishing in Baja California, Dr. Charles Mather, a professor at Los Angeles City College and a good friend of mine, told me he had written a book on the pursuit of the billfish.[3] He wanted to use a photo of a marlin that I had caught. (On August 8, 1964, I was fortunate enough to have landed a striped marlin that weighed 220 pounds. It was one big marlin!) In return for the favor, he gave me some etchings he had done of the black and blue striped marlin.

Dr. Mather recommended that we go down to the Canal Zone in Panama. He said he could make some arrangements for us through the "Zonians," which is what they called the Americans living there. Thus we rented a boat with a crew of two or three and cruised south to fish at Pinas Bay, a great place for black marlin fishing because it was where the fish went to spawn.

Our trips to Panama were great expeditions! Normally we left Los Angeles International Airport, flew to Guatemala, and then on to Panama City. We would take a taxi down to the Canal Zone, where we would have a leased boat waiting for us. Immediately, usually at night, we would cruise south to Pinas Bay. Our leased boat was named the Cayman II. Of her, a skilled fisherman wrote:

*"Boats, like people, have distinct personalities. Some are gay and frivolous; some are sleek, chic, and sophisticated; some are overweight, heavy sterned dowagers; some are truly elegant; some are honest workmen; and a few, like the Cayman II, are square-jawed, broad shouldered, lean hipped, muscular, and completely dedicated to a single goal." The Cayman II was not a 'cruiser.' She was not a 'yacht.' She was not a 'sport fisherman.' She was a marlin fisherman in every fiber of her being.*

*Built in the late 1930s, she is 40-feet long with a 12-foot beam – solid, sturdy, and seaworthy. Diesel power provides range and safety. She cruises at eight knots; high speed was made unnecessary because of her location in the center of the world's best marlin fishing.*

---

[3] Charles O. Mather, *Billfish: Marlin, Broadbill, Sailfish* (Saltaire Publishing, Inc., 1976)

*Her fighting chair has a right armrest lower than the left to provide a comfortable position for the long fight with the big one. The transom is only about twelve inches above the water and is completely open (except for railing) to permit easy hauling aboard of a giant fish. She is perfectly capable of finding, fighting, weighing, butchering, freezing, and storing a thousand pound marlin with no outside assistance. She can sleep and feed up to seven people in reasonable comfort while carrying them to wherever the marlin are feeding.*

*She has found and boated more black marlin than any other boat in the world, and she is utterly contemptuous of any other fish. She trolls two hand lines continuously for bait fish (preferably 10-15 pound tuna) to attract the marlin to the hook and regards sailfish, dolphin, rainbow runners, yellowtail, wahoo, snapper, and all other small fish as bait thieves and nuisances which delay her in the pursuit of her primary goal. Days are numbered and categorized by the number and size of marlin boated and by absolutely no other standard.*

*At the sound of "strike" she crouches, springs, and fights with the fury of a tiger. At that moment she becomes a thing alive, exultantly resilient, and implacably committed."*

The heroic Cayman was anchored by the wharf in the Canal Zone. Usually she would have a crew consisting of a captain and two deck hands plus the four of us. The Cayman had a fish freezer, a fighting deck in the stern, and one head. At night we would lay our sleeping mats on the bulkheads, stretching a tarp four feet above and over the deck of the boat to keep us dry. (There was heavy rainfall in Panama.)

As soon as we boarded the Cayman, we were introduced to the crew and the captain. They gave us a set of rules: Seek each other's safety; obey the captain; get along with the crew and each other as we are all equal. This provides harmony.

They had stocked enough food to provide meals for our ten-day expedition. As we cruised along the coast to Pinas Bay, we fished much of the time. At that point, we weren't catching any marlin, but we hooked the occasional wahoo, which is a large fish that looks somewhat like a big barracuda. We might also catch a mahi mahi and perhaps a small tuna along the way.

When we arrived at Pinas Bay, we would anchor in a lagoon surrounded by jungle. It was a beautiful, peaceful, and quiet area for the captain to prepare dinner for us. He would either barbeque steak or bring out some of the meals that had been prepared in Panama for the trip. It might be stew or pot roast or pasta. Also the crew prepared a number of special dishes themselves. The fresh barbequed marlin was great.

We arose about four the next morning, ate a quick breakfast which the captain had prepared, and headed out to sea. Usually it was rainy and windy. Hating to leave my sleeping mat, I would ask myself, *What in the name of God am I doing this morning in a place like this?*

Our first task was to catch the bait, either bonito or small tuna. They were kept alive by putting them in a tank until we attached them to the lines on our outriggers. Once we caught the live bait the hunt began.

Two fishermen would sit on the fighting deck chairs. The lines from their poles went out to the outriggers on each side at the back of the stern and then down into the water. The bait had a leader string through the top of its eyes that allowed it to swim about twenty feet below the surface of the water where the marlin lurked, waiting for a nice small fish to catch. As this took place below the surface, we very seldom saw the strike.

We had to be very careful to keep our eyes on the outrigger to determine whether its movement indicated a strike in progress. When a marlin tried to take a fish, normally he would hit it with his bill first, then check it out before he softly took it in his mouth. If he then decided it was A-Okay, the marlin gulped it down, and that was the time we set the hook. If our timing was bad, we either jerked the bait out of the marlin's mouth or ensured a bad hook up. Then the marlin would usually get away.

The most delicate thing in marlin fishing is the "hook up." If we set the hook in his stomach, the marlin will not struggle too long as he will bleed a great deal. The hook up may last an hour or two. If we hook the fish through the lip there will be very little bleeding involved and we will have a fighting fish on our hands, struggling for hours and hours.

Over the fighting deck were carved these words: "The price of a marlin is eternal vigilance." One always has to be on the alert. In the course of our fishing trips, all of us had experienced lost marlin hook ups because of distractions.

One normally fished one hour on and one hour off. When relieved by the other fisherman I could rest for an hour before returning to my rod.

I remember some tremendous fish that we caught down there…

One day Father Emmett McCarthy hooked a big marlin, and he fought the fish for about an hour. Then it sounded and went down to the bottom. He worked that fish, trying to bring it up, until it finally surfaced about forty-five minutes later. What a surprise! It wasn't the marlin he had hooked but a shark! It had eaten the big marlin and its carcass was now in his belly. The shark was hooked via the marlin!

Of course, our difficulty then was to get rid of the shark. Since the leaders and hooks cost seven and a half dollars apiece, we didn't want to cut off the leader and release the shark. We wanted to get the leader out of the shark's mouth and salvage the leader and the hook. It was pretty dangerous business.

Normally one would pull the shark up to the side of the boat. We would place the end of a broomstick type of shotgun between the shark's eyes and then detonate it, but typically the shark would not die right away. Sometimes we would pierce the shark's eyes and try to avoid the teeth and jaws while cutting and removing the hook from its mouth. But sharks are very tough animals, always in motion. Even after that, the shark often was still alive and swam off although it usually wouldn't get very far. By that time other sharks had gathered, and there would be a bloody foaming mess of water as they ferociously consumed their wounded buddy.

Sometimes we fished in very rough seas, which was quite difficult for us. On time Father Dick Murray foul hooked one real tough fighting marlin. Because it was foul hooked, Father Murray did not have much control over the fight. Dressed in shorts, he fought that fish for a couple of hours in a driving rain before finally bringing it in. It was a tremendous fish – over 450 pounds.

One always felt like a conquering hero upon landing one's fish.

I remember one day I got the guys really upset because, having started out about eight o'clock in the morning and gotten our bait, I made a hook up right away with a marlin. Fortunately, I made a lucky one in the sense that I caught him right through the upper lip; thus there was little blood involved.

By around six o'clock it was getting very dark, and the captain was uneasy because the sea was turbulent. Even with a fifty pound test line, the marlin was tireless, and I was unable to bring it in. He had come up to the boat three or four times, the leader in plain sight, but then he would take off again before the crewmen could grab the leader. Perhaps the other guys who were better fishermen could have brought it in, but I couldn't.

After about the first five hours I had gotten my second wind, the only time in my life that I recall doing so. It was really a tremendous experience. I felt fresh, like I could have gone all night.

When one has a hook up, no one can help or touch the fisherman. If assisted, I would not have been eligible for the record book. Thus I was on my own. Anything I drank had to be poured into my mouth; food was consumed without anyone touching me.

I fought that fish until my hands were bloody and blistered. After nine and a half hours the captain finally said, "You have to bring that fish in or break him off," so I tightened the fifty pound drag. That's when he snapped the line and swam off into the darkness. I had just blown landing it.

It was now fully dark, and I was really exhausted. My hands and buttocks were sore and bleeding. I wanted to go into the jungle because there was a waterfall where I could take a natural shower.

After we fished, a native usually would come out in a wooden canoe and take us back to shore. Just off the shoreline there was a magnificent jungle waterfall cascading down, but to reach it we had to go through shark infested waters. Then we had to work our way through the rocks while avoiding little poisonous snakes. If one of them bit us, we'd be dead men, but I told them, "I want a shower no matter what happens."

Father Murray went with me. When I finally got under the waterfall, it was so soothing to my aching body, oh, I never wanted to leave!

It took me a full day to get back in shape for more fishing.

Every fish was a different challenge—a real test of one's skills. To keep peace on our boat wasn't easy, especially with four guys like McCarthy, Murray, DeJonghe, and O'Callaghan, plus a crew of three, all with different personalities. To obtain good cooperation from the crew, we treated them with the utmost respect. We knew how much we really needed the crew's support and expertise. After all, they could be our lifeline in case of trouble.

It was very good that at mealtime everyone sat together at table. We had one rule for the crew. They too enjoyed "hooking up" to a marlin so we made it clear: "Don't you in any way ever touch our rod when we are fishing because we want to make the catch ourselves. We didn't come all the way out here to have you hook up and land the fish for us." They knew that rule, and they abided by it.

To avoid arguments we priestly brothers also had a rule for when we left the Canal Zone. It was simply this: "No one at any time, under any circumstance, for any reason, and any condition would complain about anything." We meant it, and we kept it. Keeping this rule was the only way we could survive. We blew off steam when we returned to the Canal Zone at the trip's end, venting our feelings and frustrations and celebrating a good trip.

One time Father McCarthy hooked a big marlin. He fought the fish beautifully, finally bringing him in so that the deck hand could grasp the leader. Instead the deck hand lashed at the leader, severed the line and the marlin swam off. All McCarthy said was, "Oh, shit." He left, went up to the top of the cabin, and sat there. After an hour or so he cooled off and came down again.

After ten days of fishing, we cruised into Pinas Bay and saw awesome scenery. At times there were literally thousands of dolphins and porpoises darting on the surface of the water. It was incredibly beautiful! We thanked God for being there.

When we landed a fish, it would sometimes weigh four hundred pounds or more. We would butcher it on deck, cut out all the good meat and put it in the boat's freezer, and then kick the carcass overboard. Once that carcass hit the water, sharks would come from everywhere, and the sea would be turbulent with them biting and tearing it apart. In a moment's time there would be one less marlin and a few less hungry sharks out there.

In the evening we usually had a wonderful dinner, and then we would sit around, play music, and have a few drinks. Oftentimes the natives would visit us in their kayaks. The father with his children or a group of kids would paddle out. These youngsters were very much aware of the dangers of the jungle. If the kayak overturned in a shark infested area, they would get that kayak back on top of the water immediately. The older youngsters were very protective of their younger brothers and sisters.

The kids liked to fish within the reflecting light from our boat. They wouldn't eat our marlin steaks. Sometimes we would invite them up on deck and then to dinner. It was amazing how the older boys wanted the younger ones to be fed first. They obviously had been taught to look out for their younger brothers and sisters. It was so different from what we often saw in the States.

One of the area's most well-known hunters and fishermen, Morito, was friendly, competent, and well respected. We admired him, too. He had a family of nine kids that he often brought out to the boat. He kept telling me, "I want to go to Miami. It is *paraiso*." I would say to him, "Hey, Morito, Pinas Bay is *paraiso* not Miami," but he thought Miami would fulfill his dreams.

One day we decided to enter Santa Dorothea, which was a small village tucked away in the jungle just south of Panama. To get there our boat had to first skim over a net that was used to keep sharks away from the kid's swimming area and then race to the shore with the incoming tide.

The four of us found it a picturesque village. Its thatched roof chapel had been built in honor of Santa Dorothea and housed a bronze statue of the saint. The natives had kept the chapel clean and nicely decorated, but there was no priest. They went to the chapel for devotions and prayers, but there wasn't a blessed sacrament present either.

There were about fifty or sixty kids on the beach, and when they heard we were priests they got very excited and asked for instructions. All of them had been baptized, I believe, save one. They were saying to us, "Padres, stay with us! Teach us so we can make our First Communion; we have no Confirmation either." We really felt sad for these kids because Panama was in dire need of priests and sisters. I thought, if only an adventuresome priest would come down and minister to them. The Diocese of Panama could provide him with a boat and crew of two. He then would service all of the villages in the area. It would be wild and marvelous for some young priest with lots of vigor and zeal. For us old guys the adventure would be a little too much.

The natives, young and old, were wonderful, gracious people. We had a tremendous time with them. In the evening, we priests and the crew listened to tapes, as well as talked a lot. About nine o'clock at night we just sacked out because we were tired and four o'clock was awfully early in the morning.

Days would go by without us seeing any other boats in the entire area. For security reasons, the Canal Zone would wireless our boat every morning about nine o'clock and every evening about six. Of course, if they did not receive a return message from us as to our fate, whatever it might be, they would either send a plane or in some way find out how we were surviving. Communication was very important when we were out there all by ourselves.

I remember one day a sudden storm blew up out of nowhere and the sky became almost ceiling zero. At the last moment, our experienced captain was suddenly not available so we had engaged an inexperienced captain who had just gotten his license. There was also a crew of two. Late in the afternoon both diesel motors on the boat unexpectedly died out.

As far as the captain knew, there was no sea anchor. Suddenly, we were beginning to wallow. As the night became darker, the storm was getting worse, and the water was breaking over the bow so we decided we'd better get help.

Since we thought there might be some boats fishing a few miles away, we decided to send up an emergency flare. McCarthy tried shooting the flares, but they were duds, fizzing out and never really getting off the boat. Finally, the last flare worked. By this time it was getting very exciting. Father Harry DeJonghe, who couldn't swim, went up to the bow of the boat where we kept the liquor. "What are you doing up here?" I asked him.

"If the boat goes down this is the last place that will go under. I'll be the safest for the longest time."

"Like heck you will! Do you see all those sharks out there? Even if you could swim, they'd eat you up."

Of course, I was very much aware of the sharks. We were drifting more and more toward the rocks, and it was a very precarious situation. I kept thinking, *they will read about this in The Tidings.* "Four priests lost at sea. Four parishes open."

Then, thank God, a boat appeared on the horizon. It had seen our last flare and soon approached. Its crew threw out a heavy rope that was attached to the capstan, and they drew us away from the rocks and other dangers. In the meantime, we found out that we did have a sea anchor on board, but the captain hadn't known where it was. It really is very important to have a wise and savvy crew; otherwise, it can be a matter of life or death.

When we finally completed our ten-day hunting quest, we returned to the Canal Zone and Panama. On the occasions we had a fishing trip and caught no marlin, we would cruise into the Canal Zone with the straw of broomsticks facing the sky on our mast. This meant we had been skunked! Geez, it was an awful feeling. On the other hand, if we had a "good fish" we would have a flag flying for every marlin we brought in. Sometimes we went into Panama with several flags flying. We experienced such a tremendous feeling of victory and success that it was as if we had climbed Mount Everest or discovered a new continent! Of course, the crew also always enjoyed this because they wanted our trip to be very successful. This enhanced their tip.

These were wonderful, exciting times. It was always a great adventure. McCarthy, Murray, DeJonghe and I, along with the crew, felt united after ten challenging days. We got to meet a number of the "Zonians," hear their stories, and meet some of their families. It was a wonderful way of life for these people, and what a change for us priests, too!

I remember one plantation that was owned by a Catholic man; his wife was a hard-nosed Protestant. We sent word that we would like to say Mass on the veranda of his shore side hacienda. His wife pressured him not to because she didn't want any priests offering Mass at her home. So, we decided the heck with that! We tied up the Cayman to the pier, got out two oil drums and put some two-by-fours on them, thus setting up an altar. By God's divine plan it was great! The four of us concelebrated Mass, facing the sea from the pier. Suddenly filtering out of the jungle and boating on the water floated canoe after canoe filled with kids and adults. They respectfully participated in the liturgy, loving being there for the holy sacrifice of the Mass. Even though we didn't say it in Spanish, they knew what was going on. They appreciated what we were doing, and they loved us for doing it. Maybe God had decided, *"This is where I want you to offer Mass rather than on that rich man's veranda."*

We had wonderful days, and these were great priests; we enjoyed ourselves very much. Thinking back now, I realize our trips were real adventures and well worthwhile! God certainly blessed us on these trips. We brought back so many rich and wonderful experiences.

Although we tried to bring some of the fish home, it was difficult so instead we would bring the frozen marlin back to Panama and give the fish to the poor. We tried to bring maybe seventy or eighty pounds of marlin in our suitcases, get them through customs, and bring them home. Sometimes the fish would unfreeze and cause a real smelly mess. However, we did manage to get some through customs and had some delicious marlin for home consumption.

The Panama days were some of the greatest. The camaraderie, scenic beauty, and its people shall never be forgotten.

## NOTHING IS EASY IN BIRD HUNTING!

We priests also loved hunting in Chihuahua, Mexico. After traveling to Delicias and Gómez Farias to hunt for duck, dove, mallards, gurus [sic], and whatever else flew on the wing, we bunked in a little dilapidated kind of motel. The proprietor, a Mexican woman with a large family, would cook meals for us. The diet was strictly Mexican food–homemade and good.

We arose early in the morning when it was cold as could be. There was a potbelly stove in the corridor of the motel, but the heat from burning kindling would die out at about one o'clock in the morning so we were actually freezing when we got up. The toilets weren't working–whatever toilets they had–because the plumbing was frozen. The only showers we could take were under a big steel cylinder adjacent to our motel, across a muddy stretch of adobe. Someone would heat up this big tank, and when the water was warm we would take showers for about two minutes apiece or less, but it soon ran out. We usually showered in the afternoon, having waited for the day's heat to warm up the water.

We'd leave early in the morning to hunt. After we drove our truck out to the lake and lay down in our foxholes, we'd wait for the geese to come off of the water. We could not let the birds suspect we were there. One hunt I was half frozen in my foxhole at about five in the morning. Bishop Bill Johnson was about thirty yards down from me in another foxhole. Because my fingers wouldn't operate, I was unable to put shells in my gun. So as not to give away my position to the geese, I crawled over carefully to Bishop Johnson's foxhole where he was rubbing his hands in this hand warmer. I said, "Willy, could I use your hand warmer as my hands are frozen and I can't put the shells in my gun."

"You cannot have it," he said. "This is for my hands! I have to keep my hands warm; I gotta be ready!"

I was furious. I went back to my foxhole and had to wait for my hands to thaw out. That afternoon we finally we got home with a number of birds, but I had shot rather poorly.

The next morning Bishop Johnson came to me and said, "By the way, Jim, our toilets are frozen. Can I use your toilet? The toilets won't be thawed out until about ten o'clock, and we can flush them then."

I said, "You cannot! You will not use my toilet. Go back to your little place and face your problem. The next time I ask for your hand warmer perhaps you will give it to me." It should be give and take.

Hopefully the geese would fly over our hiding places so we could shoot and bring down as many as possible. When we took them back to the little motel, the owner would cook them.


One of the local birds, a dark, big goose called a guru, was difficult to shoot. They were very suspicious and wary. We would lie in our mud hole near the lake's shoreline and hope for the gurus to come in.

I remember one evening when Bishop Mike Driscoll, Bishop Johnson, Emmett McCarthy, and I were prone in our foxholes near the shore of the lake, hoping the guru would descend to the lake to rest. It was very cold and getting dark when suddenly the guru flew in. Then, of course, we all got up and tried to bring one down. Fortunately, with the help of God I knocked a guru down, and so did Bishop Driscoll. We had our picture taken; two men glorious in our victory after bringing down two big gurus.

Bishop Driscoll was a fine hunter. At this time he is a bishop of Boise, Idaho–a hunters' and fishermen's paradise! Bishop Johnson also was an ardent hunter, and, of course, McCarthy, our "*jefe*," was the finest hunter of them all.

I recall one morning at the lake in Delicias when we were in a boat cruising up to the duck hole from where the duck and mallards sometimes flew out in swarms. Bishop Driscoll was on my right, I was in the middle seat, and Bishop Johnson was sitting at the prow of the skiff. Unfortunately, I'm not a good hunter and didn't have the safety on my shotgun. As we were coming into the mallard hole my gun went off, and Bishop Johnson said, "What's going on?"

I answered, "There is a goose over there."

But the fact of the matter was that I nearly killed him. By the grace of God I didn't blow his head off! I thought to myself, *How would we ever have gotten his body back to the U.S. if I had killed the bishop? It's bad enough just to get across the border!* He never knew he had been so close to death.


I was ribbed by the guys because I wasn't a good hunter. We would see the geese or duck coming off the lake, and I would often fire and miss. Then McCarthy would come right behind me and take them down. One day, however, when we were out hunting, three ducks flew by in a tight pattern. Incredibly, I knocked all three down with one shot. Hunters call it "a triple." I said, "How about that one, guys?" Of course, the birds had flown right into my shot pattern.

Some mornings, McCarthy might be driving the truck while individually Billy Johnson and I would be saying our Divine Office. McCarthy would say, "Gobble, gobble, gobble, gobble." He was that kind of a guy! We would ignore him until we got to the hunting spot.

On a typical day, we'd return in the afternoon, shower from the tank, and eat the dinner which had been prepared for us. Then we would sit down, rib each other, have a few drinks, put more wood in the stove, and regale each other with stories. A lot of give and take took place.

One day our truck broke down as we came to a Mexican junk yard not far from Delicias. There is nothing worse than a Mexican junk yard! It was an absolute hole of a place, with parts of cars and trucks everywhere. When we were entering to look for parts, Bishop Johnson said to McCarthy, "Since you guys can take care of the truck, I think I'll walk over to the motel and get some rest."

"Like hell you will," McCarthy said. "You are not a bishop here! You are just one of the guys. You get lunch ready while we get the parts for the truck."

"Yes, Sir!" Bishop Johnson said.

It was all democracy among us, and the bishop knew it.

We had some very wonderful times in Mexico! Because it was a lot cheaper, we would fly down from Tijuana and land at one of its little airports. Sometimes as we flew in we'd wonder how in the name of God pilots and planes could survive in these parts.

I have one picture which I keep in my bathroom. It shows Bishop Johnson standing with his back to me while he's overlooking one of the *lagos*. I'm pointing towards his rear end, saying, "Look at the squarest ass I have ever seen on any man in the world." As a matter of fact, when Bishop Johnson saw it he said, "Give me that picture!"

I refused to give it to him so he grabbed it. Bishop Driscoll got it back from him and I have that picture now as a keepsake. Bishop Johnson, a good friend and a great priest, died too soon.

May we all hunt together again in the Kingdom.

## IRANIAN MONARCHY

Many years ago Cardinal Francis Joseph Spellman had a secretary named Father Shea. On his summer vacation, this priest often flew out from New York to visit Hollywood, where he would spend some time ministering to the actors, stage hands, and others on the film set. While there he met Hermes Pan who was the choreographer for RKO. They both became good friends.

During the course of Cardinal Spellman's episcopate in New York, a highly placed Muslim couple in Iran had become converts to the Catholic faith. It was an almost instant conversion that had occurred when they were traveling in Jerusalem to visit the Holy Land. Their reception into the church was done secretly because if it had become known in Iran, their lives and freedom could have been endangered.

This couple decided to come to New York for a vacation. Of course, Cardinal Spellman was aware of their conversion through his Rome connections. Knowing they were going on to Hollywood to check out the film industry and meet some celebrities, the cardinal asked Father Shea, "Is there anyone there to whom I can entrust this couple because I don't want them getting into the wrong hands."

Shea told him about Hermes Pan.

The couple flew out and met Hermes. To keep their identity unknown, they were introduced to film people as a dance couple from Iran. Since I was a close friend of Hermes's, I soon met them.

They were a very fine, lovely young couple, very cultured. Hermes and I had dinner and long conversations with them, especially at Hermes's home. We all got along well, and after a few months we were at ease with each other. In time they returned to Iran.

A few years later, as their family began to increase and grow, they moved to the United States. They maintained two homes here–one in Bel Air and another in Montecito, California. (They also retained their place in Teheran.) The couple's three children all had been baptized Catholics and raised in the faith.

Princess Shams Pahlavi was the elder sister of the Shah of Iran. He knew that she and her husband, Mehrdad Pahlbod, had converted to Catholicism, but all three wanted this to be kept secret because they believed the Muslim people would be incensed. The princess feared someone might try to assassinate them or endanger some of their family; therefore, this couple concealed their identity while attending Mass and religious services. There was always a coterie of Iranians plus a lady-in-waiting around them. The princess was called "Her Highness" and treated with utmost respect. Mehrdad, her husband, was very solicitous about her well-being and anticipated most of her needs.

Some years later they visited Iran and sent invitations to Hermes and me to come over and be their guests. I dovetailed my vacation schedule to align with Hermes's time off. We then flew from Los Angeles to Rome to Teheran. It was a very precarious trip over high mountain peaks in a KLM airplane, especially when we got fogged in. At times we felt we would never make it, but, thank God, we safely arrived at the airport in Teheran.

They had sent a limo to take us to the palace of the Princess Shams. I couldn't believe the luxury. Hermes and I, thank God, had a hotel suite on the outskirts of the city.

Our hotel at Darbon [sic] was high up in the mountains. The people obviously lived in abject poverty. Their water came from above the city and ran along the streets in gutters. The people used this water for drinking and washing clothes.

Although it was great and more relaxed to be outside of the palace, we were soon brought into the private life of the Royal Family.

Within a week of our arrival, we had dinner with the Shah at his palace. It was a wonderful and interesting occasion. I found him to be very athletic, very much in charge, very dignified. He spoke at least five or six languages; his English was precise and eloquent. When the Shah first entered the room, everyone stood to show their respect for his office. When he sat down, they did, too. At the end of the meal when the Shah stood, everyone would rise to their feet. He was always referred to as "His Highness."

In those days there wasn't TV, but as he was most interested in film, he did have a projection room. He had movies brought in, but if he didn't like the movie that was playing, he would say, "Turn it off! Bring in a new one."

We had lots of conversations about movies, American sports, and politics. (At this time, he didn't know I was a priest. I had entered Iran as a coach and a teacher.) The royal family had assigned a Dr. Hadjazi to be our guide and interpreter. He told Hermes and me not to go into any Muslim temple because we could be killed by some fanatic. So we traveled around casually, keeping out of the Muslim places of worship and avoiding any Catholic churches or schools.

When I went to Mass with the Princess and her husband, we were driven by a trusted servant who picked us up in an old car. Once we passed through the palace gates the driver would cruise around the city to avoid detection. When we came to a certain walled compound–the home of Tehran's Catholic bishop–a gate would open, and we would quickly enter. Mass would be celebrated inside his home with the princess and a few other trusted individuals. After Mass we would cautiously go back to the palace.

Hermes and I found the long wait to meet with members of the royal family exceedingly tiring. The princess frequently had her hair done in the morning, followed by a manicure, pedicure, and finally a massage. We would spend time with her family, visit the sights of the city, and occasionally have dinner with the Shah.

Princess Sham loved dogs, birds, and especially parrots. The palace had two rooms specifically for her pets. She actually had a general from the army who was in charge of them, her dogs especially.

As I got to know the Shah better, I was tremendously impressed with his knowledge, courage, and class. He knew much about Thomas Aquinas, Saint Augustine, Francis of Assisi, and church history. While discussing these subjects with him one time, I said, "You know an awful lot about Christianity. I am amazed that you have not become a Christian."

"I am the Shah," he said. "I am the head of the Muslim state; that is out of the question."

That took care of that. He knew where he stood and where his responsibilities lay.

In 1949, the Shah had been standing on the steps of a government building, when an assassin, Fakr Arai, pulled out a gun and fired five bullets. Though the shots were at point blank range, the Shah was only wounded in the face and shoulder. The Shah said, "Don't kill the man," so the police took him captive.

The Shah once showed me a mannequin dressed in the same blood-drenched uniform he had worn that day. It was on display, protected and encased under glass, to illustrate his courage. He believed that Allah had spared him from that particular assassination attempt.


During our stay, the body of the deposed Rezā Shah, his father, was brought over from Egypt for interment in Teheran.

The funeral entourage processed for miles. The casket was drawn down the main street on a gun carriage with the Shah walking directly behind. He strode erectly and proudly in procession, totally exposed. I thought, "What a courageous man!" He could have been assassinated at any moment for he had many enemies in Iran, yet he walked boldly as emperor and son.

In the meantime Hermes and I were in the wailing room, as they called it, with Princess Shams, her sisters, and other members of the royal family. There were also hired wailers–women who were crying and sobbing at will. During this time, the princess turned to me and said, "Isn't it awful to have these wailing people? They don't have any idea of our grief nor our belief in love, resurrection, and immortality that we have as Catholic Christians."

After the funeral procession and burial we returned to Princess Shams' palace for a luncheon. The family was close-knit and loving.


The Shah had royal hunting grounds for picnicking and athletic games. Believing I was a coach and teacher, he invited Hermes and me to accompany the royal family to the soccer field where I was urged to play.

"I don't play soccer," I said.

"Be the goalie and just block the soccer ball," his brothers said.

The male members of the family were very competitive, and they almost beat me to death as I tried to keep the soccer ball out of the goal. I did not do too well!

After competing we sat down on Persian carpets and ate lunch. They really ribbed me about my lack of goalkeeping skills!


As I had gotten into the country under the subterfuge of being a coach and teacher, Dr. Hadjazi said to me one day, "The Iranian basketball team is preparing for the Olympics. Do you know how to teach the fast break?"

"Yes."

"We'll take you to the large gymnasium where the Iranian Olympic basketball team is practicing, and perhaps you could teach them."

He conducted me there, and thank God I was able to teach the Iranian Olympic team the fast break. It enhanced my coach identity.


We had so many wonderful times just sitting and talking with the royal family. They were definitely interested in the needs of the people, but unfortunately the Shah was not allowed to reign long enough to accomplish some of the ideals and plans he had in mind. The Shah, knowing of the Catholicity of his sister and brother-in-law, was understanding and compassionate enough to protect them by keeping the fact from going public. This aided them to quietly and humbly attend Mass and raise their children as Catholics.


The Shah's first wife had been the sister of King Farouk of Egypt. The Shah and his wife had not been blessed with a son and he wanted an heir, so he divorced her and later married a young Iranian woman. When it became apparent she couldn't have children, he married a third time, with more success. They had four children. Of the oldest boy he said, "I want this boy trained by men because they will make him strong and hopefully build him to be a future leader and Shah." He was a man of tremendous vision.

The Shah was a congenial and family-oriented person. He had a number of brothers and sisters, and, of course, Princess Shams, his sister, was very close to him. One younger brother was mentally challenged. The emperor oftentimes had this young man at his side and expected the greatest respect to be shown him, and it was! He really loved his brother.

There was another brother called Mohammad who was a general in the Iranian army. He was about six foot one, a big air force pilot. I later heard that after I had left he had flown into the mountains on an errand of mercy. A shepherd had a burst appendix and needed to be brought to a hospital. Unfortunately, Mohammed's plane crashed on the way back and both lives were lost.

The Shah himself was a great pilot who loved to fly. He, too, had had a number of scrapes with death. He asked me one day, "Would you like to take a flight with me?"

"No."

"What do you mean?"

"I don't fly with amateurs."

"I am the Shah."

"But you are not a professional pilot.

"Allah will protect me."

"I'm going to pass that one up."

I had no desire to fly with an amateur, Shah or no Shah!


When we attended dinners, I oftentimes observed he was very abstemious. He would eat and drink sparingly while entertaining his guests. (He was about one hundred and sixty-five pounds in weight.)

He was also very competitive. At times he would say, "Let's see if you can arm wrestle me."

Of course, I was a little bit bigger than him, but he always beat me at the arm press. He would also say, "Put your knees between my two legs and see if you can spread them," so he could show the power of his legs.

I said, "Well, you ride horseback, and I don't have that kind of power in my legs."

I was never able to beat him in those contests.


I was very concerned about the state of the Catholic Church in Iran. I recall one night when I actually slipped out of the palace unobserved and went into the streets alone, looking for a nearby Catholic church that I'd heard about. (I think it was staffed by Claretian missionaries.) When I encountered one of the priests, he spoke English and seemed delighted to meet me. "Who are you?" he asked.

"I'm an American from California," I replied, "and I happen to be a Catholic priest. How is the Catholic faith here in Iran?"

"To tell you the truth," he said, "I have been here for ten years, ministering to the people, and I have had ten converts, but I doubt the security and strength of the conversions. I don't know whether they will last under pressure."

"Then why are you here?"

"It's frustrating, but remember that Saint Paul said some people will plow the ground, some must water, some will sow the seed, and many years later there will be a harvest. We feel that by having our Catholic schools train and teach Iranian boys, at least they are getting some knowledge of the Catholic faith. Even if we have no Muslim converts, it will help the church later on because they are going to be the judges, the lawyers, the politicians, and the doctors. These men will certainly have a better perspective of the Catholic Church. After all, many Iranians think if you are loyal to the church and the pope, naturally you cannot be loyal to Iran or the emperor. Hopefully, we are going to dissipate that over the years."

He had tremendous faith, and he was very right in that.


One day the Royal Family held a party for various important groups, and some United States embassy officials were present. They wanted to know who Hermes and I were and how we were connected with the Royal Family. Hermes and I said nothing. It was strictly our business.

Another day Dr. Hadjazi said, "The Shah would like you to see the treasury of Iran."

He took us to the Iran's version of Fort Knox. The treasury area was unbelievable, the gold and jewels hanging and stacked everywhere was a thing to behold. The walls were covered with strands of beautiful pearls. There was a pyramid of diamonds stacked on a counter; also one emerald box they stated was priceless. The value of these jewels and treasures no doubt backed up their economy. It was an enormously treasured vault–one had to see the actual sight to believe it!

At one point during our visit the Shah found out that I was a Catholic priest. He was most cordial and caring about it. One night some guests were playing a game with the Royal Family, along with some lovely Persian girls and young men from the official staff. Everyone played this game in which one person passed oranges under his or her chin to another. Fortunately, I was seated between two lovely young Persian women. As I was getting ready to play the game, Princess Shams came over and said, "You can't play this game because you are a priest."

"Wait a minute," I said.

"No, you can't, as you have to take the orange under the chin of the young lady next to you with your chin and pass it on to the other young woman next to you."

She cut me out of that game, much to my disappointment!

During our holiday Hermes said, "I'd like you to meet the Shah's mother, the queen mother."

She was the queen under the old Shah. Hermes told me, "When you see her be sure you kiss her hand."

"I don't wish to do it."

"You have to because she is the queen mother."

I did kiss her hand when I met this amazing person. She had the most expressive, dark blue, penetrating eyes. I saw in her face and her body the suffering and fatigue she had endured over the years. Her enormous strength was equally apparent. No doubt it was from her the Shah had received much of his determination, grace, and love.

As the days went on, Hermes and I found that waiting around for the Royal Family to be available was very tiring. It also was hard to obtain privacy with servants everywhere. Finally I told Hermes I had to get back to my parish duties.

When we told the Shah that we had to leave, he said, "No, I want you to stay longer."

"I've got to get back," I said.

Hermes added, "We have to return home. Our vacation time is over."

"I am the Shah and you cannot leave Iran without my permission. I want you to stay here longer."

So, we had to stay, and finally, thank God, he allowed us to fly back to Rome. From there we returned to the United States.

Although the Shah lived in luxury, he did want to industrialize Iran and upgrade the lives of its people. I believe he really had their welfare in mind.

When the Ayatollah Khomeini came into power, the Shah was exiled from Iran. We could have done a much better job of working with and caring for the Shah of Iran while he was dying of cancer and had very few places to go.

It's a shame when the challenging time came during the Carter administration, the United States did not back him as well as we could have.

In the United States I had the privilege of celebrating the fiftieth wedding anniversary of Princess Shams and Mehrdad in Montecito near Santa Barbara. This was just a short time before Princess Shams died of cancer. She was a woman of enormous faith and courage who had raised her children "undercover" in the Catholic faith. I also had the pleasure of baptizing one of her ladies in waiting who had been a Muslim and accompanied Princess Shams to the United States. Through the influence of Princess Shams her conversion was made possible. Who would have known what would have happened to the Royal Family had the Muslims found out?

Princess Shams was grateful to receive this tremendous gift of faith granted when she and her husband had been in Jerusalem. It's amazing that the Shah's mother-in-law–who was Farouk's mother–also received the gift of faith as she was making the Stations of the Cross while in Jerusalem. She then became a Catholic Christian. I had the privilege of participating in her burial at Saint Paul's in Westwood near Los Angeles. She used to say to me, "Augustine made a saint out of Monica, and maybe my son will make a saint out of me." She prayed and prayed that King Farouk would be converted. Instead, pleasure driven, at a young age he collapsed and died on the streets of Rome, a victim of amorality and opulence. There is a price to be paid for everything.

## ON RETREAT

I have never been able to eloquently express my approach to my spiritual life. It has been and still is difficult. I have advanced somewhat spiritually in my fifty-nine years as a priest; however, I find that my prayer life is one based on discipline and the conviction that I must spend time with God. Hopefully, during that time God will speak to me in His own way and let me know where I am going and what I should be doing. I can't prove this, but I do know that when I spend time with God before the Blessed Sacrament, as tedious as it may be sometimes, thoughts often go through my mind which no doubt are inspired by the Holy Spirit.

Recently, I spent seven days at the Camaldoli Hermitage in Big Sur. This gorgeous place, built on a hill rising about twelve hundred feet above the ocean, has an hermitage, a chapel, and seventeen guest rooms.

Nine guests have private rooms on a level overlooking the ocean. Each of these rooms has a bed, a little bathroom, a couple of chairs, drawers for one's clothes, and a beautiful view of the ocean. On the front of each room there is a little patio and a chair. Private showers are available in a little area near the kitchen.

On the outskirts of the retreat compound, there are additional guest hermitages overlooking the mountains and the sea. These are reserved for people who have better ambulatory skills than I.

The diet of the Camaldoli Hermitage is vegetarian, and the food is plentiful. The monks are excellent cooks and bakers.

One making this retreat spends much time in silence and prayer, trying to blend in as much as possible with the monks' daily lives and their spiritual liturgies. One arises for the 5:45 a.m. office vigil followed by an intervening break, and then lauds at 7:00 a.m. Eucharist is celebrated at 11:30 a.m. Vespers takes place at six o'clock in the evening. This is followed by a voluntary half-hour of silent group meditation in the church rotunda. Guests are welcome to participate in these religious prayer services.

Their beautiful chapel is octagon in shape and has a pervading aura of reverence. I had the tremendous privilege of concelebrating Mass with the monks. Their chanting gives one an awareness of the supernatural and a real sense of God's presence. It's an amazing help to one's spiritual life.

Although I always have had difficulty leaving an active life to spend some quiet time with God, over the years I have learned that a Holy Hour spent with God enriches the rhythm of my daily life. His sacred presence gives greater meaning to my life.

The beauty in the simplicity of their lives is inspiring. The monks are available for spiritual direction and confession. One may select a monk, apply for his availability, and make an appointment for advice and guidance.

One can walk, bicycle, or jog for two miles up and down the main road. Highway 1 stretches above Big Sur. The wild life is absolutely magnificent. One may hear deer thrashing among the thickets. Little foxes come out along the road, and often one sees a covey of quail scurry by. Doves, hawks, birds, blue jays, pelicans, and all sorts of other winged creatures soar. Those who stay in one of the trailers can become very good friends with them by handing out bread or other edibles. The deer even wander up to the trailers. I saw one with twin fawns. It is an incredible scene, and God's animals make one aware of His presence through the beauty of His creatures.

The sunsets are absolutely unparalleled. One evening I remember asking Almighty God to give me the strength and grace to do what was right. The theme I had for this retreat was from 1 Chronicles, Chapter 4:9-10: In it, Jabez called on the God of Israel, saying, "Oh Lord, increase my boundaries."

As the retreat was coming to a close I was out on the bluff overlooking the ocean while the sun was setting. No artist could do justice to this magnificent scene or the colors of the sky as the sun slowly dropped into the ocean. I was thinking of the poet, Joyce Kilmer, who said, "Poems are made by fools like me but only God can make a tree."

Magnificent paintings had been made by Raphael, Van Dyke, and other great artists in the world, but only God could make a sunset like this. No artist could truly duplicate the colors I witnessed.

For some reason or other I had the thought: "My life is now at four o'clock as far as the clock goes. Perhaps only two hours exist till the sunset in my own life occurs." I then prayed that Almighty God would increase my boundaries and let me have a productive elderly life filled with challenges and people, that I would not offend the Lord, and that I, hopefully, would help others. It was a tremendous feeling.

I told my friends who made the retreat with me – Irma Martz, Sister Joann of the Carondelet Sisters, and Valerie Sinkus – that I had some thoughts about the clock and our lives. I mentioned to Valerie, "You are at eleven o'clock; Sister Joann, you are at your high noon; Irma, you are at 1:30; and I am at 4:00 p.m. Let all of us be as productive as we possibly can and do all we can for Christ in our lives."

When spending some time at the Hermitage, I view the world from a different perspective, aware of God's presence and moved by the inspirational lives of these monks. One retreatant asked two of them, "Why are you here? Why did you leave what you had?"(Some of them had been in society as professionals, laborers, members of religious communities, etc.)

One answered, "We wanted more." When I am up here I begin to understand what that more is: being more present to God and to all that God has to offer us.

I had to learn this the hard way.

One has to give oneself some space. We busy American people will head to Las Vegas, Hawaii, Mexico, or Europe. We will make the time for a vacation, or a necessary medical leave, but the average Catholic will carve out little time to make a retreat for him or herself. That is one of the greatest tragedies of our lives. We don't see the value of being alone with God, being open to His graces, and just being silent in His Presence. Try it – God will speak to you!

One feels refreshed and strengthened after seven days at the Camaldoli Hermitage. Upon returning to the secular world, one can better bring Christ to others.

The retreat prepared me for some eye surgery and gave me peace. Before I left, I was anointed by one of the monks in the presence of my friends. I thank God for directing the hands of the surgeon, and pray that my one eye will come out well. Hopefully, God will allow me to be active and productive in carrying out His will, until six o'clock and the sun sets.

# EPILOGUE

# FAMILY REMEMBRANCES

## MICHAEL KEVANY, BROTHER-IN-LAW
## AND MICHELLE KEVANY, NIECE

### INTERVIEW BY
### MAUREEN O'BRIEN KROCK

Six o'clock chimed and the sun set on Father O's life on October 26, 2002. A three-day bout with peritonitis had ended his nearly six-decade long priesthood.

He had received his calling early in life and never wavered. A favorite baseball cap was embroidered with these heartfelt words: "A Call; Not a Choice." Although we knew with absolute certainty that the church was Father O's number one priority, he was always careful to include us in his pastoral family. One special memory is Midnight Mass on Christmas Eve, when family members filed into reserved front row seats at St. John Vianney Church. Parishioners treated us as though we were a presidential first family.

Another favorite memory is the many family baptisms Father O celebrated. He would boisterously welcome yet another grand-niece or nephew into the faith and start clapping his hands—off beat—as he sang, "*He's got the whole world in his hands...*" The family would join in, each one teasingly adding their own discordant beat.

As pastor of St. John Vianney, Father O took upon himself to celebrate an additional evening Mass on Thanksgiving, Christmas Day, and Easter—holidays which are traditionally celebrated in the morning. While his associate priests took those nights off to spend time with friends and family; Father O celebrated 5:30 p.m. Mass before hurrying over to join us, his other family, for dinner.

The first Christmas Eve following his retirement, he was able to come over much earlier than usual. After a couple hours of the chaos typical of our large family gatherings, he disappeared, obviously overwhelmed, for a long restorative nap.

As both priest and friend to many celebrities, it's important to know Father O didn't seek them out—rather they sought him. His zeal for his faith and priesthood acted as a magnet, attracting public figures, fellow priests, and parishioners, and made him an endearing family member.

# REFLECTIONS

# MONSIGNOR KEVIN KOSTELNIK

## PASTOR
### CATHEDRAL OF OUR LADY OF THE ANGELS

Monsignor O'Callaghan wasn't into titles. We just knew him as Father O, a simple priest of Jesus Christ, and in the tradition and likeness of his favorite patron, St. John Vianney, Father O was simply a parish priest.

I first met this parish priest in 1975 when I made an appointment to see him. I was escorted to his office by his secretary and as I waited for Father O to come in, I marveled at the oversized glass-top desk that enshrined photos of all the people of importance in his life and all the trophy photos of the great marlin fish that he had caught. When Father O walked in, I quickly stood at attention. He looked at me and barked, "Put those shoulders back and stand up straight, Man." And those pleasantries exchanged, we sat down to do business.

I informed him that I was 20 years old and worked full time at a ski and sporting goods store, that I went to school at Mt. San Antonio College and my girlfriend wanted to get married someday. And yet I was troubled because I kept thinking about the priesthood; I kept thinking about becoming a priest. "Father O, what should I do?"

His eyes stared me down and he responded, "Kevin, just keep thinking about being a priest, being a soldier for Christ." He got up to leave the room and it was then apparent our appointment was already over. I asked him if we could maybe talk about it. He leaned over the desk, pointed his fingers the wrong way, the vein popping out on his neck, and repeated, "Just keep thinking about it."

The whole meeting was about two minutes and thirteen seconds. I left rather bewildered and confused. Was I signing up for the priesthood or the army?

It turned out to be the best and most concise advice. I just kept thinking about it.

Father O became for me and for many others a friend, mentor, and spiritual father, and we loved him very much.

The gospel portrays Jesus as the Good Shepherd. And what a good shepherd we were given in Father O for over 59 years. He was a shepherding priest, always attentive to the flock, tirelessly working to meet our spiritual needs. Like a shepherd he reverenced solitude and silence, and like a shepherd whose inherent disposition is rugged and individualistic, such was Father O's. I remember those many congregation parties: his 25th, 35th, 40th, 50th, his retirement, and when he became a monsignor. Before I left the Cathedral, I would tell Cardinal Mahoney I was going to a party for Father O, and he would say, "Another party for O'Callaghan?"

At one such event I remember a collage of slides depicting Father O's memories crisscrossing many video screens—all the pictures were accompanied by Frank Sinatra's song, *"I Did it My Way."*

Father O always did it his way and that's what we admired about him. You always knew where he stood. He didn't mince words. It was either black or white, with little room for gray, and plenty of room for confrontation.

His scrupulosity kept his routine true, faithful and disciplined. He was authentic. He did what he said, and he lived what he preached.

Father O was a sacramental priest. Everyday life centered on the Mass. He was Eucharistic through and through.

He witnessed your marriages, he baptized your children, and he buried your loved ones. He was the first to arrive at the bedside of a sick or dying parishioner at the hospital or at their home.

He was always making sure that people were properly prepared to meet the Lord—one last confession, Viaticum, and the last anointing.

Before he went into surgery on Friday, he must have set the record because we think he was anointed at least four or five times, all by different priests. He was—in the words of St. Paul's scripture—well prepared to give an account of himself to God.

Father O was a priest who prayed. And in this church Jesus Christ had a brother priest who spent much time in prayer.

He lived the truth of St. Paul's words, "If we live, we live for the Lord." Father O's longing and thirst for Christ was satisfied by making that daily holy hour and by a huge amount of spiritual reading. His worn-out breviary offers testament to his faithfulness to the hours of the Divine Office.

He meditated daily on the Stations of the Cross, both inside the church and out in the parking lot. And if you think about it—walking those Stations outside, at a brisk pace with leash in hand—he wore out about three or four dogs.

In his life, he probably went through dozens of rosary beads, for in this church, Mary, the Mother of God, had a son who knew his mother well.

Look around and admire this great church that Father O built along with so many of you. Now look around and admire one another, this community of faith that Father O built up by teaching us how to pray. He often said that we must pray, because to pray is to know Christ so that when we die and arrive at the gates, Jesus will say, "I've been waiting for you."

Father O was a manly priest. He celebrated life as an avid golfer, fisherman, hunter, coach, and teacher—his shoulders back, standing straight, and always looking forward. He was Irish in heritage and fanatically Irish in support of Notre Dame football.

His chronological years of 85 plus would define him as an elderly priest; however, we never got to see him old. He never let on to the pain in his back or legs because he was tempered with a mind and a spirit that was always so young. Even up to his last week on this earth, I always thought of him as a quarterback who on the snap of the ball steps back and with keen acumen quickly surveys the broad scope of the field and makes instant decisions, and then lives with those decisions. He was doing that even at 85.

Father O was a priest of the Word, the Word of God. He loved to preach. He spent hours working on his homilies. They were often sermons — orthodox in content, didactic and dynamic in delivery, confronting, challenging, filled with stories of faith, and always experiential, encouraging us with practical examples of how to walk out of the doors of this church and live the gospel.

From the church pulpit, to retreat houses, to the seminary, he always offered a zealous and enthusiastic response to Christ. That was the purpose, the meaning of his delivery in homilies. Father O was a sacramental priest, Father O was a manly priest, Father O was a prayerful priest, Father O was a priest of the word of God.

On Saturday morning I arrived at the hospital five minutes after he died. Father O's sister, Mary, his brother- in-law, Mike, his doctor, and a couple of family members gathered around his bed while we offered the prayers of the church for those who had just died. And then we stepped into the hallway and did what so many of us have done these past few days—we told O'Callaghan stories.

Before I left the hospital, in my last private moment with him, I went into his room, bent down to his lifeless body, and whispered, "Thanks for my vocation; I'm glad I just kept thinking about it. On behalf of the priests and people who would like to be here now, thanks. I paused and then continued, "By the way, right now Notre Dame is beating Florida State." I paused again, realizing his new perspective, and added, "But you already know that. It's the second quarter and you already know the outcome of the game."

Tonight and tomorrow, we will assemble and we will pray. And with confident faith in the promises of God, we know the outcome. For us Father O was a parish priest; now, with the Good Shepherd, Father O is eternally a priest of Jesus Christ, forever and ever. Amen, amen.

## FATHER JACK STOEGER
### CARDINAL MANNING HOUSE OF PRAYER FOR PRIESTS
### AUGUST, 2012

*For me to be a saint means to be myself. Therefore the problem of sanctity and salvation is in fact the problem of finding out who I am and of discovering my true self. Trees and animals have no problem. God makes them what they are without consulting them, and they are perfectly satisfied. With us it is different. God leaves us free to be whatever we like. We can be ourselves or not, as we please. We are at liberty to be real or to be unreal. We may be true or false, the choice is ours. We may wear now one mask and now another, and never, if we so desire, appear with our own true face....If we have chosen the way of falsity we must not be surprised that truth eludes us when we finally come to need it.*

Thomas Merton, *New Seeds of Contemplation*, 31-32

It has been several weeks since Father O's brother-in-law, Mike Kevany, called me to ask if I might like the original dining room table from St. John Vianney's Rectory for the House of Prayer for Priests. Mike could think of no more appropriate place since countless priests had sat around it over the many years when Father O was pastor. Now that tradition will continue with more priests sharing food and experiences of God and the numerous people who cross our paths.

The acquisition of this table has sparked renewed memories of five wonderful years—we called them "Camelot" years—sitting around this table and drinking deeply of the exceptional qualities and personality of one very unique man and priest: James Aloysius O'Callaghan. The stories of his life and ministry that he shares in his book witness to his unique and true self!

I will never forget the Friday night when I first came to St. John Vianney. Father O welcomed me with excitement and a flurry of enthusiasm. Apparently, the entire parish had been praying for the right priest to come because another priest's assignment had not materialized at the last minute.

My years with Father O brought me a truly new zeal for what parish priesthood is really all about and encouraged me on my journey to being my true self. For example, he wanted me to be more courageous and not such a "feeler." He kept telling me, "I want to see steel in your eyes," and "I want to develop the killer instinct in you." I assured him I could never be a killer.

However, I must admit that over the years since then—especially when it came to administration and decision-making—I have become more assertive, more forthright, and more courageous to speak my truth and not just say what I believe the other person wants to hear. He encouraged gifts in me I didn't even know I had because he set a tone where I could be myself by creating an empowering atmosphere of affirmation, joy and camaraderie.

His enthusiasm and dedication to priesthood and the people 24/7 was contagious. When I left SJV in 1986, Father O gave me his picture inscribed with these simple words: *Jack, Be Free! Jim.* I treasure it to this day and I am attempting to do just that: Be free!

This amazing, one-of-a-kind man was his "true self." He always said what he thought. That trait sometimes got him in trouble with archdiocesan authorities and some parishioners who wanted priests to live an imposed role rather than letting God use them for his purposes. I have lived in too many situations where there were unspoken rules of what could or could not be shared. Father O was often at odds with the "party line" in some clerical circles, except when it came to liturgical matters and the traditional basics of a disciplined spiritual and priestly life.

He loved taking new and more assertive approaches to ministry, challenging the people to a deeper spirituality and a more vigorous integration of their faith with their daily lives. He was utterly convinced of the importance of personal integrity and living out the moral implications of being a disciple of Jesus. He wasn't afraid to say if something was "nasty bad" but then he would compassionately yet firmly help the person find a way out or a way through the situation.

He wanted to get to know us priests. After I remarked that exercise was important to me as a way of nourishing my need for solitude and replenishment so I could be truly present to the people in ministry, he always asked if I had gotten in my exercise.

He was a sports nut himself and loved to play (in his younger years) golf and basketball. For ten years he was the championship football coach at St. Anthony's High School in Long Beach. He loved to watch sports on TV, was always on the sidelines for the football games at Los Altos High School across from the church on Turnbull Canyon, and devoured the sports page of the LA Times at breakfast, fighting with Father Joe Shea over that section. He went hunting and deep sea fishing with his priest buddies. Right up to the end, because of his horrible back problems, he pushed himself to swim two miles every day.

When I was assigned to the seminary as Spiritual Director, he told me that the quality he most looked for in a candidate for priesthood was "balance." He modeled that balance. He used to say that it's like the tripod of a camera: unless the three legs are locked and in position, the camera can't focus. The three legs represent body, mind and spirit. If they are not attended to and kept in balance, we can't focus and the quality of our ministry with people will be compromised.

The only time I would experience Father O being a little unreal was when he would have to meet with Monsignor Hawkes or Cardinal Manning. Father O would put on a kind of bravado and wear his clerical shirt with #1 embroidered on his left sleeve.

He would sometimes come on strong, as if ready for war, because he knew the others thought differently than he did and he wanted to make a point and share his conviction about this or that issue. If it looked as if he might not get the associate priest he wanted, he had a letter of resignation ready in his coat pocket to pull out for extra emphasis. Every meeting of priests on the deanery or priests' council level was certainly interesting because he was not shy or reticent to express what was on his mind. He was a true maverick in many ways.

I could tell endless stories but back to the table! What was shared there bespeaks so much of what I admired about Father O. He always said there was nothing that could not be talked about at the table. Nothing! That was true, and anyone who tried to censor the topic was immediately challenged. What was most important was priestly fraternity and honesty.

I can certainly imagine how some might have felt intimidated by him because he was such an imposing figure who, by his own admission, might be "seldom right" but was "never in doubt." Father O was committed to fostering fellowship and support. He would wait until every priest was at the table before he said the blessing and if they weren't there he would call them in their offices and ask, "Aren't we (priests) as important as the parishioners?"

Father O tried to be a true father to us priests. He could certainly be overbearing at times, perhaps even perceived as militaristic by some, but he was interested in us and what we really thought about everything.

He was open to new ideas and ways of doing things and if we could convince him, he would support us 110%. "Risk" was one of his key words. Apparently it wasn't always that way. Not that he was closed-minded, but he needed a strong argument to convert him to another point of view. He loved to be challenged but sometimes he would be too strong a presence and we priests would say that he needed to get away for a week or so for his own good and to give us a break. We could be totally honest with him.

Those were wonderful days and it is a real joy to write about them. The walks around the parking lot with the dog after dinner…especially Saturday nights. The camaraderie with Doug Ferraro and Joe Shea and Monsignor O'Duignan, each unique individuals in their own right, yet they complemented, supported, and played off each other in marvelous ways.


Father O was one authentic person; you either liked him or you didn't, principally because he was daring and honest and didn't beat around the bush. He also was faithful and zealous. Even though he took off two days a week for his health, no one really noticed because he was so present the other five days.

He was always available, at a moment's notice literally dashing off to the bedside of a sick person or someone who had been away from the Church. We had a policy that if someone was sick or had died, one of us priests would call the person or family, if not visit them, before the end of the day.

He truly cared about the moral fiber and character of people and would challenge the heck out of people, speaking the truth even if it hurt. He was convinced of his vocation to call people to integrity and the full living of the Gospel. He would often dismiss the people at the end of Sunday Mass with: "Go in peace to love and serve the Lord with courage, vigor and a great deal of enthusiasm!" And the veins would be popping out of his neck! Once you experienced that dismissal you never forgot it or him!

I firmly believe that his authenticity and zeal, like that of St. Paul, came from his strong personality and work ethic, his total love of priesthood but, most especially, his incredible relationship with Christ evident in his pattern of personal prayer.

His spiritual discipline included one hour a day in front of the Blessed Sacrament (non-negotiable!), making the Stations of the Cross and saying the Rosary daily, as well as pondering arduously over Scripture in preparation for his insightful and rousing homilies which the people often applauded.

He was noted for the power of his message and its relationship to the reality of peoples' lives, bringing the Gospel message down to the level where every person, no matter what age, could relate. His commitment to the daily Holy Hour and his fidelity to Mass and the Divine Office were part of the discipline he practiced about almost everything.

People sought him out for advice because they knew they would get honest input. And the legacy of one Monsignor Bernard J. Dolan, his first pastor at St. Anthony's in Long Beach, lived on in the daily availability for confession before the 5:15 p.m. Mass. After all, how could a parish named after a parish priest, St. John Vianney, who often heard confessions for 16 hours a day in Ars, France, not offer frequent confessions? People came from all over—especially high school and college students—to avail themselves of the sacrament because they could talk about what was going on in their lives and learn how to have a deeper relationship with God.

The only exception to this disciplined manner of Father O was in his role as master to his successive Irish Terriers. They were hopeless, helpless and hapless. He couldn't get them to obey for anything. So ironic! Whether it was "Rory" or "Parnell" they could never be let off their leash. Citations even appeared in the local paper about his habit of driving around the parking lot holding the leash out the window as he exercised the dog.

Father O's days at RKO Studios with Fred Astaire, Hermes Pan, Ginger Rogers and Ricardo Montalban were legendary. His friendship with Frank O'Connell, Martin Giordano, Cristobal Arellano, Mary Toneck, Sisters Joann Heinritz, Theresa Harpin, Lydia Sandoval and Mary Ann Scanlon, along with countless others, created a really exciting family atmosphere.

He always counseled us to make time for *the little people*–those who were on the margins or those who worked around the parish and could easily be taken for granted. But he was always himself, and that is what made him so effective and so sought after by people of all ages, whether in a moment of crisis, after Sunday Mass, or arranging for a wedding or baptism.

Even though the church Father O built so lovingly and of which he was so proud tragically burned down at the beginning of Holy Week 2011, the spirit of the parish family soars...it is not centered on buildings but people. When I heard the shocking news, I immediately thought of what Father O might say. He would, no doubt, proclaim his oft-repeated dictum, one of the famous "planks" upon which he built his life: "I work for God and no man; I can function in disaster but I always finish with style."

Needless to say, Father O was not a "maintenance" pastor; he was a visionary one. He loved to try new things, and he loved for his associates to suggest new approaches or processes to enhance the faith life of the people. His many religious education/formation opportunities were legendary and the best, he was always trying to improve the quality and content of what was offered.

The famous Renewal Program (1979-1984) during which he suspended the religious education programs for the children and focused on evangelizing the adults because "For too long we have educated the children and played with the adults; now it's time to educate the adults/parents. If the parents are truly to be the first educators of their children in the ways of faith, we have to help them grow in their faith so they can pass it onto their children."

Needless to say, that did not go over well with the authorities in the Archdiocese, but it worked. There was an amazing rejuvenation of faith in thousands of adults that resulted in an enormous and lasting impact on the children.

Father O truly cared about us priests. I looked forward to gathering in the kitchen at 9:30 or 10 p.m., after all our meetings and appointments. He would put on a pot of tea and have some toasted Il Fornaio bread and honey. I would sit on the sink while we talked over the day's activities and challenges and pretended we were solving all the problems!

Once a month we went down to his sister's San Clemente beach house for a team day with the three Sisters of St. Joseph. We would assess the needs of the parish in terms of liturgy and spirituality, etc. There was time for quality prayer together, and time to go off by ourselves for a swim or walk on the beach. We would end the day with a wonderful dinner together, regaling each other with stories and doing crazy things like "let's tell what kind of dog we remind each other of." We all agreed that Father O was a Doberman!

As I keep saying, if that table could talk!!!!!! It was truly an extension of Eucharist: sharing stories, always in the context of God, and breaking bread together! It was and continues to be a sacred table around which to gather and keep telling stories and remembering all who have sat around that table in the past and who are still with us in one way or another. I know for certain there will be a day when we all gather around the heavenly banquet table and are reunited in the Kingdom. I can't wait! Will we have stories to tell!!!!

I am truly grateful for the marvelous and graced experience of knowing and living with Father O. Although sometimes misunderstood and even disliked by some of his own peers, there was no question that he was one unique, dedicated, and honest man and a priest of integrity. His presence in my life now and the memories of what we shared together continue to challenge me to strive to be even half the man and priest he was and is! I often wonder what he would say about where we are in the Church and world today. Probably, "Pull up a chair and gather around the table!"

He absolutely loved being a priest and he used to say that his only disappointment in life was that he didn't have many more years left for priestly ministry. May he continue to live in and through us who have been indelibly touched by his life and ministry and who are striving to walk in his footsteps, becoming our true selves in Christ so, just like Father O, we can zealously lead others to Him.

## BISHOP SYLVESTER RYAN
### BISHOP EMERITUS OF MONTEREY

While attending City College in Long Beach, California in 1948-49, I played basketball for the CC basketball team. We used the St. Anthony gym because CC did not have one of their own. I would show up early, before 5:00 p.m. practice. I met Father O'Callaghan and fell under the spell, and we talked fairly often about sports and about the priesthood. He encouraged me to give it lots of prayer and thought. At the end of the year I approached my parents on the subject, and my mother was very opposed—I was an only child. My father thought I should wait until after college. I spoke with my pastor and he told me to pray and let God take care of what would happen.

Well, almost at the last minute my mother and father said I could go. I gathered together my papers and sent them in, and I was accepted. God had answered my prayers.

Flash forward to my twenty-fifth anniversary as a priest at Our Lady of Lourdes parish in Sunland Tujunga. Many of my family had gathered in the rectory dining room. Father O'Callaghan arrived early for the Mass and came to the rectory. As I started to introduce him to my mother, she blurted, "I know you..." And immediately Jim replied, "And I know you, too, Charlotte." I was baffled. I didn't know they had already met. But things were moving fast for the celebration and I did not get a chance to bring it up until a couple of days later. When I asked my mother how she had met Father Jim, she told me that the summer before I entered the seminary she and my father went to Saint Anthony's to meet Father O'Callaghan and discuss the seminary business. My mother told him flat out that she was not going to give me permission to attend the seminary. Father Jim told her flatly she had no right to make that decision for her son. So the two of them (with my father watching this battle) went at it. She did not mention how it all ended. But afterwards my father and mother spoke together about it and decided they would give me permission.

All along I thought it was my prayers that changed the day, but it was O'Callaghan!

# ACKNOWLEDGMENTS

With much appreciation for the many contributors who aided Father O in getting this book ready for publication.

Carol Lambert
Toni Aja
Michael Kevany
Michelle Kevany
Dom and Sandy Niccoli
Bianca Niccoli
Maureen O'Brien Krock
Janet Dovidio
Valerie Sinkus
June Schwarz
Marie Manahan
Jerry and Lynne Mook
Sister Joann Heinritz
Yvonne Rochester
Bob Altman
Ann Dunbar
Wilma Dela Cruz
Father Joseph Shea
Father Jack Stoeger
Monsignor Kevin Kostelnik
Bishop Sylvester Ryan